# Mercantilism, Account Keeping and the Periphery-Core Relationship

AF735184

Mercantilism and accounting remain two dynamic and debated concepts in terms of definition and scope. This volume brings together the research of international scholars from a wide variety of disciplines – accounting, anthropology, native studies, economic geography, economic history and management – to reflect on alternative approaches to the study of these concepts.

This book focuses on how individuals across space and time negotiated and navigated systems of exchange and trade, especially when confronted with world views and cultural systems that conflicted with and disrupted perceptions of their own. Through this, the volume offers a helpful reinforcement to the view that the analysis of mercantilism must be more highly contextualised to time and place, with a deeper focus on the local actors involved. It is these local actors who negotiated, exchanged and navigated differing world views and who enable us to tease out the longer-run global economic and social processes and the impacts of these encounters.

Complementing the growing interest in mercantilism, Indigenous studies and the relationships between colonists, traders and their counterparts in colonies and trading ports, this work provides a cross disciplinary examination of the subject area. Furthermore, it encourages a renewed interest in the use of archival documents and documentary sources in novel and innovative ways.

**Cheryl Susan McWatters** is the Father Edgar Thivierge Chair in Business History and professor of accounting at the University of Ottawa, Canada. She holds a PhD in Management from Queen's University, Canada, and her research interests span accounting, business and economic history, management accounting and control, and operations management. She is also the editor of *Accounting History Review* and associate editor of the *Journal of Operations Management*.

**Perspectives in Economic and Social History**
Series Editors: Andrew August and Jari Eloranta

**A History of Professional Economists and Policymaking in the United States**
Irrelevant Genius
*Jonathan S. Franklin*

**Merchants and Trade Networks in the Atlantic and the Mediterranean, 1550–1800**
Connectors of Commercial Maritime Systems
*Edited by Manuel Herrero Sánchez and Klemens Kaps*

**Property Rights in Land**
Issues in Social, Economic and Global History
*Edited by Rosa Congost, Jorge Gelman and Rui Santos*

**Working-Class Community in the Age of Affluence**
*Stefan Ramsden*

**Culture, Philanthropy and the Poor in Late-Victorian London**
*Geoffrey A. C. Ginn*

**The Economic and Business History of Occupied Japan**
New Perspectives
*Edited by Thomas French*

**An Urban History of The Plague**
Socio-Economic, Political and Medical Impacts in a Scottish Community, 1500–1650
*Karen Jillings*

**Mercantilism, Account Keeping and the Periphery-Core Relationship**
*Edited by Cheryl Susan McWatters*

For more information about this series, please visit www.routledge.com/series/PESH

# Mercantilism, Account Keeping and the Periphery-Core Relationship

Edited by Cheryl Susan McWatters

Routledge
Taylor & Francis Group
LONDON AND NEW YORK

First published 2019
by Routledge

2 Park Square, Milton Park, Abingdon, Oxfordshire OX14 4RN
52 Vanderbilt Avenue, New York, NY 10017

*Routledge is an imprint of the Taylor & Francis Group, an informa business*

First issued in paperback 2020

Copyright © 2019 selection and editorial matter, Cheryl Susan McWatters; individual chapters, the contributors

The right of Cheryl Susan McWatters to be identified as the author of the editorial material, and of the authors for their individual chapters, has been asserted in accordance with sections 77 and 78 of the Copyright, Designs and Patents Act 1988.

All rights reserved. No part of this book may be reprinted or reproduced or utilised in any form or by any electronic, mechanical, or other means, now known or hereafter invented, including photocopying and recording, or in any information storage or retrieval system, without permission in writing from the publishers.

Notice:
Product or corporate names may be trademarks or registered trademarks, and are used only for identification and explanation without intent to infringe.

*British Library Cataloguing-in-Publication Data*
A catalogue record for this book is available from the British Library

*Library of Congress Cataloging-in-Publication Data*
Names: McWatters, Cheryl S., editor.
Title: Mercantilism, account keeping and the periphery-core relationship / edited by Cheryl Susan McWatters.
Description: Abingdon, Oxon; New York, NY: Routledge, 2018. | Series: Perspectives in economic and social history; 53 | Includes bibliographical references and index.
Identifiers: LCCN 2018008058 (print) | LCCN 2018010044 (ebook) | ISBN 9780429485428 (ebook) | ISBN 9781848936058 (hardback: alk. paper)
Subjects: LCSH: Mercantile system—History. | Accounting—History. | Economic history.
Classification: LCC HB91 (ebook) | LCC HB91 .M4265 2018 (print) | DDC 330.15/13—dc23
LC record available at https://lccn.loc.gov/2018008058

ISBN: 978-1-84893-605-8 (hbk)
ISBN: 978-0-367-66611-8 (pbk)

Typeset in Bembo
by Apex CoVantage, LLC

# Contents

# Figures

# Tables

# Contributors

**Yannick Lemarchand** is professor emeritus of management science at the University of Nantes, France. He is a former director of the Maison des Sciences de l'Homme Ange-Guépin in Nantes and a member of the Laboratoire d'Économie et de Management de Nantes-Atlantique. His research focuses on the history of the theories and practices of management. In 1995 Lemarchand initiated the Journées d'Histoire de la Comptabilité et du Management and is now honorary president of the Association pour l'Histoire du Management et des Organisations. His recent publications include 'Revisiting the Birth of Industrial Accounting in France, a Return to the Actors Involved', *Accounting History Review*, 26:3 (2016), *Merchants and Profit in the Age of Commerce, 1680–1830*, co-edited with Pierre Gervais and Dominique Margairaz (Pickering & Chatto, 2014) and, co-authored with Cheryl McWatters, 'Merchant Networks and Accounting Discourse: The Role of Accounting Transactions in Network Relations', *Accounting History Review*, 23:1 (2013).

**Cheryl Susan McWatters** is the Father Edgar Thivierge Chair in Business History and professor of accounting, University of Ottawa. She holds a PhD in Management from Queen's University, Canada. Her research interests span accounting, business and economic history, management accounting and control, and operations management. She is the editor of *Accounting History Review*, associate editor of the *Journal of Operations Management* and a member of a number of editorial boards in accounting and history. Her research has appeared in a wide variety of published volumes and academic journals including *Accounting, Organizations and Society*, *Accounting, Auditing and Accountability Journal*, *Accounting History Review*, *Accounting Historians Journal*, *Business History*, *Droits*, *Revue du Nord*, and *Journal of Operations Management*.

**Leanna Parker** Leanna Parker completed her PhD in native studies and environmental sociology at the University of Alberta in 2011. Her dissertation examined the effects of participation in commercial industries on Indigenous traditional economies, specifically considering the fur trade in Canada and the shore-based whaling industry in New Zealand. A portion of her dissertation formed the basis of research for her chapter in this volume. Dr Parker's research interests include Indigenous history, economic history, and Indigenous resource use and management.

**Arthur J. Ray** is professor emeritus at the University of British Columbia. His major publications include *Aboriginal Rights Claims and the Making and Remaking of History* (McGill-Queens University Press, 2016), which was awarded the 2017 Canada Book Prize of Humanities and Social Sciences Council of Canada, *An Illustrated History of Canada's Native People: I Have Lived Here Since the World Began* (McGill-Queens University Press, fourth edition, 2011), *Telling It to the Judge: Taking Native History to Court* (Montreal, 2011), *The Canadian Fur Trade in the Industrial Age* (University of Toronto Press, 1990), *Indians in the Fur Trade: Their Role as Trappers, Hunters, and Middlemen in the Lands Southwest of Hudson Bay, 1660–1870* (University of Toronto Press, second edition, 1998). He also co-authored with D. B. Freeman, *Give Us Good Measure: An Economic Analysis of Relations Between the Indians and the Hudson's Bay Company Before 1763* (University of Toronto Press, 1978).

**Mario Schmidt** is currently a post-doctoral researcher at the a.r.t.e.s. Graduate School for the Humanities, University of Cologne, where he works on a project exploring local understandings of money and quantity in Western Kenya. His research interests include the history of anthropology (especially the Durkheim School, Claude Lévi-Strauss and British social anthropology), anthropology of food, economic anthropology, corruption and democracy. Geographically he focuses on Eastern Africa, especially Kenya, and Native North America, especially the North-Eastern Woodlands. His doctoral dissertation provides an analysis of the cross-cultural use of wampum as a currency inspired by Marcel Mauss' 'Essay on the Gift'.

**Frank J. Tough** is a historical geographer (PhD, York University) and professor at the University of Alberta. Tough published *As Their Natural Resources Fail: Native People and the Economic History of Northern Manitoba, 1870–1930* (1996), which received two book awards. His academic curiosity concerns three odd empirical/disciplinary pairings: (1) history and law; for example, a legal history of the dispossession of Indigenous peoples; (2) history and geography, such as the historical geography of Aboriginal people's participation in frontier capitalism; and (3) history and economics, as in the case of an economic history approach to the Individualisation of collective property rights. These themes are usually tinged with some political economy, but his approach is heavily based on archival sources, including accounting records. He has published on Indian economic behaviour, the transfer of Rupertsland, the commercialisation of native fisheries, and the economics of Indian treaties and Métis entitlements (scrip). Often the empirical findings dispute the conventional thinking of both lawyers and historians.

**Richard W. Unger** (PhD, 1971) is professor emeritus in the History Department of the University of British Columbia, where he taught medieval and early modern history for four decades. An economic historian, he has published on the technology of shipping, the brewing industry and on Renaissance cartography. His most recent book, co-authored with John Thistle, is *Energy Consumption in Canada in the 19th and 20th Centuries: A Statistical Outline* (2013). Recent articles include 'Trade, Taxation and Government Policy in the High Middle Ages', *Viator*, 46 (2015) and 'Ships and Sailing Routes in Maritime Trade Around Europe, 1300–1600', *The Routledge Handbook of Maritime Trade Around Europe, 1300–1600* (2017). He is the former president of the Medieval Academy of America.

**Frederik Vermote** is an assistant professor of global history at California State University, Monterey Bay, and a research fellow at the USF Ricci Institute for Chinese-Western Cultural History. His research interests include Jesuit finances and travel between Europe and China during the fifteenth to eighteenth centuries. His forthcoming and most recent publications include 'Travellers Lost and Redirected: Jesuit Networks and the Limits of European Exploration in Asia', in *Itinerario: The Journal of the History of European Expansion and Global Interaction*, two book chapters on financing Jesuit missions in edited volumes published by Brill and Oxford, and an article in *The World History Connected* journal, 'Dangers and Limitations of Jesuit Travel Throughout Eurasia During the Seventeenth and Eighteenth Centuries'. Vermote's book manuscript *Moving Money and Missionaries in a Global World: The Jesuit Financial Networks Between Europe and Asia* is under contract with Brill.

**Petr Vorel** is a Czech historian and full professor of history at the University of Pardubice (Czech Republic). He is a graduate of the Faculty of Arts at Charles University in Prague (1986). From 1986 to 2000 he worked as a historian and numismatist at the East Bohemia Museum in Pardubice. Since 2000 he has worked within the Faculty of Arts at the University of Pardubice. There he held positions as head of the Historical Department (2000–2006), vice dean for research (2006–2007) and dean of faculty (2007–2015); since 2015 he has been vice rector for development of the university. He is a member of the Association of Historians of the Czech Republic (chairman 2005–2011), the Czech National Committee of Historians (chairman since 2011), the Learned Society of the Czech Republic (Prague), the Collegium Carolinum (Munich) and the Comenius Academic Club (New York). In his research he focuses on central European history of the late medieval and early modern era, on economic history and the history of monetary circulation.

# Acknowledgements

At the XVI World Congress of Economic History in Stellenbosch, South Africa, we invited international scholars from a wide variety of disciplines – accounting, anthropology, native studies, economic geography, economic history and management – to reflect on alternative approaches to the study of mercantilism and account keeping. Since the Congress, we have updated, revised and reviewed individual chapters to incorporate comments from the session participants, other colleagues and manuscript referees. This volume represents the results of this endeavour to bring our internationally comparative and interdisciplinary research to a broader audience. The final chapters have benefitted from the meticulous and enthusiastic efforts of Dr Ignaz Cassar who edited all contributions to maintain the integrity of their varied research traditions and norms while harmonising their presentation. I owe him so many thanks for taking on this critical role. Lastly, I wish to thank especially my colleagues whose studies appear within these pages for their patience as the project evolved, and our editors and production team at Routledge for their interest and ongoing support for this project.

Cheryl Susan McWatters

# Introduction

## Mercantilism and accounting across space and time

*Cheryl Susan McWatters*

Mercantilism and accounting remain two dynamic and debated concepts in terms of definition and scope. Putting aside debates about their conceptual validity and arguments of historicism, this volume puts forward an alternate path. It brings together a collection of studies by authors who share a common starting point: how did individuals across space and time negotiate and navigate systems of exchange and trade, particularly when confronted with world views and cultural systems that conflicted with and disrupted perceptions of their own. Grounding our work in terms of mercantilism underscores that we are indeed examining trade relations and how these relations were part of global networks of exchange. While trade relations might have been operationalised on an individual basis, they were not isolated transactions given their connections to larger networks and differing cultural understandings.

Accounting might conjure up ledgers and debates about the emergence of double-entry bookkeeping, credits and debits. However, we interpret accounting much more generously in terms of 'making account' – the practice of reckoning and providing an explanation, often in the form of narrative descriptions, of one's actions.[1] In terms of trade, this accounting could take the form of records and sophisticated systems yet also included simpler processes to track and note everyday transactions, providing thereby an enduring 'record' of them.

The sixteenth to eighteenth centuries saw the creation of a number of major merchant trading firms (e.g. the Dutch East India Company, la Compagnie des Indes, the Dutch West India Company, the Hudson's Bay Company and the Russian American Company) that were granted charters to explore, trade, raise taxes, enlist private armies and, importantly, generate profits for their shareholders. As quasi-states, they played key roles in colonial expansion. Arriving in distant territories, agents of these trading firms came into contact with Indigenous peoples whose systems of property assets and whose market models did not align with economic concepts grounded in 'Western views' of rational behaviour. In significant ways, these entities are early examples of the multinational enterprise and have been the frequent focus of research into mercantilism. As such, the analysis of their accounting records and those of other, even 'bit' players offers insights into the long-term outcomes of their operating decisions and actions, as well as glimpses into the individual choices made by actors at a point in time when confronted with the dynamics of these exchange relationships. Given parallels with present-day enterprise, these analyses remain an important basis on which to examine comparatively current models of international markets, trade and development.

In this volume we focus on less frequently told stories of this periphery-core relationship, including a reminder that the periphery could be geographically distant or close at hand. First, we are interested in the outcomes for those situated at the periphery, as opposed to the usual research emphasis on the returns to the centre/empire. Second, we analyse the means by which non-European trade actors reacted to the mercantilist system, especially in spatially extended trade networks. In this manner, we reverse prevalent thinking that non-European players did not act rationally, highlighting the dominance and mediation of non-economic factors that motivated the conduct of these actors. Inadequate attention to and frequent misinterpretation of these factors have led to the simplistic view that these players 'failed' to respond in a manner aligned with economic concepts of rational market behaviour. Third, we are interested in the outcomes of these mercantilist activities in different economic, political, cultural and spatial contexts, including the effects of changing political and economic policies established at the core, which affected the profitability and stability of operations in far-flung settings.

Additionally, we wish to examine the behaviour and conduct of actors who were involved in these exchange relationships yet often were characterised as rather minor players or mere cogs in the wheel. For example, merchant companies competed with small traders, other Europeans who arrived in these settings along with traders and merchants, for example, missionaries, bankers and colonial agents. These actors included importantly local players who were the necessary ingredient to make these exchanges operate and function – players who equally were caught up in these economic and cultural exchanges through interaction with those who had sought and pursued global opportunities. All of these individuals together were part of and created this periphery-core relationship. However, while much attention has been paid to the advantages and economic returns to the core players, far less attention has been paid to the perspective of those participants who were not part of the merchant and controlling group. Our objective is modest, given the nature of the exercise, with no offering up of generalised arguments or theories. Rather, the chapters are presented as contextual studies as opposed to macro-level analyses. Each one, in different ways, demonstrates how these relationships were forged and conducted, anchored in their economic, social and cultural setting. All of the studies[2] rely on primary sources and archival materials.

## Translating mercantilism

Invoking mercantilism as a basis to examine global exchange requires not surprisingly some elaboration of what exactly we mean by the term. Beuve, Brousseau and Sgard note that standard definitions of mercantilism – taken-for-granted 'clichés' along with analytical limitations – neglect historical experience. In their view, these definitions can be summarised as 'a broad period of European history during which absolute monarchs followed illiberal policies based on false premises: protectionism, widespread monopolies, and the confusion of wealth, money, and power'.[3] They further note that such definitions leave out policy preferences and bureaucratic mechanisms that were required to implement them.[4] Yet while casting aside the 'liberal and generous' mercantile system of Adam Smith[5] and others, we can explore more richly the historical record. As argued eloquently by Reinert with respect to political economy more generally:

> By almost exclusively devoting themselves to the study of a small handful of canonical texts, historians and their audiences in other disciplines run the risk of convincing themselves that these texts are somehow representative of their times. [. . .] We must study the canon historically, not history canonically.[6]

Importantly, in our case, Reinert encourages the examination of 'historical practices', not 'canonical ideas'.

Magnusson also argues for the need to treat mercantilism historically, 'as a series of written texts; pamphlets, tracts, books [. . .] a literature, discourse, on trade and economics [. . .], but linked to [. . .] the polity and economy of the "real" world'.[7] It is well known that mercantilism, as encapsulated within broader developments of political economy, did not emerge in one place at one time. Rather, its discourses were translated and 'emulated', as Reinert argues, as these tracts and treatises were transmitted and reinterpreted in Europe and the New World. In this spirit, we focus on this real world and how the mercantilist system did play out in various contexts. Moreover, we do view mercantilism as a system in which there was a market for goods, money and exchange, a market in which economic agents engaged in concrete actions to pursue their economic interests.[8] We also would agree in broad terms with the analysis of Foucault in which mercantilism is linked to governmentality, the rise of the administrative state and social control.[9]

## Translating accounting

At this juncture, let us return our attention to accounting. While it is trite to say that accounting is the language of business, underlying this phrase is the essential concept of accounting as discourse. Accounting discourse refers to accounting transactions as presented in written texts and the analysis of these texts within their social and historical context.[10]

This discourse contains an inherent duality, the accounting *by* someone for something *to* someone else. It also underscores the notion of reciprocity. The ability of accounting to translate this reckoning across space and time was critical to many market exchanges. As well recognised, 'exchange relations depend on some measure of give and take, trust, and a belief in fair play'.[11]

Ongoing exchange was based on shared understandings of the rules of the game; exchanges were not always profit-seeking but furthered the development and maintenance of social relations within and across social strata. Accounting records also provided means to mitigate weaknesses in agency relations on many levels; these records, their inscriptions[12] and transcriptions promoted accountability to multiple partners. They also introduced elements of control given that they often were re-presented and transmitted to other commercial partners or individuals to whom an account of transactions was required. Thus, these accounting records – as formal or informal as they might have been – enable us to assess the social relations behind them. 'By teasing out the interactions between parties, we see how this discourse supported and sustained the dynamic social relations between actors across space and time.'[13]

## Accounting for mercantilism

In bringing accounting to bear on mercantilism, our objective is to underscore that mercantilism involves both social and economic exchange – the basis of accounting discourse. Those not familiar with accounting might discard too readily journals and ledgers as mere numbers difficult to interpret and lacking in intellectual interest. Yet within these accountings was a rich interplay of social actors revealed through the exchange mechanisms that brought them together. The accounting inscriptions represented the underlying reality of the exchange process well beyond the financial. These inscriptions crossed time and space – often thanks to the ability of accounting to represent a shared language or understanding – ways-of-doing – such that those in one locale could understand and act upon the account offered by another. In this way, accounting is another means to bring mercantilism from the abstract to the social reality of those engaged in trading activities.

Whether these trades were purely local or crossed borders or continents, they were undertaken similarly in terms of records kept, transmitted and acted upon. For example, time spent examining and comparing the records of the Hudson's Bay Company with those of slave-trade merchants reveals that many of the underlying logics of these accountings and recordings were the same. Yet, beyond the mechanisms and the accounting themselves, in both cases, these records reveal social relations which enable us to tease out how these mercantilist systems were constructed and sustained over time. These analyses go well beyond the debits and credits to engage with what underlies these entries.[14]

## Studies of spaces and times

This collection brings together the research of global scholars whose original studies were part of an interdisciplinary session at the XVI World Economic History Congress (WEHC). This session explored, from an interdisciplinary perspective, issues of mercantilism, its antecedents and impacts. The studies represent research approaches from a variety of disciplines to counter usual tendencies which frame the discussion of mercantilism around the tenets of neo-classical economics. Rather, our interdisciplinary approach led to a rich exchange of opinions and ideas, especially on the nature of evidence, which are reinforced in the individual chapters. Contributors range from history, management, geography, anthropology, accounting and native studies. Post-conference dialogue and manuscript review ensured that the final versions corresponded to the overall theme, its global emphasis and plurality of approaches.

Part I, 'Pre-market intermediaries and Indigenous players', examines contexts of early contact and how actors negotiated cultural divides. Frederik Vermote brings to life the account books of the seventeenth-century Jesuit missionary François de Rougemont, his local interactions in China and his disconnection from the global economic networks of the Jesuits. Thus, these local exchanges indicate the ways in which both copper and silver circulated in this local setting, but also how the global economy played out in terms of localised socio-economic relations. This theme of monetary exchange is examined by Mario Schmidt in a very different setting, that of New Netherlands and the Coastal Algonquians. His analysis of the differing understandings of money by the Dutch colonists (a political problem) and the Coastal Algonquians (an economic opportunity) illustrates the deeper cross-cultural interaction in which mercantilist dogma conflicted with what Schmidt describes as the pragmatism of the Native Americans.

Part II, 'Encounters with the periphery', investigates merchant trading in two different settings, Europe and Africa. Petr Vorel reminds us that the periphery need not be some far-flung region but rather that the periphery-core relationship can be applied readily to the markets for precious metal in the Kingdom of Bohemia of the sixteenth century. The struggle for dominance in the mining and exporting of precious metal paralleled the striving for political control at both the local and international level. From a very different angle, Cheryl Susan McWatters and Yannick Lemarchand pick up the 'trade, truck, custom and barter' of Adam Smith to drill down into the accounts of French slave-trade cargoes, specifically the accounts of the merchandise on these vessels destined for African markets. The relations between French traders, their African counterparts and various intermediaries demonstrate how terms of trade were developed and negotiated over time and place, and how each side reacted to a market for global commodities but did so within the vagaries and idiosyncrasies of local exchange dynamics. The use of accounting records of the time enables a precise drilling down into the socio-economic relations that were forged over time.

Part III, 'Production, consumption and management of the colonial economy', places us directly into the colonial and Indigenous economy of the nineteenth and early twentieth centuries. Leanna Parker provides an extensive analysis of the consumption and production patterns of Indigenous peoples in the fur trade and whaling industries of North America and New Zealand respectively. Her analysis of changing consumption patterns presents strong evidence of how Indigenous players – mostly Dene, Cree and Métis in the North

American case and the Maori in New Zealand – were drawn into an increasingly colonial capitalist economy. This adaptation led over time to a dwindling self-sufficiency and a growing dependency on the commercial industries introduced by colonial interests. Arthur J. Ray delves further into the role of the Hudson's Bay Company (HBC) and its management records introduced in the nineteenth century at the district level. These analyses reveal how HBC managers assessed market conditions and distilled market and competitive intelligence to facilitate long-distance monitoring and control. Beyond economic intelligence and management control, these reports convey rich detail of the trading behaviour of local native people and the complex exchange relations in which these individuals engaged. Through the analysis of one seemingly inconsequential accounting record contained in the York Factory accounts of the HBC, Frank J. Tough provides a compelling case of how Indigenous trappers were connected over time and space – to the fur markets of London and to a rich variety of merchant goods. His conclusion reinforces the link of mercantilism and colonialism and how periphery players were captured within increasingly globalised commodity chains where economic growth in the periphery was contingent on the consumption needs of the core.

An initial assessment of our approach and its outcomes is offered by Richard W. Unger who joined this project and took up the challenge to provide a synthesis and general conclusion. His examination offers his own perspective on our study of mercantilism and accounts. For our part, we expect that this volume will complement and align with recent and growing interest in mercantilism, Indigenous studies and the manner in which relationships between colonists, traders and their counterparts in colonies and trading ports were forged, conceptualised and constructed. It also contributes to the increasing interest in studies that cross disciplinary boundaries and encourage renewed interest in the use of archival documents and documentary sources in novel and innovative ways. With the growing interest in commerce, trade networks and relations, in history writ large, we re-visit models and perspectives, such as the periphery-core debate, to take advantage of new sources, new approaches and importantly, to examine these analyses from the perspective of those in the periphery, instead of emphasising impacts on those in the core. The volume offers a potentially helpful reinforcement to the view that mercantilism emerged much earlier than has frequently been argued. The analysis of mercantilism must be more highly contextualised to time and place, along with deeper focus on the local actors involved. It is these local actors who negotiated, exchanged and navigated differing world views who enable us to tease out the longer-run global economic and social processes and the impacts of these encounters.

## Notes

1 From the Old French *aconter*.
2 Apart from the concluding chapter.
3 J. Beuve, E. Brousseau and J. Sgard, 'Mercantilism and Bureaucratic Modernization in Early Eighteenth-Century France', *Economic History Review*, 70:2 (2017), pp. 529–58.

4 Beuve, Brousseau and Sgard focus on post-Colbertian France. This specificity further underscores the need to contextualise any definition to the case at hand.

5 A. Smith, *An Inquiry into the Nature and Causes of the Wealth of Nations*, Book IV, ed. E. Cannan (London: Methuen and Co. Ltd., 1904), chapter IX. *Library of Economics and Liberty [Online]*, available from www.econlib.org/library/Smith/smWN19.html; accessed 3 November 2017.

6 S. A. Reinert, *Translating Empire: Emulation and the Origins of Political Economy* (Cambridge, MA: Harvard University Press, 2011), p. 72.

7 L. Magnusson, *Mercantilism: The Shaping of an Economic Language* (London: Taylor and Francis, 1994), p.VII.

8 Magnusson, *Mercantilism*, p. 11; P. Gervais and C. S. McWatters, 'Globalisation', in A. de Jong, S. Toms, J. Wilson, and E. Buchnea (eds.), *The Routledge Companion to Business History* (London: Routledge/Taylor and Francis, 2016), pp. 316–30.

9 For further insight into this aspect of Foucault, see M. Foucault, *Security, Territory, Population: Lectures at the Collège de France, 1977–78* (London: Palgrave Macmillan, 2007); K. Hoskin and R. Macve, '"L'État c'est moi" . . . ou quoi? On the Interrelations of Accounting, Managing and Governing in the French "Administrative Monarchy": Revisiting the Colbert (1661–1683) and Paris Brothers (1712–1726) Episodes', *Accounting History Review*, 26:3 (2016), pp. 219–57; see also the brief examination by Beuve, Brousseau and Sgard, 'Mercantilism and Bureaucratic Modernization in Early Eighteenth-Century France', p. 534.

10 N. Fairclough, 'Discourse Analysis in Organization Studies: The Case for Critical Realism', *Organization Studies*, 26:6 (2005), pp. 915–39; J. Ferguson, 'Analysing Accounting Discourse: Avoiding the "Fallacy of Internalism"', *Accounting, Auditing & Accountability Journal*, 20:6 (2007), pp. 912–34; C. S. McWatters and Y. Lemarchand, 'Merchant Networks and Accounting Discourse: The Role of Accounting Transactions in Network Relations', *Accounting History Review*, 23:1 (2013), pp. 49–83; C. S. McWatters and Y. Lemarchand, 'Accounting as Story Telling: Merchant Activities and Commercial Relations in 18th-Century France', *Accounting, Auditing & Accountability Journal*, 23:1 (2010), pp. 14–54.

11 McWatters and Lemarchand, 'Merchant Networks and Accounting Discourse', p. 76.

12 K. Robson, 'Accounting Numbers as "Inscription": Action at a Distance and the Development of Accounting', *Accounting Organizations and Society*, 17:7 (1992), pp. 685–708.

13 McWatters and Lemarchand, 'Merchant Networks and Accounting Discourse', p. 77.

14 We are not interpreting accounting narrowly as double-entry bookkeeping and thus focussing on its role in the emergence of capitalism. Moreover, as seen in this volume, our accounting stories do not rely in all cases on double-entry records to create reciprocal relations.

# Part I

# Pre-market intermediaries and Indigenous players

# 1 Jesuit account books and their role in connecting worlds

*Frederik Vermote*

In the study of the history of globalisation and its myriad connections, world historians sometimes compare the evolution of this process to the Buddhist image of Indra's net.[1] It is hard to find a better metaphor or more convincing visualisation than a giant web with reflecting nodes at every intersection, a symbol for a world of interconnectedness where interdependent entities and their reciprocal interactions affected everyone and everything. Globalisation during the seventeenth and eighteenth centuries was not as encompassing as its perfect Buddhist analogy. If globalisation had any resemblance to Indra's net, or could be understood as an earthly, imperfect shadow of the idea, then it seems logical to assume that it grew more connected throughout the period we are looking at – call it the early modern world 1500–1800. While new knots were appearing as more people and regions were tied into a global net, the degree of connectivity grew similarly. As new connections and threads were spun, the density of the existing threads increased, which fortified the connections along yet other axis.

The process of globalisation shaped the Jesuit missions in China in a continuous way, not just as the missionaries started out and travelled along the maritime network that the Portuguese sailors had established in the early sixteenth century, but also later on, in the seventeenth and eighteenth centuries, as multiple European states and companies provided networks from Europe to east Asia. At that time the Jesuit missions in Asia operated no longer 'in an era of first contacts', but rather in an 'age of sustained contact', where first encounters 'were turned into places of repeated meeting'.[2] The aim of this chapter is to examine the process of globalisation in this period and the ways in which it affected the finances of the Jesuit missions in China.

World historians such as Peter Stearns and Robbie Robertson, who have studied the process of globalisation (including its historical roots and the development of a global consciousness), do not include the seventeenth or the eighteenth centuries as significant turning points that marked an increase in 'global history'.[3] According to them, the year 1492 – the first time humanity's interconnections assumed global proportions – and 1850 – the second wave of globalisation – are milestones that do deserve a historian's attention. These two dates did not end the debate within the field of world history as to when the process of globalisation began or generated revolutionary transformations: different world historians have taken the position that globalisation was a phenomenon that became significant after 1500 (Jerry Bentley), during the sixteenth century (Immanuel Wallerstein), somewhat before 1500 (Janet Abu-Lughod) or a long time before 1500 (Andre Gunder Frank and Barry Gills). Meanwhile, economic historians have understood the concept of 'globalisation' as 'the integration of international commodity markets'.[4] According to O'Rourke and Williamson this definition of the economic phenomenon of 'globalisation' is in line with 'the way all economists are trained' and places the birth of 'globalisation' somewhere in the nineteenth century.[5]

O'Rourke and Williamson are convinced that economically *significant* globalisation did not start before the nineteenth century no matter how many galleons, junks or caravels sailed between Europe, Asia and the Americas. Just as in the field of world history, the debate has not been resolved in economic history either. Monetary historians with a focus on specie flow such as Dennis Flynn and Arturo Giráldez have rejected the narrow approach of O'Rourke and Williamson.[6] Others, such as G. Balachandran and Sanjay Subrahmanyam, have similarly criticised O'Rourke and Williamson's 'gross caricature of world trade in the sixteenth and seventeenth centuries, which derives entirely from a slanted reading of European trade in the epoch'.[7] In another article Subrahmanyam regrets that economic historians often ignore non-European actors and economic movements, thereby misrepresenting the overall early modern period. As such, O'Rourke and Williamson's evidence places the birth of globalisation 'under the (probably benevolent?) aegis of the British empire'.[8] Rather than proposing yet more landmark dates that could resolve the debate on the birth of globalisation or facilitate the construction of a periodisation of the past 500 years, this chapter examines some insignificant dates. These dates are insignificant in the sense that they do not delineate a historical period. However, the dates are tied to very rich sources, snapshots or keyholes, through which I will write a global micro-history of Jesuit finances in China.[9]

## Snapshots or keyholes to world historical time[10]

My snapshot is taken in 1676. This date is not significant in either the bigger Asian or European history narratives. It is the date or short period – 1674–1676 – that was covered by a Jesuit account book of missions in the southern Chinese province of Jiangnan. I will analyse the local, regional and global elements, and the overall historical context of the account book to improve our understanding of the relationship between local histories and global connections, and to reveal how globalisation may have affected Jesuit missions in China. I argue that although the Jesuits are often portrayed as global avatars with successful methods, knowledge and intercultural sensibilities to organise their distant missions, their finances betrayed a dependence on mostly local economic sources and benefactors.

The account book, written by the Jesuit missionary François de Rougemont (1624–1676), is a keyhole that bears semblance to a high-resolution image. No other sources on Jesuit finances in China match its detail. Nearly all his accounting entries illuminate local and regional interactions, and illustrate the degree to which he was disconnected from the global Jesuit financial network. His records therefore throw light onto the complex local economy and can help us understand that, in the highly monetised economic region of Jiangnan, silver was more pervasive than scholars previously assumed, even among the poorest layers of Chinese society. By reconstructing economic networks, this snapshot and account book of a person with global connections illustrates how de Rougemont balanced his finances thanks to local real estate investments, combined with rent from assets in India and Macau.

Jesuit account books of their missions in China are a rarity. The bibliographical section on Western primary sources of the *Handbook of Christianity in China* includes only three, two in Western languages and one in Chinese.[11] Most Jesuit account books were destroyed upon the author's death because enemies of the Society could use this type of document to critique the Jesuits' management of their financial affairs, which was a very delicate issue. The three that survive seem to have been preserved almost by accident. Each of the sources in Western languages is a draft version of a more complete account book or 'major ledger' that has been lost. The reason François de Rougemont's account book survived was that, after his death, his friend Philippe Couplet, who was a missionary in the nearby Shanghai missions, decided to take it with him when he visited Europe during the early 1680s. Couplet most likely wanted to use it as a propaganda tool to re-emphasise that the missions in China still needed money from rich European benefactors. After that the account book was forgotten only to be unearthed from the archives in 1992, when Noël Golvers, realising the value of this source, deciphered, translated and analysed the manuscript and wrote a thorough study about his findings.[12] De Rougemont's account book is without doubt the most complete and extensive of its kind, consisting of nearly 150 pages of text with over 800 entries that cover his daily expenses and other financial transactions. The manuscript itself is 'a small in-12° codex of 230 single pages (14.8 by 8.5 cm), of Chinese paper'.[13] The manuscript received a new cover when it arrived 'into the collections of the Koninklijke Bibliotheek (Royal Library)' of Brussels. It is relatively well preserved apart from a hole through several pages, its ripped open fold and the fact that just over twenty pages are cut out. Most of the text is written in Latin, Portuguese, Chinese and Dutch.

The account book information was framed within a bifurcated balance of debit and credit. Numbers prevailed and because of their often incomplete and mathematical nature even economists or economic historians have to go through great pains in order to puzzle together their detailed renderings of who owed whom such and such goods and money. Despite this, historians without a knack (or passion) for numbers are often amazed at the information penned down in these Jesuit account books. Perhaps this is because, just like

Indra's net, every entry in an account book was connected to a certain degree. Even the most basic and short account books hinted at a human network (behind the numbers), through which, at the very least, money and goods were exchanging hands. The relationship between two parties was often more entangled than a simple material exchange. Take, for example, the following entry made during April or June 1675: '[. . .] Yam, the great-*hsiang kung* [secretary-catechist], sent me 4 ounces of pure silver – 4.000t. – which were spent to print and bind books, (both) sacred and profane, as for example (*T'ai-hsi*) *shui-fa*.'[14] This entry raises many questions: Was it a regular occurrence for high-class (?) Chinese women to sponsor the Chinese Christian missions? What role did they play in these communities? Did the missionaries often use this type of funding for scientific goals (publishing books)? Was the money given in silver (instead of copper) because the printers would rather accept this currency? Who was the audience of the work – (*T'ai-hsi*) *shui-fa* – published with this grant? How was Yam thanked for her support in the preface to this work? How would Chinese readers relate to this type of benefactress (was she funding scholars or religious misfits)? Account books are lenses into local communities that constituted the tiniest node in a global network. The information they contain magnifies the degree to which its players were all interacting, to such an extent that the assimilated Jesuits and their global religion were sometimes hard to distinguish for being buried so firmly and deeply into the fertile ground of the local communities.

## Global turmoil and local solitude

Of the Jesuit missionaries active in China during the second half of the seventeenth century, François de Rougemont was 'one of the lesser known, eclipsed by such personalities as Ferdinand Verbiest (1623–1688) and Philippe Couplet (1623–1693)'.[15] While Verbiest's work took place in the Chinese high society at the court in Beijing, de Rougemont worked in the Chinese countryside in a local parish. De Rougemont was born on 2 April 1624 in Maastricht. He entered the Antwerp Jesuit college in 1635 and continued his studies in Brussels, Mechlen, Louvain, Courtrai and finally Louvain again until 1654. It took him close to four years to travel from Flanders to Jiangnan, China. He stayed several years in the nearby town of Hangzhou before being sent to the adjacent Suzhou prefecture where he arrived in July 1661. The pastoral centre of this prefecture was Changshu where, after the death of his predecessor Father Girolamo de Gravina (1603–1662), de Rougemont became the head of the Jesuit mission, responsible for the Christian communities of the whole prefecture.

From the moment de Rougemont had expressed interest in the Jesuit China missions in 1654 until his death in 1676, he worked under the auspices of the Portuguese *padroado* or patronage. As such, before leaving Europe, de Rougemont travelled to Portugal since the Portuguese king would sponsor his trip to China and provide him with an annual stipend as well. When the recruiter of Jesuit missionaries Martino Martini (1614–1661) passed through Louvain on his way from northern Europe to Rome (and Portugal) in 1654, he stayed several months in the same Jesuit residence as de Rougemont. De Rougemont was inspired by Martini and requested permission from his superior to join Martini on his way back to China and become a missionary. They left Antwerp in December 1654, and it would take the Jesuit missionaries nearly four years before they reached Macau towards the end of July 1658.

The journey to China was long and arduous. One of the many factors that prolonged their voyage was the disintegrating state of the network of the Portuguese maritime empire. Many travellers never made it to their destination thanks to inter-European competition over maritime trade routes. By 1650, the truce between Portugal and the United Provinces (the Netherlands) was on its last legs and the conflict between these two European powers was about to reach a peak during the next decade. When the first Anglo-Dutch war ended in 1654, the Dutch East India Company (VOC) focussed all its attention on appropriating the remaining nodes of the Portuguese maritime network. They first attacked every Portuguese position on India's east coast, leaving only São Tomé de Meliapor (which was also one of the last Jesuit centres on that coast).[16] After that, the VOC rushed to capture Cochin before the Portuguese state signed another peace treaty with the Netherlands. Cochin was the second most important Portuguese city on India's west coast, the site of the first Portuguese factory in India and the original capital of the Portuguese *estado do India*. It fell to the Dutch in 1663. The Jesuit alliance with the Portuguese made sure that de Rougemont and his fellow fathers destined for China were caught in the middle of this violent handover. Before reaching the Indian Ocean, however, de Rougemont and his group of fellow future missionaries travelled from Belgium to Amsterdam. This is where they met more Jesuits, namely Ignatius Hartogveldt (1629–1658) and George Keynes (1629–1658), who came from the College of English Jesuits in Liège.[17] From here all left for Lisbon in March 1655 on a Swedish ship with a Dutch captain, but just missed the Goa-bound fleet when they arrived in the Portuguese capital in April 1655. This meant they had to wait until spring 1656 for the next passage, so they made good use of this time to learn Portuguese, the *lingua franca* of the East. They finally left Lisbon on 30 March of the next year together with four Portuguese Jesuits and the Polish Jesuit Michal Boym (1612–1659). Boym was on his way back to China after an unsuccessful mission to seek the Pope's assistance for the Southern Ming in their resistance to the new Manchu emperor. However, even though Chinese Christians such as Xu Guangqi and Jesuit missionaries had facilitated the short-term and small-scale deployment of Portuguese gunners defending the Ming dynasty against Manchu raids in the north in the 1620s, no papal assistance could help the Ming by the 1650s. The Manchus conquered the Ming capital in 1644 and pushed the Ming south until they captured the last Ming claimant to the throne in Burma in 1662. The Manchus thus ended the last Han-Chinese dynasty, the Ming (1368–1644), and started China's last (Manchu) dynasty, the Qing (1644–1911). Instead of military support, Boym returned to China with a comforting missive.

The sea voyage to Goa was over in just eight months. Sailing into the port of Goa on 6 November 1656, all nine Jesuits survived the voyage, while seventy out of the 600 other passengers died of either fever or scurvy.[18] The group of Jesuits had overcome this first hurdle without casualties, but soon their luck would run out. First, the collision of Portuguese, Dutch and English interests scattered the international group of Jesuits. A Dutch fleet blocked Goa's port for an entire year. The global turmoil that was about to enclose the Jesuit travellers and send each of them along a different route was devastating. The different paths were so complex that scholars are still not sure who was aboard which ship from Goa onwards. Of the four Portuguese Jesuits only André Gomes (or Gomez) would make it to China. He eventually worked as a missionary in Cambodia, Siam and later Macau where he died in 1681. Father Boym was the most experienced Jesuit of this little cohort and decided to take the most dangerous way out of Goa.[19] As he had been delayed in so many places, Boym was anxious to get back to China to report his failed mission to the Southern Ming, so he boarded a little vessel that tried to sneak through the Dutch blockade. He made it to Siam at the beginning of 1658, where he found out that the authorities in Macau did not want him, a Southern Ming diplomatic envoy, to travel to Macau since they feared the Manchus' revenge if they found out.[20] On a Chinese ship with a Dutch pilot, Boym made it to Tonkin, and from there he managed to enter southern China, only to die before he could get into contact with the fleeing Southern Ming government. The three Belgian Jesuits decided to walk across southern India, so they could board another ship on the east coast that would eventually take them to southeast Asia and from there to Macau. They decided to leave part of their European luggage in the trust of the local British trading post to have it sent to Macau as they walked from Goa to Rajapur, Malabar, Travancore and Pescaria.[21] The luggage would make it just fine through the India-Southeast Asia-China network. Shipped across three different routes, it reached Macau before the surviving Jesuits did.

The major unknown players who affected the Jesuits' travels were the Dutch. When the Belgians made it to the east coast of India, they were cordially received in a Dutch factory before they continued their trip to Tenasserim. De Rougemont fell ill during his walk through India but recovered. In Siam the three Belgians walked from the Gulf of Bengal to the capital of Siam and then further east. The Dutch had blocked the straits of Malacca, but this was not the reason why the group avoided Malacca. The Jesuits stayed with the local VOC representative, Jan de Ryck, in Ayutthaya, capital of Siam, for about eight months and took the overland route instead of a ship to save time.[22] During their stay in the damp forests of Siam, Hartogveldt fell sick and died. From Siam Couplet and de Rougemont left for Macau aboard four Portuguese ships, of which only two arrived safely. The two Jesuit fathers did not travel together on one ship, so they were in luck that precisely their two ships made it to Macau. Keynes, the English Jesuit, was not so fortunate. He boarded an English ship set for the Philippines that sank close to his destination. Out of these nine fathers, only three would live and work as missionaries in China.

Similar Jesuit odysseys during the early seventeenth century confirmed that the toll of traveling along these global connections in turmoil was high. De Rougemont and Couplet ended up working as missionaries side by side – separated by less than 100 kilometres – in China's Jiangnan region for another two decades. While in his 30s, de Rougemont crossed oceans and continents, but once he was in China, his existence became more locally focussed. This is why it is hard to find any of his global connections at all in his account book. Contrary to his earlier global odyssey, de Rougemont's missionary life was isolated from all other European encroachment in Asia. His finances and the keyhole of his account book are such a personal document that rather than allowing us to see the world, they offer a glimpse of the local Chinese economy and the cultural and economic integration of a European missionary.

Missionaries who operated as the sole missionary of a single Christian community would receive a yearly grant of 60 taels[23] offered by their Jesuit superiors in the Japanese province. This money was either of Japanese or 'European' origin and was deposited in Macau. This would have been the first indication of de Rougemont's global finances, money that sometimes had a better chance of making it to its destination than human resources (as seen above, in case of the luggage). However, there was not a single reference to this grant in de Rougemont's account book. This may be due to the incomplete nature of the account book, but I suspect that this money never arrived during the 1670s. While the Jesuit missionaries and their possessions had been tossed around by turmoil in the Indian Ocean and the Southeast Asia region at the end of the 1650s, they were facing more conflict in the 1670s. This time the chaos that surrounded them was even more disruptive in the sense that it disconnected both de Rougemont and Couplet from any communication or financial help that came through southern China. The main reason for this was the eruption of the War of the Three Feudatories in 1673.[24]

Already in 1662, Couplet wrote that he had not received Macau's financial support for the past three years.[25] If Macau was not able to send money northwards into China during times of relative peace, what were the odds of successfully transporting money and other resources across southern China during the next two decades, when one of the bloodiest wars in the history of the early Qing was raging? A decade later, in 1674, Le Faure, a Jesuit working in Shanghai, referred to Macau as the only place whence any support was expected, but that the road was closed and missionaries like himself and de Rougemont were unable to receive their 'financial remedies'. The unrest in the whole of southern China explained then why what we can see through the account book as a keyhole is more local than regional.

## A draft of an account book and the use of silver versus copper

During the seventeenth century China's economy was bi-metallic; both silver and copper were used as monies. Ideally, it would take one sentence to explain the Chinese bi-metallic system of copper coins and silver taels during the late-Imperial period: 1 silver tael was worth 1,000 copper coins. Unfortunately it was not so simple. Inflation was an obvious factor but not the only explanation. Both silver and copper experienced different inflation rates. As for copper, there were different copper coins minted by the state and by private agents, at different times and with varying metallic substances.[26] In addition, the same copper coins' value would even change according to the local market in which the coin was used. Silver, however, was not minted into coins. It was mined domestically at first and later imported from Japan and South America. Silver would be easier to use, were it not for the fluctuations in global bullion flows, inconsistent domestic mining and the fact that, before 1435, silver could not be used to pay taxes in China. However, its popularity and pervasiveness in the Chinese economy gradually rose until, in the mid-sixteenth century, it overran the Chinese economy to such an extent that scholars speak of the Chinese 'silver century'.[27] The changing relationship between silver taels and different copper coins, and the fluctuations in value and availability, make the study of the Chinese monetary system a complex matter.

To track the movements of each currency in every different region over a period of time, exhaustive historical records would be needed. Unfortunately, as stated above, these no longer exist. Once again the study of monetary change over time and place has to be approached through alternative sources to get around the confusion concerning the multiple and coexisting currency circuits. What we do have is an extensive draft of a two-year account book that allows us to study the fluctuating relationship between silver and copper: this economic keyhole can capture exactly what was going on at one specific time, in one specific place.

Normally an account book would not be useful to describe the differences in expenses or receipts in silver and copper money (depending on whether the ledger is a summary or a running tally). The reason for this was that silver was the money of account (besides being an actual currency), which means that all accounting information was jotted down in silver taels, even if the actual expense or receipt had been in a different currency (for example gold, cowries, copper). Until the Jurchen Jin dynasty, c. 1200, copper coins were used as money of account.[28] After 1200, silver replaced copper as a money of account (with the exception of a short regression to copper from 1368 to the 1430s). From the fifteenth century onwards, silver became the standard currency in both public and private finances as an actual currency, besides being the money of account. By the time of de Rougemont's account book, silver would have been the currency used in every entry of his account book. This is also why the entries in every other Jesuit accounting sheet were written down in silver. Given that de Rougemont's account book was only a draft that he planned to copy into the 'great ledger' or official account book of the mission (that had been kept by de Rougemont's predecessor since the mission's start in the beginning of the seventeenth century), his entries were sometimes in silver and sometimes in copper. If the complete account book had survived instead of de

Rougemont's shorter draft version, we would never have been able to examine the intricate texture of the use of copper and silver in his local economy. Because de Rougemont had no time to systematically convert every expense and receipt of copper money and thus transform his draft into the prevailing (yet less grainy) contemporary accounting documents, this keyhole of a global actor is most valuable for peeking into the local Jiangnan economy and its silver and copper currency use.

Since de Rougemont was disconnected from his usual global financial patronage, and passed on most of the silver money he obtained from the Beijing fathers to pay for the expenses of certain Chinese converts, his personal finances were even more sustained by and integrated into the local economy. Additional evidence for his integration was that, even if he had received his yearly stipend (but just did not write it down in his private account book), this money would still have covered only part of his expenses to keep the mission operative. In a letter to the Jesuit General Jean Paul Oliva written on 15 September 1681, Verbiest stated,

> Surely, the yearly subsidy [. . .] does not suffice, so that the missionary could meet for one-third or one-fourth part of the year all these costs with a minimum decorum. Thus the missionaries are often reduced to a condition of extreme poverty.[29]

This letter could be interpreted as a subtle demand for more money from the higher echelons of the Jesuit organisation, but scholars generally agree that the Jesuits working in small-scale China missions were not as rich as their adversaries made them out to be. In the particular case of de Rougemont, Verbiest's estimate was fairly accurate. De Rougemont's annual subsidy from Macau was 60 taels. Golvers calculated (partly on a hypothetical basis) that de Rougemont's total expenses for the year 1675 would have been 231 taels. Golvers knows that de Rougmont's silver and copper income of nine months was 173 taels. De Rougemont did not enter anything during three months, and for this Golvers adds a hypothetical one-third of the previous 173 taels, or 57 taels, to arrive at an estimate of de Rougemont's expenses for the entire year.[30] This extrapolation based upon the expenses entered in the account book confirms Verbiest's estimate. Sixty taels is more or less one-fourth of 231.

As mentioned earlier, Macau paid the annual subsidy. But the communication lines with the south were cut off and no Macau payment was ever mentioned in de Rougemont's account book. Communication through the north was still possible and the account book does contain several references to amounts of silver from the Jesuit fathers stationed in Beijing.[31] All transactions were in silver currency. De Rougemont distributed it to other missionaries and specific Chinese Christians. Whenever de Rougemont gave them money from his own budget, he would immediately note that this sum was later to be reimbursed from the Beijing fathers. The total amount of silver that de Rougemont received from Beijing and from local sources, which are explicitly mentioned in the account book, is 149 taels. Just over 65 per cent of this number had a 'Beijing' source: this meant that either Father Buglio, Father Couplet or an anonymous member of the 'Beijing Fathers' had donated the silver. However, only a fraction of this amount (2.6 taels out of 97.5 taels) was spent by de Rougemont. Most of it was simply handed over to Chinese catechists. As Golvers points out, the silver that came from Beijing was most likely 'distributed, via de Rougemont, to native Christians who were directly and personally responsible for the management of the various Christian parishes'.[32] Does this mean that de Rougemont received similar amounts of silver for his own expenses, which he for some reason does not write down? Unlikely. He would have written this down in his draft account book. Golvers further hypothesises that the Beijing silver could be 'a substitute for a possible missed Macau grant'.[33] We would know if this were the case had de Rougemont included more information on what he personally kept from the Beijing silver (if he kept any at all). What we do know is that over 95 per cent of the silver that de Rougemont spent in his own community and further circulated via expenditures to craftsmen, printers and other Chinese people came from local donations (see Figure 1.1).

Most of the money that de Rougemont was receiving and almost everything he himself spent and circulated came from within the local economy. I do not know why this happened. There is simply not enough information to calculate precisely which silver he used for which purpose. What we do know is that while de Rougemont had travelled extensively to get to his China mission, once he was working in Changshu county, his existence depended on full integration into the local society and economy. Global patronage would pay one-fourth of his actual expenses at best. However, even this money was most likely not delivered during the 1660s and the 1670s. In addition, the silver that he obtained regionally, largely from Beijing, he would pass on to other pastors.

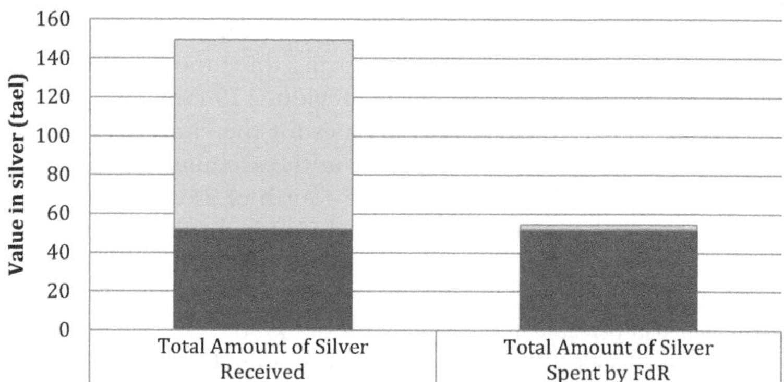


| | Total Amount of Silver Received | Total Amount of Silver Spent by FdR |
|---|---|---|
| Regional Origins | 97.5 | 2.6 |
| Local Origins | 51.9 | 51.9 |

*Figure 1.1* De Rougemont's local and regional income in silver, 1674–1676.

This meant that almost all the silver he did spend, he acquired locally. Therefore, de Rougemont's account book cannot be used to write a history of long-distance connections of Jesuit economies. However, I will use this rich source to offer a new micro-history of China's entangled regional economies and their complicated and ever-changing bi-metallic currencies.

## The pervasiveness of silver in the day-to-day exchanges of Jiangnan's economy

De Rougemont's seventeenth-century account book was not just a snapshot at an arbitrary time or location in Qing China. The time was the heart of the 'Kangxi depression', and the place was China's most vibrant and booming economic region: the Jiangnan basin consisting of the cities of Hangzhou, Suzhou, Changshu and Shanghai. During this time scholars have always assumed that China's bi-metallic economy crumbled under the lack of monies: it regressed. I will question this based upon the information from de Rougemont's source. The next section will first explain the steady rise of silver in Chinese society and then discuss how it eventually tied China's domestic economy to the rest of the world.

## Silver from the Song to the Qing

The transition to a silver economy started during the Song dynasty (960–1279) and gradually changed China's society and economy. The monetary policy of the Chinese state was increasingly losing ground to the forces of the Chinese market. This domestic process of commercialisation intensified during the Song, Yuan and Ming dynasties and sped up even more during the late Ming (1580–1644) when maritime trade, both from other parts of Asia and the rest of the world, reached China and infused the Chinese market with large amounts of foreign silver. This influx of foreign silver reduced sharply during the 1650s due to both global and local conditions. These include a so-called Little Ice Age; the conversion of bi-metallic ratios around the world in 1640; increased conflicts between European maritime empires that disrupted economic activities between Manila, Macau and China; the repeated loss of Manila galleons connecting the Americas and China during the 1640s and 1650s; and restrictions imposed on maritime trade by the new ruling Qing dynasty.[34] Less than ten years later the Chinese economy experienced the 'Kangxi depression', which lasted until 1690. The scholarly disagreement with regard to the precise start date of the depression illustrates that the exact behaviour of silver and its relation to the other money, copper, is difficult to determine. De Rougemont's keyhole could not have picked a better moment to shed light onto this issue.

The academic debate concerning the role of silver on a global scale is no less intense. Many scholars have studied the rising importance of silver and its connection to the concurrent booming commercialisation of the Chinese (and world) economy. Some have tried to explain this evolution with a rather Eurocentric view of the Chinese economy and have pointed out that foreign silver transformed the Chinese domestic economy.[35] They contend that this huge influx financed and fuelled China's commercial development. Richard von Glahn has argued that the transition to a silver economy started before the influx of foreign silver and that the demand for silver by China's domestic market caused the influx of foreign silver.[36] I agree with the latter regarding the specific position of silver in the Chinese and world economies. Some of the evidence supporting this is provided by a local gazetteer – a local history compiled by members of the local elite – of precisely the county in which de Rougemont was active (Changshu). The 1539 local gazetteer of Changshu described the customs of people regarding copper and silver in the section containing the records of food and commerce as follows:

> In past times, the inhabitants of Changshu invariably conducted trade in coin. In those days full-value coins were minted. The people, in accordance with their means, hoarded coin, just as northerners accumulate coin in order to attain wealth. Now, with counterfeiting flourishing throughout the Empire, there is a growing surfeit of coin. Any coins that enter the county are strictly used for buying or selling goods. No one accumulates stocks of coin. People are concerned that coin may be abandoned, and thus will not retain its value.[37]

As the local gazetteer illustrates, people converted their assets that were previously built up in copper coins to something more stable such as silver or silk. In between the time this gazetteer was describing changes in local customs and the time that de Rougemont wrote his draft account book, copper lost its prominence as the main currency while large quantities of silver mined in Japan and South America made their way to China. An oft-cited description was the one the Portuguese merchant Gomes Solis made in the early sixteenth century in his *Discourse on Silver*: 'Silver wanders throughout all the world in its peregrinations before flocking to China, where it remains, as if at its natural centre.'[38] Gomes' rendition was eloquent, but to economic historians the reason why China became the sink in which the silver of the world accumulated was fairly simple: the Chinese market valued silver more highly than anywhere else in the world. In the early sixteenth century, the gold/silver ratio hovered around 1:12 in Europe, 1:10 in Persia, 1:8 in India, and an impressive 1:6 in China.[39] The further the silver 'migrated' east, the more valuable it became. Until 1640, when bi-metallic ratios around the world converged, China's gold/silver ratio was well above the 'international' rate, which caused both contemporary European merchants and modern historians such as Braudel to state that silver was being 'sucked' into China.[40]

This newly available silver currency generated a boost in consumerism and sped up the financial transactions in the economy of highly commercialised areas such as the Jiangnan region (and with it Changshu, the county in which de Rougemont's mission was located). However, the differences between the European and Chinese gold/silver ratio eventually balanced out, and the two-decade-long disturbance that accompanied dynastic change from Ming to Qing in 1644 cut off (or at least severely diminished) the bullion flow into China. The Qing's conquest was not primarily aimed at fighting all maritime trade, but, in an effort to defeat opponents with maritime bases such as the Zheng family, the Qing decided to forcefully evacuate the littoral population of certain southern provinces such as Fujian in an attempt to eliminate their advantage. The Qing also declared a ban on foreign trade that was not lifted until 1684.

This brings us to the second half of the seventeenth century when the Kangxi depression hit the Chinese economy. Silver influx had diminished since the 1640s, and no one is quite sure what happened to the role of silver as a currency in any regional Chinese economy at that time. Silver became scarce; food prices were low, so copper gained in popularity when it came to daily economic exchanges. Silver in turn stopped circulating, since rich merchants and those who had a reserve of silver (such as the Qing government) started hoarding it.[41] As such, Japanese economic historians' ideas of Chinese economic behaviour during this depression (hoarding silver, using copper coins or even bartering) is remarkably similar to an even older paradigm in history that assumed that the Chinese economy was not as advanced as the contemporary European economy in the sense that Chinese people easily regressed to a pre-monetised socio-economic state.[42] Even late-Imperial China historians who have battled and reversed the knowledge of historians who worked under earlier paradigms (with incorrect assumptions such as the one that the Chinese economy was not as monetised or advanced as the Western one) are convinced that silver as a means of exchange left circulation during the 1670s when the depression was most severe.[43] The overall impression is that silver was so scarce that even rich merchants, who had hoarded it in previous years, were slowly losing it and became impoverished.

Based upon the information of de Rougemont's draft of an account book, it is clear that in the Changshu and wider Jiangnan regional economy, the circulation of silver did not stop. If we peek carefully through the keyhole, it is even possible to argue that silver was more pervasive in this regional economy than historians such as Kishimoto and Golvers have concluded. Before looking at the data I have extracted from the account book to support this, I will explain where the line was between the two currencies and for what kind of expenses each currency was used.

## The use of silver in payments above and below one *shi* of rice

Historians drew a line between the use of copper and silver based on a source written by Tang Zhen 唐甄 (1630–1704). Tang kept notes and observations that have provided historians with textual evidence for the assessment of whether or not silver was still in circulation in the early Qing. He noted that the quantity of silver (in circulation) decreased daily and that there was simply not enough silver for daily transactions. Silver was scarce and, as a result, grain and hundreds of other unsold commodities piled up at the market centres in Suzhou.[44] Although Tang Zhen and de Rougemont were contemporaries and even bought their goods in the same markets (Suzhou was less than 50 kilometres from Changshu), there is no reason to suppose that they ever met.

Through the sources that both left, it is clear that both used copper and silver in the same regional circuit, and, though Tang Zhen did not leave an accounting sheet through which we could calculate for what goods he used either currency, he did jot down his opinions on the pros and cons of a bi-metallic economy. Tang Zhen further wrote that 'though cash [copper] is now used, it is only for transactions in fish, meat, fruit and vegetables. For a *shi* of rice and above, or a roll of cloth and above, silver is always used.'[45] The price of a *shi* of rice refers to the actual price of a certain amount of rice, and it can also be read as a symbolic reference to the pervasiveness of silver in the economy of the Yangtze delta. Based upon this reference, scholars such as Kishimoto, Golvers and Brook conclude that daily transactions or small-scale purchases were paid for in copper, whereas un-minted silver was the medium of larger scale purchases such as purchases in bulk (above one *shi* of rice) and luxury products.[46] In the following paragraphs I will show that this generalisation is still useful but may need to be modified slightly in specific regions.

The price for one *shi* of rice in Suzhou in 1669 was between 0.6 and 0.9 tael.[47] Mi Chü Wiens, who worked with the same data as Kishimoto (the *Yue shi bian* 閱世編 written by Ye Mengzhu 葉夢珠, 1624–?), comes to similar prices, namely between 0.9 and 1.3 tael per *shi* during the year 1670, 0.63 tael during the fall of 1673, and 0.73 tael in 1678.[48] Wang Yeh-chien includes values of 0.83 tael per *shi* of rice in 1672 and 0.93 for 1678.[49] Golvers, who calculated the price of rice based upon several entries in the account book, comes to a price of 0.9–1 tael per *shi* of rice.[50] Golvers also calculated the conversion rate between silver and copper from 1674 to 1676: 1 tael was worth 2,500 copper coins, or 1,000 copper coins equalled 0.400 tael. All these scholars conclude that the prices for one *shi* of rice were somewhere between 0.6 and 1 tael.

The depression was draining silver from all layers of society but especially the poor, thus I decided to investigate de Rougemont's interactions with the poorest among his parish first and compare his monetary exchanges with them. Alms or charitable relief to the poor constituted about 5 per cent (more or less 15 taels) of the total amount of expenses noted in the account book.[51] De Rougemont gave these alms to a broad range of people who were poor, sick, physically disabled, female (widowed) or any combination of these factors. I expected all of these entries to be in copper, since even rich merchants no longer dared to use their silver. Of the 60 entries for alms that I encountered, only 19 entries included the alms' receiver, and only three individuals could be clearly identified as Chinese Christians. The smallest amounts were given in copper (30, 40 or 50 coins), but silver was also given in relatively small amounts, such as 1/5 of a tael and even 1/20 of a tael (equal to 125 copper coins). Alms were also given in kind, for example in rice or cotton. Food and clothing would be the most logical item to be distributed among the poor. What is surprising is that 34 of the alms were given in silver, and only 26 of them in copper coins (56 per cent of the number of alms in silver, 43 per cent in copper). I expected all entries to be in copper, since no one was willing to use silver for large or small expenses.

However, if we look at the mean amount of alms in silver that de Rougemont gave to the poor (0.361 tael), then we see that it is well below the price of one *shi* of rice (0.6–1 tael, see Figure 1.2). This average even obscures that 28 of the 34 alms given in silver were amounts below 0.500 tael, and 20 of those were even below 0.200 tael. Without the six entries that were above 0.500 tael, the average was 0.260 tael. The poor people who received de Rougemont's silver probably used most of this silver to buy daily necessities, since several of the entries explicitly state that these poor people were in grave need. If de Rougemont gave them silver, this indicates that these poor people could effectively buy something with this silver; it is unlikely that this financial help was similar to handing over a bar of gold to a homeless person. Instead de Rougemont gave them lots and lots of (silver) change. De Rougemont himself was yet another link in the circulation chain: he got the silver he spent from local sources (he was disconnected from Macau and did not spend the silver he received from Beijing himself), and he was not afraid to donate (thus circulate) it to other people as well.

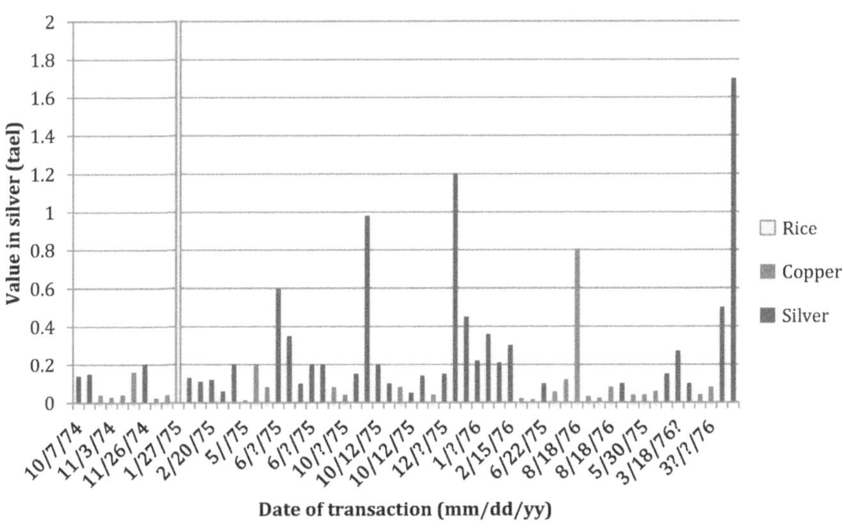


*Figure 1.2* Alms given in silver, copper and rice.

Apart from this category of 'very poor people', de Rougemont had several other categories of expenses that involved specifically lower-class people. In interactions with common people such as bearers, the data of the account book confirm Tang Zhen's assessment of the use of copper and silver. The majority of times de Rougemont paid the bearers for their services such as carrying his sedan chair or luggage (30 of the 36 entries) in copper. This suggests that daily wages were paid in coin. In contrast, work on a seasonal or annual basis was paid in silver.[52] Most of the payments in silver were entered towards the end of the account book. However, it would be too hasty to conclude that a gradual change of currency occurred. Copper may have prevailed as the most popular currency to pay for this specific interaction, but again all the amounts of silver were below 0.250 tael. The silver payments were made in much smaller quantities than what one would expect from Tang Zhen's remarks.

Another daily expenditure that was entered 55 times in the account book was the distribution of tips (called *xam fum*, *shang feng* 賞封) or monetary rewards that were given to a social inferior.[53] One would expect these data to comply with the daily wages of the bearers, in the sense that these were daily expenses paid out to a worker or server. Only in 19 entries was the word 'servant' (domestic or not), 'skipper', 'clerk' and 'workmen' entered, but several other entries indicate that some sort of service had been performed in order to receive the tip (see Figure 1.3). Slightly more tips were distributed in copper than in silver (30 versus 25), but again over half of the silver tips (16 of the 25) were distributed in amounts less than 0.270 tael, and five of the nine tips that were above this amount (corresponding to the 0.450, 1.325, 0.980, 0.400 and 0.700 tael) were in fact given out for various combined tips, or combined with other services. Including the combo-tips mentioned above, the mean amount of silver given was 0.394 tael.[54]

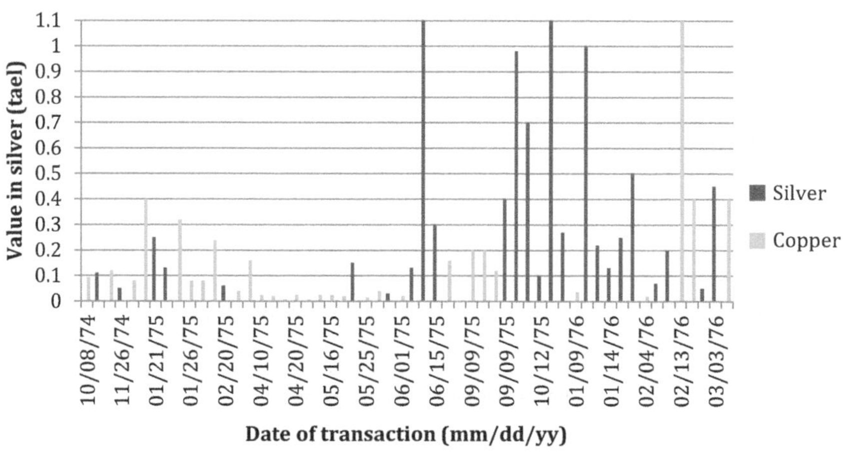


*Figure 1.3* Tips given in silver and copper.

A last daily expenditure that exposed the pervasiveness of silver in the regional economy was the distribution of travel money and the fares that de Rougemont paid for his – and converts' – many journeys to the different cities and villages of the lower Yangtze area. Most of de Rougemont's fares were paid in copper (seventeen copper entries versus nine silver). In six of the seven times de Rougemont entered the cost of the fare between Changshu and Suzhou it was in copper, with an average cost of 253 copper coins (or converted in silver: 0.101 tael).[55] Only once did de Rougemont pay in silver, an amount of 0.300 tael, which is exactly three times the usual fare. As Golvers suspects, this could represent the fare of three persons.[56] This would indicate that the skipper who received the money of the fare dealt in both currencies and was accustomed to accepting fares in silver and copper. Of the nine fares that de Rougemont paid for in silver, six involved a journey to Hangzhou. Since Hangzhou was outside of de Rougemont's local circuit, it made sense to pay in silver, as copper coins were tied to their local currency circuits (whereas silver transcended these boundaries more easily).

In contrast to the fares, the quantity and type of 'travel money' that de Rougemont distributed to converts and other Chinese for regional travel indicates the pervasiveness of silver in this expense category (nineteen entries in silver, five in copper). On no less than six occasions, travel money for Nanjing or Hangzhou was distributed in silver currency. However, silver was also used for destinations within the regional market in which de Rougemont and his converts were operating (such as Suzhou, Chongde, Taicang and Shanghai). It is also significant that certain silver payments for travel money were in amounts as low as 0.060 tael. All this evidence supports the claim that silver was preferred over copper to pay for fares and donations of travel money within and outside the regional market. Local skippers were able to make transactions and receive payments in both currencies, accepting amounts of silver below one *shi* of rice (0.6–1 tael).

## Conclusion: copper and silver, Jesuit and Chinese sources

Besides de Rougemont's draft of an account book, there are several Chinese contemporary sources that discuss the Jiangnan regional economy as well. From the Ming onwards, the socio-economic changes that occurred in Jiangnan have fascinated Chinese, Japanese and Western scholars, and an entire generation of China historians has used the abundance of sources on the Jiangnan region to refute earlier notions of 'Chinese stagnation'. Looking at both Chinese sources – such as Tang Zhen's and Ye Mengzhu's comments on the changing role of silver in economy – and Western sources – such as de Rougemont's account book – allows us to view a more diverse picture of the use of copper and silver in that regional economy. By setting side-by-side information on the role of copper and silver from both sources, it becomes clear that silver could be used on an everyday basis, despite being 'a primitive, indeed regressive form of money', that 'constituted a mediocre instrument of exchange'.[57] I agree that this is a correct assessment at the dawn of the age of silver in the fifteenth and early sixteenth centuries, but at the time of the early Qing in the regional market of Changshu, the main focus of this chapter, many external factors influenced the use of silver and copper. In an economic crisis, the use of either silver or copper may have been random depending on what type of currency the buyer had at hand. It may not always be true that silver was used for expenses well above one *shi* of rice. Perhaps the transaction costs involved in using silver currency – it was still uncoined, so it had to be cut with special scissors – and the cumbersome measurement of its weight and purity were not as serious an impediment as assumed earlier.[58]

In comparing Chinese and Western sources one last note on the historical context of Tang Zhen's source is of importance. As Kishimoto acknowledges, Tang Zhen was not just a radical thinker but also a member of an 'anti-silverist group'. Tang Zhen was opposed to the accumulation of wealth and actively promoted the abolition of silver as a currency. In his opinion it would have been better to use copper since 'like a fountain, [it would] never be exhausted'. Out of concern for the wellbeing of society, Tang Zhen tried to help by promoting the interests of the anti-silver lobbying group of which he was a member. Tang's background and his perceptions of how the Chinese Confucian elite could remedy the disorder caused by rising commercialism dictated the way he thought people ought to use silver and copper.[59] De Rougemont's accounting draft or keyhole does not necessarily adjust our understanding of whether silver was used only for expenses above one *shi* of rice or not. To do so, more account books or other similar sources that comment on monetary affairs during the early Qing are needed, preferably covering multiple regions in combination with an interval of dates that could help us understand the development and waves of monetary cycles before, during and after the Kangxi depression. However, using de Rougemont's account book as an example, I do believe that an approach that uses Jesuit sources and seeks ways to contextualise them can add something to our understanding of the global economy and its many players and to the specific socio-economic interactions of a very local setting. In this case, de Rougemont's account book elucidates the complexity of China's bi-metallic economies in one specific region during the 1670s. This way world history – and a historical source such as the account book of a missionary who has travelled far and wide – has the ability to engage at a deep level with local history.

## Notes

1 T. Brook, *Vermeer's Hat: The Seventeenth Century and the Dawn of the Global World* (Toronto: Penguin, 2008), p. 123.

2 Brook, *Vermeer's Hat*, p. 8.

3 P. Stearns, *Globalization in World History: Themes in World History* (New York: Routledge, 2010); R. Robertson, *The Three Waves of Globalization: A History of a Developing Global Consciousness* (London: Zed Books, 2003).

4 K. O'Rourke and J. Williamson, 'When Did Globalisation Begin?', *European Review of Economic History*, 6 (2002), p. 25.

5 K. O'Rourke and J. Williamson, 'Once More: When Did Globalisation Begin?', *European Review of Economic History*, 8 (2004), p. 109.
6 D. O. Flynn and A. Giráldez, 'Path Dependence, Time Lags and the Birth of Globalisation: A Critique of O'Rourke and Williamson', *European Review of Economic History*, 8 (2004), pp. 81–108.
7 G. Balachandran and S. Subrahmanyam, 'On the History of Globalization and India: Concepts, Measures and Debates', in J. Assayag and C. J. Fuller (eds.), *Globalizing India: Perspectives from Below* (London: Anthem Press, 2005), p. 19.
8 S. Subrahmanyam, 'Historicizing the Global, or Labouring for Invention?', *History Workshop Journal*, 64 (2007), p. 330.
9 I have borrowed the concept of global micro-histories from Tonio Andrade and Sugata Bose. Andrade points out that world historians have 'made great strides building powerful models of global historical structures and processes: global silver flows, strange parallels, divergences great and small'. However, these great social scientific models tend to ignore people. Andrade believes that we 'should adopt microhistorical and biographical approaches to help populate our models and theories'. T. Andrade, 'A Chinese Farmer, Two African Boys, and a Warlord: Toward a Global Microhistory', *Journal of World History*, 21:4 (2011), pp. 573–91. Bose's approach similarly aims 'to avoid the high degree of abstraction that characterises so much of global, oceanic, interregional and comparative histories in which real human beings and their agency vanish from view'. S. Bose, *A Hundred Horizons: The Indian Ocean in the Age of Global Empire* (Cambridge: Harvard University Press, 2006), pp. 22–23. Besides my enthusiasm for Andrade's and Bose's rationalisations for a global micro-history approach, I use the concept of global micro-histories because it incorporates and defines both sides of globalisation: its limits and its extent.
10 T. Brook, 'Time and Global History', *Globalizations*, 6:3 (2009), p. 381.
11 N. Standaert (ed.), *Handbook of Christianity in China, Volume One: 635–1800* (Leiden: Brill, 2001), pp. 290–93.
12 N. Golvers, *François de Rougemont, S.J.: Mission in Ch'ang-Shu (Chiang-Nan): A Study of the Account Book (1674–1676) and the Elogium* (Leuven: Leuven University Press, 1999). I would like to thank Dr Golvers for introducing me to this source.
13 Golvers, *François de Rougemont, S.J.*, p. 31.
14 Golvers, *François de Rougemont, S.J.*, p. 237.
15 Golvers, *François de Rougemont, S.J.*, pp. 3–18.
16 D. Alden, *The Making of an Enterprise: The Society of Jesus in Portugal, Its Empire and Beyond, 1540–1750* (Stanford: Stanford University Press, 1996), p. 188.
17 Hartogveldt wrote a journal on this trip from Amsterdam to Lisbon. Museum Plantin-Moretus (MPM), Ms. 269. P. Demaerel, 'Couplet and the Dutch', in J. Heyndrickx (ed.), *Philippe Couplet, S.J. (1623–1693): The Man Who Brought China to Europe* (Nettetal: Steyler Verlag, 1990), pp. 91–94.
18 N. Standaert, 'The Jesuit Presence in China (1580–1773): A Statistical Approach', *Sino-Western Cultural Relations Journal (SWCRJ)*, XII (1991), p. 5; F. A. Plattner, *Jesuits Go East* (Dublin: Clonmore and Reynolds, 1950), p. 108.
19 P. Pelliot, 'Michel Boym', *T'oung Pao*, 31 (1935), pp. 95–151.
20 Pelliot, 'Michel Boym', p. 131. According to Plattner, Boym embarked on an English ship in Goa, perhaps together with Keynes, and set sail for Burma. In this case the Jesuit party split up in Burma rather than in Goa. Plattner, *Jesuits Go East*, p. 108.
21 Golvers, *François de Rougemont*, p. 15.
22 Plattner, *Jesuits Go East*, p. 109; Golvers, *François de Rougemont*, pp. 16–17.
23 The tael consisted of 37.3 grams of silver, with a ranging fineness. See H. U. Vogel, 'Chinese Central Monetary Policy, 1644–1800', *Late Imperial China*, 8:2 (1987), p. 5.
24 This suspicion is put forward by Noël Golvers.
25 Golvers, *François de Rougemont*, p. 587.
26 A. Kuroda, 'Copper Coins Chosen and Silver Differentiated: Another Aspect of the "Silver Century" in East Asia', *Acta Asiatica*, 88 (2005), pp. 65–86.

27 R. von Glahn, *Fountains of Fortune: Money and Monetary Policy in China, 1000–1700* (Berkeley: University of California Press, 1996), chapter 4.
28 R. von Glahn, 'Monies of Account and Monetary Transition in China from the Twelfth to Fourteenth Centuries', *Journal of the Economic and the Social History of the Orient JESHO*, 53:3 (2010), p. 464.
29 Golvers, *François de Rougemont*, p. 588; H. Josson and L. Willaert (eds.), *Correspondance de Ferdinand Verbiest de la Compagnie de Jésus (1623–1688) directeur de l'observatoire de Pékin* (Brussels: Palais des académies, 1938), p. 354.
30 Golvers, *François de Rougemont*, p. 596; ARSI, JapSin 145, ff. 41–44: letter from Ferdinand Verbiest to Jean Paul Oliva, Beijing September 15, 1681. '[. . .] non sufficit ut missionarius haec omnia cum aliquo decore per tertiam aut quartam anni partem sustineat.'
31 Account book, p. 201, p. 166, p. 154, p. 150 and p. 12.
32 Golvers, *François de Rougemont*, p. 589.
33 Golvers, *François de Rougemont*, p. 589.
34 A. Giraldez, *The Age of Trade: The Manila Galleons and the Dawn of the Global Economy* (London: Rowman and Littlefield, 2015), chapter 4. The precise point at which the influx of silver declined is under debate.
35 For example, W. Atwell, 'Notes on Silver, Foreign Trade, and the Late Ming Economy', *Ch'ing-shih wen-t'i*, 3:8 (1977), pp. 1–33; W. Atwell, 'International Bullion Flows and the Chinese Economy circa 1530–1650', *Past and Present*, 95 (1982), pp. 68–90.
36 von Glahn, *Fountains of Fortune*, chapter 7.
37 von Glahn, *Fountains of Fortune*, p. 103; Kuroda, 'Copper Coins Chosen and Silver Differentiated', p. 70. Changshu xianzhi (Gazetteer of Changshu County), 1539, 4.15b.
38 Cited in V. Magalhães-Godinho, *L'économie de l'empire portugais aux XVe et XVIe siècles* (Paris: S.E.V.P.E.N., 1969), p. 531.
39 von Glahn, *Fountains of Fortune*, p. 127. This gap in regional ratios closed by the middle of the seventeenth century.
40 F. Braudel, *Civilization and Capitalism, 15th–18th Century*, vol. 3 (London: Collins, 1981), p. 490.
41 M. Kishimoto, 'The Kangxi Depression and Early Qing Local Markets', *Modern China*, 10:2 (1984), pp. 227–56. See also M. Kishimoto, 'On the Fluctuation of the Price of Rice in the Chiang-nan Region During the First Half of the Ch'ing Period (1644–1795)', *Memoirs of the Research Department of the Toyo Bunko (The Oriental Library)*, 37 (1979), pp. 56–90.
42 M. Weber, *The Religion of China: Confucianism and Taoism*, trans. H. H. Gerth, intr. C. K. Yang (New York: Macmillan, 1964).
43 M. Kishimoto and T. Brook do not share the exact same opinion on this matter. Brook sees the withdrawal of silver as partial to certain regions, without a serious impact on local economies. He has yet to publish his findings. See personal correspondence March 2012.
44 Kishimoto, 'The Kangxi Depression', p. 231. This observation matches up with a popular idea amongst economic historians that the size and number of economic transactions within an economy is dependent upon the quantity of money available. If silver was not available, people would use copper or barter, or goods would simply not sell.
45 1 shi = 10 dou = more or less 100 litres. For a discussion on the shi as measure for rice, see H. Chuan and R. Kraus, *Mid-Ch'ing Rice Markets and Trade: An Essay in Price History* (Cambridge: Harvard University Press, 1975), p. 62 and pp. 79–99.
46 Kishimoto, 'On the Fluctuation of the Price of Rice', p. 62; Golvers, *François de Rougemont*, p. 563; Brook, 'The Fall of the Ming and the Price of Grain: A Simple Correlation?' (unpublished, February 2008), p. 5.
47 Kishimoto, 'On the Fluctuation of the Price of Rice', p. 68.
48 M. Chü Wiens, 'Cotton Textile Production and Rural Social Transformation in Early Modern China', *Xianggang Zhongwen daxue Zhongguo wenhua yanjiusuo xuebao [The Journal of the Institute of Chinese Studies of the Chinese University of Hong Kong]*, 7:2 (1974), p. 531.

49 Wang Yeh-chien in T. G. Rawski and L. M. Li (eds.), *Chinese History in Economic Perspective* (Berkeley: University of California Press, 1991), p. 40.
50 Golvers, *François de Rougemont*, p. 610.
51 Golvers, *François de Rougemont*, p. 314.
52 I would like to thank Richard von Glahn for making this very valuable comment.
53 Golvers, *François de Rougemont*, p. 330.
54 During the months of April and May 1675 de Rougemont was travelling in Hangzhou and systematically exchanged silver for copper coins to pay all his expenses. Towards the end of the account book de Rougemont paid slightly more often in silver than in copper. Whereas throughout the entire account book both currencies are intermingled, Golvers noted the same two deviations. See Golvers, *François de Rougemont*, p. 562. Golver also calculated that of the '818 monetary indications (divided over 806 separate entries), 478 or 58.44 per cent are expressed in silver, and 340 or 41.56 per cent in copper'.
55 On several occasions de Rougemont entered the price of an article in both silver and copper. As Golvers pointed out, 'Such unexpected internal proof is found in the price for the fare ("naulum") for the distance between Changshu and Suzhou, as a rule set at about 250 copper coins or 0.100 tael.' Golvers, *François de Rougemont*, p. 565. This also explains why Golvers opted for a silver/copper exchange rate of 1,000 copper coins: 0.400 silver tael.
56 Golvers, *François de Rougemont*, p. 609.
57 von Glahn, *Fountains of Fortune*, p. 83.
58 Von Glahn agrees with this assessment. He also commented that later evidence does show that whenever coin was available in sufficiently abundant quantities (bronze coin in the mid-eighteenth century and Spanish pesos in the late eighteenth century), there still was a decisive preference for using coin over sycee silver, and this preference was surely related to the transaction cost problem.
59 For more information on the Chinese elite's reaction to the upcoming consumerism during the fifteenth and sixteenth centuries, see T. Brook, *The Confusions of Pleasure: Commerce and Culture in Ming China* (Berkeley: University of California Press, 1998).

# 2 'But whatever were the honey in the mouth of that beast of trade, there was a deadly sting in the tail'

## New Netherland's monetary policy and the Coastal Algonquian pragmatic response during the seventeenth century

*Mario Schmidt*

The sentence cited in this chapter's title is taken from William Hubbard's *A General History of New England* (1680) and the phrase 'beast of trade' refers to the beaver that, in Hubbard's assessment, caused many of North America's seventeenth-century disasters. For the historian, it is clear that the European fancy for beaver hats had

> brought our people to the knowledge of *wampampeag* [small white and violet shell beads]; and the acquaintance therewith occasioned the Indians of these parts to learn the skill to make it, by which, as by the exchange of money, they purchased stores of artillery.[1]

Hubbard sketches out a simple causal chain here: as a consequence of their 'beaver fever', the Europeans' interest in Native Americans gained traction, which triggered the production of sewant (*wampumpeag*),[2] with which the Indians procured weapons that they subsequently used to cause trouble in the English colonies. This chapter attempts to test Hubbard's argument in a historically and geographically related context: the colony of New Netherland. By focussing on the intricate relation between New Netherland's adoption of sewant and beaver as legal tender and the colony's economic decline, it analyses the political authorities' oscillation between mercantilist dogma and economic liberalisation on the one hand, and the relations between the colony's downfall and Coastal Algonquian pragmatic approaches to money on the other.

After carving out how sewant was adopted as currency and appropriated as a cornerstone of New Netherland's monetary system, I demonstrate that the liberalisation of New Netherland's economy had changed how colonists, political authorities of the West India Company (WIC)[3] and merchants perceived and dealt with money. These changes did not only fuel conflicts between Native Americans and New Netherlanders, as Hubbard's hypothesis would suggest, but also between richer and poorer segments of the colonial society. The following analysis of diverse and contradictory strategies of dealing with this intricate situation suggests that, in the wake of the economic liberalisation, money had suddenly become a *political problem* for the colonial authorities, which they, as mercantilists, believed could be solved by introducing new laws. These laws, judicially implemented from the 1640s until the surrender of the Dutch colony to the English in 1664, were, however, unable to reconcile the contradictory notions of money circulating: while the company's merchants understood money as a *form of capital*, many colonists considered it as a *prosaic lubricant*, a mere tool of getting on with daily life.

The examination of these different understandings of money circulating in the colonial society sets the stage for a cross-cultural comparison arguing that Native Americans, in this case the Coastal Algonquian, who are too often still perceived as economically illiterate lovers of gewgaws and reciprocity,[4] might have had competitive advantages due to their more flexible and pragmatic understanding of the role of money in an economy.[5] I will, therefore, conclude by suggesting that, while the Dutch authorities considered money as a *political problem*, the Coastal Algonquian perceived it as an *economic opportunity*.

## Mercantilist projection – introducing sewant as legal tender

While everyday economic transactions in the seventeenth-century Dutch Republic were based on trust,[6] social relations between New Netherlanders and Native Americans were initially not characterised by mutual understanding. The leaders of the Dutch colony, however, assumed that they could rely on something else: the certainty that even uneducated Native Americans, called *wilden* ('savages') by early Dutch explorers and politicians, would use a medium of exchange in which their religious, economic and cultural values were enmeshed and which therefore, from their perspective, possessed the highest intrinsic value of all objects. Although in principle agreeing with the judgement that 'wild' people do neither have a king, a law nor a faith ('*ni roi, ni loi, ni foi*'), they considered it inevitable that the Native Americans possessed some form of money whose value was based upon the value of the scarce material of which it was made. In other words: they were sure that the 'savages' were also mercantilists, merely mercantilists with a different type of species – in this case not silver, but sewant.

As this expectation was further enforced by what Dutch explorers had learned by experience in other parts of the world, it is not surprising that it seemed obvious for the secretary of the colony, Isaack de Rasiere, to close the gap of trust between the Indigenous population and the Dutch settlers by introducing an object, which, due to its objectively high value, could mediate economic exchanges and make them more predictable. In a letter to the Amsterdam Chamber of the WIC, dated 23 September 1626, de Rasiere reported that he had sold 'beads' to the colonists, '[. . .] because they [. . .] can buy for them from the Indians maize, fish, and various other things'.[7] These beads, most probably sewant, fulfilled all requirements of a medium of exchange. They were durable, partible, and at least initially quite rare, accepted by the Native Americans and had low transportation costs. Taking into account these advantages, it is not surprising that the Dutch colonists themselves appropriated sewant as currency and thereby attempted to solve the problem of having no coins.[8]

While the New Netherlanders used sewant almost exclusively as a medium of exchange, it was employed for a variety of purposes in Coastal Algonquian societies during colonial times. They used it as payment for religious specialists, as bride-wealth and blood-money, deposited it in graves, exchanged the beads in transactions with Europeans and displayed sewant in the form of nicely strung ornaments symbolising the authority of their political leaders (*sachem*).[9] Although the absence of sewant could therefore definitely threaten the success of any transaction throughout seventeenth-century Northeastern Woodlands, it is necessary to acknowledge that many Native Americans just viewed it as one among many suitable trade goods. Reverend Jonas Michaëlius, first minister of the colony, enumerated some of these goods in a letter dating 11 August 1628: '[. . .] wares, such as knives, beads, and the like, or seewan [. . .]'[10] to which bread, gun powder, beer, cloth and others could be added. Although the data in the account books analysed by the Dutch scholar Kees-Jan Waterman cover a different geographic area and time span (an area around Albany in the years 1695–1726), they confirm this impression: only 1.2 per cent of the transactions in the account books include sewant.[11] Although sewant was thus sought after by many, it might not have been an unparalleled and unique medium of cross-cultural exchange as often claimed.

I therefore suggest that it was not only as a consequence of the Native Americans' demand that sewant became a valuable medium of exchange between colonists and Native Americans and between colonists themselves, but also because it materially resembled currencies with which the Dutch had become acquainted in other inter-cultural situations, and because it lacked a precise use-value in the Coastal Algonquian societies. What I try to indicate is that the Dutch mercantilist fantasy that people all over the world needed a currency similar to their own was more influential for the rise of sewant than the Native American belief in its inherent and superior value. The credibility of the Dutch assumption might have been reinforced further by the fact that Dutch merchants were sure to make the bargain of their life by receiving valuable beaver for valueless beads. However, it is well known and epitomised in the following quote that Native Americans were analogically assuming that they were receiving valuable knives, weapons and kettles for valueless beaver:

> I heard my host say one day, jokingly, Missi picoutau amiscou, 'The Beaver does everything perfectly well, it makes kettles, hatchets, swords, knives, bread; and, in short, it makes everything.' He was making sport of us

> Europeans, who have such a fondness for the skin of this animal and who fight to see who will give the most to these Barbarians, to get it; they carry this to such an extent that my host said to me one day, showing me a very beautiful knife, 'The English have no sense; they give us twenty knives like this for one Beaver skin.'[12]

Before I can shed further light on the historical development of sewant's role in the colony's economic system, it is necessary to outline this system more abstractly. It will become clear that it was not the Native American demand for sewant that secured the stability of the value of the colony's main medium of exchange, but the mercantilist fur trade monopoly.

## New Netherland's mercantilist currency system and its relation to the fur trade monopoly

While the colonial authorities and settlers of New Netherland used the Dutch *gulden* as the unit of account, the main medium of exchange for small and interethnic transactions was sewant, which was also used to pay employees of the WIC as well as for promissory notes and IOUs. Apart from circulating internally (by being exchanged among colonists),[13] sewant also circulated externally (by being bartered for beaver and other goods).[14] Due to their unhandiness, indivisibility and high value, beaver pelts served as a medium of exchange in transactions involving more expensive objects. Furthermore, they were used to redeem accumulated debts. At first glance, it seems that such a dual currency system must be inherently volatile because fluctuations in one currency could easily lead to a *de facto* demonetisation of one of the two currencies in case people would collectively withhold the more valuable currency and/or reject payment in the less valuable one. This threat was even more severe in the present case of the Dutch colony whose political authorities never endogenously controlled the money supply.[15]

In combination with the strong position of the political sovereign and a small and easy-to-govern settler population, the fur trade monopoly, however, assured that the monetary system operated smoothly for several years.[16] By legally binding colonists to sell their beaver pelts to the WIC at rates considerably below their real value, the profit rate of people engaging in the beaver trade could be kept at such a low level that the company's profitability was never endangered.[17] At the same time, the company's authority over the value of beaver, achieved by political force, the pillar of any mercantilist doctrine, enabled it to politically control the exchange rate between the two currencies and thereby to stabilise the value of sewant regardless of the latter's amount. Even if the amount of sewant had suddenly increased, it would have made no sense to resort to beaver pelts in daily transactions as these could only be sold for a price, probably paid in sewant, which was fixed by the company.

The monetary system thereby not only fulfilled economic purposes but, at least initially, disguised an important difference between the ways merchants and colonists understood money: while the first depended on sewant being 'invested' as a *commodity* in inter-cultural exchanges, the second used it as a *lubricant* for the facilitation of everyday exchanges such as the purchase of beer, bread and other necessities. As will be shown in the next two sections, it was the abandonment of the fur trade monopoly that laid bare the contradiction between these two understandings of sewant and made it impossible for the colonial authorities to continue to balance between them. Although it had been relatively easy to politically inhibit the sale of beaver pelts to agents apart from the WIC, it turned out to be impossible to coerce people to accept a fixed exchange rate between beaver and sewant as soon as people were permitted to barter beaver according to its real value.

## Economic liberalisation, political democratisation and fetishisation of the beaver

Partly as a response to emerging political demands for democratisation, the WIC opened the fur trade to all colonists in 1640 and thereby not only disentangled political influence and economic interests, but also destabilised the currency system. Although the authorities did not abandon the fixed exchange rate between sewant (now a commodity independently exchanged against beavers by any *burgher* of the colony) and beaver *de jure*, sewant immediately began to be bartered below its legal value. The exchange rate *de facto* became a floating one. The economic liberalisation thereby led to an increase of the nominal value of the beaver and a decrease of sewant exchange value. The level of inflation can be roughly estimated by looking at the actual quantity of beads exchanged for a beaver pelt. It rose from 960 white beads in 1656 to 1,920 in 1659 to 2,560 in late 1660; compound inflation rates of 25.99 per cent for the three years from 1656 and 27.79 per cent for the four years to 1660.[18] This inflationary process was, however, already well underway much earlier as the following letter of a colonist dating from 17 December 1649 exemplifies:

> We, who have come to New Netherland, are unfortunate men, for it grows from bad to worse. [. . .] poor people have scarcely enough to eat, for no supplies of bread, butter, beef and pork can now be had, except for beaver or silver coin.[19]

These disturbances of the everyday economy led to three independent but related re-evaluations of the media circulating in the monetary sphere: money became (1) a political problem for the colonial authorities because (2) sewant had lost its ability to mediate everyday transactions. The small beads no longer functioned as the prosaic lubricant on which colonists depended. On the contrary, it became more and more common to increase the sewant price of goods or even to decline payments in sewant. At the same time, however, more and more colonists attempted to legally enforce their right to pay outstanding debts in sewant instead of beaver.[20] These internal disputes about repaying debts, triggered by the vicious circle of sewant devaluation and appreciation of beaver pelts, created an atmosphere of civil disorder. It was indeed a situation in which what the nineteenth-century economic historian William Weeden had named the 'magnet'[21] of capital accumulation had become 'villainous'[22] as the WIC Directors called wampum in a letter – dated 22 December 1659 – to Petrus Stuyvesant, director of the colony from 1647 to 1664. Although everybody wanted to pay with sewant, nobody wanted to accept it.

All this led to (3) a concentration on participating in the beaver trade that encompassed all members of society. If somebody wanted to remain able to buy the daily necessities, the individual was suddenly coerced to understand sewant as a commodity to be invested in the beaver trade. The difference between money as capital and money as a prosaic lubricant had dissolved. As a consequence of this development, the ability to 'earn one's beaver' was elevated, albeit only rhetorically, to a 'civil right' by the *geemenen handelaers* (common traders) of Fort Orange in a petition dating 17 June 1660.[23] This equation is an apt expression of the emerging democratic demands and simultaneously a sign of the deteriorating economic situation, which not only led more and more people to focus on obtaining beaver, but created and exacerbated antagonistic feelings between the rich and the poor, between wealthier merchants (*principaelste handelaers*) and all colonists who, in one way or the other, aimed at profiting from participating in the beaver trade.

The ongoing inflation of sewant, allegedly the Native's gold, the ongoing concentration on beaver, doubtlessly the new New Netherlander's gold, and the fact that the WIC paid its employees in sewant, whose nominal value was much higher than its real value, had thus endangered the political legitimacy of the colony and led to a mutual reinforcement of monetary destabilisation and loss of political sovereignty. This intricate situation is the background of the political authorities' introduction of new laws concerning the colony's currency system that are explored in the next section.

## Squaring the circle – money as a political problem, a lubricant or capital?

A radical solution to solve the problems of the currency system would have been the issuing of some form of fiat money. As this option would have presupposed a complete abandonment of the belief in the necessity of an intrinsic, natural value of specie, a fundamental belief of mercantilist dogma, the implemented laws oscillated between the three following options:

- Commoditise sewant and introduce a system solely based on credit and beaver. This option would have favoured the richer inhabitants of the colony who were controlling the fur trade.
- Re-arrange the rate between sewant and *gulden* in accordance with the prevalent economic situation and thereby act *de jure* after market pressures had changed the economic situation *de facto*. This option would have affected merchants possessing huge amounts of sewant as well as small-scale

savers. It would further have been tantamount to a confession of the political impotence of the colony's authorities.

- Force people to accept overpriced sewant and/or introduce fixed prices for specific commodities, thereby favouring poorer colonists and employees of the WIC.

While the authorities had initially attempted to re-arrange the rate in accordance with the economic situation,[24] the ordinances of 5 June 1651 and 19 December 1653 employed a harsher tone and fixed the sewant prices of both locally produced (for example, bread, wine and beer) and imported commodities (for example, soap, salad oil, candles, nails and cloth).[25] Despite these measures the authorities, in the ordinance of 3 January 1657, still noted that 'some greedy people do not hesitate to sell the most necessary eatables and drinkables'[26] for an amount above the official exchange rate and hence felt obliged to once more instruct craftsmen and shopkeepers to accept the rate. The ordinances that followed[27] are awkwardly ambiguous, probably a sign of growing uncertainty and helplessness – the faith in the political controllability of money was obviously on the wane. The ordinance of 11 November 1658, for instance, demonetised sewant for transactions above the value of 24 *gulden* and reduced its value for transactions below this amount.[28] This 'solution', an introduction of a dual exchange rate system inside of a dual currency system, exacerbated confusion and furthermore was difficult to govern. As Johan de Deckere, New Netherland's supervisor of finance, noted, it would lead to 'the absurdity and contradiction, [. . .] that sewant is declared a commodity at one place, and at another place sewant as money is reduced in its value'.[29]

This oscillation between inconsistent strategies allows for two conclusions. First, it exemplifies a lack of a clear political agenda. Instead of either protecting poorer colonists who perceived sewant as a thing that helped them living their lives or favouring merchants who exploited sewant's ability to serve as a form of investment, the authorities continuously attempted to reconcile these contradictory goals. Second, and more fundamentally, they ignored that the economic reality of the colony could no longer be influenced by non-economic actors at least since the liberalisation of the economy had been accomplished. Petrus Stuyvesant and the directors in Amsterdam failed to realise that their strategies were bound to remain futile without a deliberate re-establishment of the former politico-economic system of trade barriers and a strict monopoly on the fur trade. This option, though, depended on a tight political grip on the colony and could have never been aligned with the increasing demands of further democratisation.[30]

The argument so far seems to build upon the assumption that liberalisation and mercantilism historically contradict each other as the first presumably does not acknowledge the second's assumption of the primacy of the political.[31] The case of New Netherland, however, presents itself as more intricate and shows that the ideological attachment to mercantilism can survive the disappearance of the legal and political scaffolding that supports it. Although the authorities had, themselves, created a situation in which the level of their own influence had clearly diminished, they still believed in the primacy of political over economic power. The concentration on the beaver,[32] although embedded in anti-mercantilist ideas about opening the trade for all burghers, might have further exacerbated the attachment to mercantilist thought by strengthening the belief that it was beneficial to amass value in one specific good (the beaver) instead of focussing on the development of an economy characterised by division of labour and a diversity of branches of trade. In fact, however, they faced a situation where their own political powerlessness, combined with the demand of political democratisation, had led to the emergence of a liberalised economy with a *de facto* floating and politically no longer controllable exchange rate between sewant and beaver.

The advocates of political democratisation, who had hoped that an increasing political participation of citizens would be made possible by liberalising the economy as advocated by, for instance, Pieter de la Court's 'commercial republicanism',[33] however, had to witness how one non-democratic actor was replaced by another. The trickle-down effect for which they had yearned never did take place as shown by Oliver Rink's illuminating analysis of how a few Amsterdam merchant families, much less blinded by a belief in an inherent value of either sewant or beaver, more or less took over control from the WIC after the latter had started to liberalise the colony's economy. In light of this 'secret colonialism'[34] it is highly questionable that the economic liberalisation, which was on the surface closely entangled with the demand for further democratisation, resulted in a better life for most colonists who, on the contrary, suffered from the destabilisation of sewant value set in motion by the liberalisation. Furthermore the colonists were now, instead of being openly ostracised from the fur trade, secretly excluded.

In the next section, I wish to compare the inflexibility and inability of the Dutch authorities to align the different monetary demands of the population (prosaic lubricant versus medium of investment) with the economic pragmatism of the Coastal Algonquian. Before I can substantiate the assumption that the Coastal Algonquian exploited the economic disorder in the colony, as well as explore how they accomplished this, it is necessary to understand that their monetary pragmatism had its basis in a difference between two transactional modes.

## Nanoue *and* anaqúshento – *two transactional modes among the Coastal Algonquian*

Descriptions of the economic behaviour of the Coastal Algonquian are replete with seemingly irresolvable contradictions. On the one hand, Roger Williams, founder of Rhode Island, keen observer of the customs of the Coastal Algonquian and ethnographer *avant la lettre*, compares them, without hesitation, with European merchants: 'They are as full of businesse, and as impatient of hinderance (in their kind) as any Merchant in *Europe*.'[35] On the other hand, he evokes images of eternal friendship and brotherly love: 'It was not price nor money that could have purchased Rhode Island. Rhode Island was purchased by love.'[36] What allowed Williams and other observers to switch so effortlessly between portraying Coastal Algonquian as paragons of generosity and as competitive hagglers? Why were their perceptions of the economic behaviour of the Coastal Algonquian so contradictory? In what follows, I assume that it was the European misrecognition of the existence and importance of two independent transactional modes in the Coastal Algonquian society that led to the ambivalent perception of economic behaviour and subsequently multiplied cultural misunderstandings. I further suppose that Coastal Algonquian were highly profit-oriented in one of these transactional modes, while in the other they tended to behave generously and with care.

Although this dual structure is never mentioned explicitly by Williams or other observers, one can attempt to reconstruct the two transactional modes by focussing on two opposing semantic fields that are clearly discernible in the contemporary sources. In his *Bloody Tenent*, a theological examination of the relation between the religious and secular aspects of power published in 1644, Williams translates *nanoue* as 'Giving their Commodities freely'.[37] In Trumbull's dictionary of the Natick language one finds '*nannowe, nanouwe*' translated as 'freely', 'safely', 'voluntary' and 'of free will'.[38] Williams, however, gave a second translation of *nanoue*, which stands in stark contrast to the first one: 'They adde *Nanoue*, give me this or that, a *disease* which they are generally infected with'.[39] As this contrast immediately reminds one of Marcel Mauss' famous *Essay on the Gift* where he argues for the universality of a transactional mode in which exchanges between two or more actors are enacted voluntarily and obligatory simultaneously,[40] it seems valid to conclude that *nanoue* and semantically related words referred to transactions that were embedded in reciprocal gift relationships. People engaging in these transactions felt secure enough to 'beg' for whatever they needed and happily gave to whomever was in need.[41]

This conclusion is substantiated by traces of a second transactional mode that stands in opposition to the *nanoue* one. The term '*anaqúshento*' is translated by Williams as 'Trading'[42] while '*Anaqushaog*' and '*Anaqushanchick*' are translated as 'Traders' and the phonetically derivative '*Mouanaqushaúog*' as 'Chapmen'.[43] Another contemporary observer of Coastal Algonquian culture, William Wood, translated the Massachusetts '*unkesheto*' as 'will you truck'[44] and Trumbull gives '*anaqushaü*' as 'he trades, traffics'.[45] If my comparison with the dichotomy between gift and commodity exchange is valid, one can conclude that *anaqúshento* referred to purely economic transactions, whose endurance beyond the time of the actual transaction was not desired, maybe even thought of as at best prevented. As a reaction to the existence of this second transactional mode, Williams' *Key* is full of phrases aiming at getting better prices and includes plenty of others that aim at helping his fellow colonists to bargain toughly with Coastal Algonquian traders: 'Cosaúmawem./You aske too much. [...] Wuttunnautu./It is worth it. [...] Cosaúmakese./You have told too much. [...] Mamattissuog kuteaúquock./Your Beads are naught.'[46] While in *nanoue*-relations one was expected to be as generous and charitable as possible to distinguish oneself from other members of society, *anaqúshento* relations might have been characterised by cold calculation, sometimes even fraud and deception. It is reasonable to assume that both types of relationships tended towards self-reproduction. While generous actions prolonged the relationship, tough bargaining and calculation inhibited a continuation of the relationship beyond the satisfaction of profit-motivated and commercial interests.[47]

Although a great deal more could be said about the two transactional modes what is of importance for the argument made in this chapter is that apparently a transactional mode existed among Coastal Algonquians that, similar to modern profit-oriented exchanges, was not hindered by any tribalistic, aesthetic, social, legal or religious influence. On the contrary: the *anaqúshento* mode allowed actors to focus on gaining as much as possible. One common strategy employed during *anaqúshento* transactions was to reject specific beads whereby one aimed at getting better prices. An incident that happened during Williams' journey to the Coastal Algonquian *sachem* Ousaemquin is illustrative in this regard:

> offered him but fifteen fathom of white wampum (*it being a time when white wampum only was current*; and which we knew he only would accept). But he desired to have commodities and wampum, and at last we agreed upon ten fathom of white wampum, four coats of English cloth, six of the best Englisch hoes and English axes, and twelve great knives; which wampum and commodities *he desireing speedy pay of*, we went, all of us over to Portsmouth to procure the said wampum and commodities [. . .]. We brought him the wampum which he accepted of, the coats also, which he accepted of and received the cloth, choosing out of two parcels, but of twelve knives he choose eight; out of six hoes, he chose one, we promising to procure the rest of the hoes and hatchets and knives to his liking, which he was fully content. Afterward going to sleep he *begged* two coats of us, which we promised to give him; yet in the morning, some of us refusing to sell him shot, as also our all refusing to give him four coats more, he took forth our money and goods again to us, which we refused, not being willing to countenance such dealing in the barbarians; and having before in their payments and a coat to his councellour which he desired, and some other small gifts unto them layed out, *the value of about forty fathom of wampum*, we were not willing to wrong our country in granting his desire of four coats, and so unreasonably to raise the price of such parcels of land in this barbarous wilderness.[48]

This episode indicates that Coastal Algonquian presented themselves as tough exchange partners who, in case they were dissatisfied with the offered objects, sent colonists away to procure goods that they considered more suitable. Instead of absorbing valueless beads, Ouasemquin demanded specific payment. For him it was the current and future exchangeability of diverse goods that counted; he was merely interested in sewant's market value. It was hence neither the law as in the case of New Netherland whose authorities had fixed the ratio between white and violet beads (two white beads equalled one violet bead) nor religious feeling as assumed by scholars such as Snyderman[49] that backed up the value ratio between white and violet beads. This detachment from any legal or cultural obligation was the basis for Coastal Algonquian economic pragmatism. They could decline payment in sewant due to its quality or quantity and alter the value ratio according to the situation. If, for instance, sewant's economic value decreased, which, as I have shown earlier, it did continuously from the 1640s, Coastal Algonquian, acting in accordance with the *anaqueshento* mode, just refused to accept it. They considered sewant a mere fiat money without an intrinsic value beyond its usability in actual exchanges. This stands in stark contrast to the legalism of the Dutch authorities who tried to uphold the value of sewant by codifying specific quality, quantity and ratio standards, whereby they were only able to react after the market situation had already changed, which – a consequence of the specific temporality of the beaver trade and the geographical vastness of the colony – happened regularly and was unforeseeable.[50] In contrast hereto a group of merchants acknowledged the Native Americans' ability to quickly adapt to new prices during a meeting in New Amsterdam on 8 January 1657: 'The Indians, who will know it immediately, will charge more for everything and will enrich themselves, and consequently can never be brought to the previous rate, of which there are examples.'[51] All these examples show that both the price of goods and the value of wampum were negotiable, expressed in abstract terms (fathom,[52] hand, etc.) over which serious interpretative conflicts could emerge, which suited the flexibility of the *anaqúshento* transactional mode.

## Conclusion

All the discussed examples suggest that what presented itself to the political authorities of the Dutch colony as an intricate and ultimately irresolvable political dead end supplied the Coastal Algonquian with a pool of opportunities. The conclusion that can be tentatively drawn is that, while the political authorities of the colony tended to confuse sewant's mere symbolic with an intrinsic value, the Amsterdam merchant families as well as the Coastal Algonquian might have realised and exploited that the value of sewant was grounded in the cross-cultural acceptance of it – a fact that the colonists of New Netherland had to learn the hard way after the liberalisation of the economy had dissolved the artificial attachment of beaver and sewant value.

In light of both the relatively inflexible understanding of money that the political authorities of New Netherland possessed and the Coastal Algonquian pragmatism, I wish to end this chapter by suggesting the exploration of similarities and differences between the New Netherland example and the ways in which other North American colonial authorities dealt with Indigenous pragmatic approaches towards money and the politically complex economic situations of their own colonies with special focus on monetary innovations.[53] Are there other Indigenous actors who, like the Coastal Algonquian, exploited the monetary system, which had been imposed on them, by productively instrumentalising the difference between unit of account and medium of exchange, by ditching off money of minor quality or by only accepting high-quality currency? In contrast to this Indigenous pragmatic and innovative handling of the situation, the colony of New Netherland had ultimately been unable to find an appropriate substitute for its dual currency system, which had proven to be indefensible without the fur trade monopoly, its mercantilist backbone. The encompassing concentration on the beaver, the simultaneous devaluation of sewant and the loss of political control did indeed make the colonial authorities aware of the Coastal Algonquian economic pragmatism and the beaver's 'deadly sting'.

## Notes

1 W. Hubbard, *A General History of New England* (Boston: Little and Brown, 1848), p. 100.

2 'Sewant' is the Dutch and 'wampumpeag', often abbreviated to 'wampum', the English term. Neither 'sewant' nor 'wampum' was used to designate glass or any other beads.

3 The WIC was a chartered company of Dutch merchants with a highly bureaucratised structure. It had five offices (*kamers*) in Amsterdam, Rotterdam, Hoorn, Middelburg and Groningen that sent directors, equipped with massive political power, to the different colonies. See H. den Heijer, *De geschiedenis van de WIC* (Zutphen: Walburg, 1994). J. Jacobs, *New Netherland: A Dutch Colony in Seventeenth Century America* (Leiden: Brill, 2005) is by far the most comprehensive work on the Dutch colony.

4 G. R. Hamell, 'Mythical Realities and European Contact in the Northeast During the Sixteenth and Seventeenth Centuries', *Man in the Northeast*, 33 (1987), pp. 63–87.

5 In contrast to another published study in which I discussed Iroquian–Dutch relations, in this chapter I focus on Coastal Algonquian economic expertise, see M. Schmidt, 'Entangled Economies: New Netherland's Dual Currency System and Its Relation to Iroquoian Monetary Practice', *Ethnohistory*, 62 (2015), pp. 195–216. I reuse material from that chapter in the sections that deal with the colony's currency system.

6 Partly achieved by reminting the diverse circulating species, which was executed by the 1609 established Bank of Amsterdam (Amsterdamsche Wisselbank) and inhibited monetary confusion. See J. de Vries and A. van der Woude, *The First Modern Economy: Success, Failure, and Perseverance of the Dutch Economy, 1500–1815* (Cambridge: Cambridge University Press, 1997).

7 I. de Rasiere, 'Letter from Isaack de Rasiere to the Directors of the Amsterdam Chamber of the West India Company', in A. J. F. van Laer (ed.), *Documents Relating to New Netherland 1624–1626* (San Marino, CA: Henry E. Huntington Library and Art Gallery, 1924), pp. 171–254.

8 E. S. Peña, 'Wampum Production in New Netherland and Colonial New York: The Historical and Archaeological Context' (PhD dissertation, Boston University, 1990), and L. Ceci, 'The Effect of European Contact and Trade on the Settlement Pattern of Indians in Coastal New York, 1524–1665' (PhD dissertation, New York, 1990) extensively discuss sewant-mediated encounters between Europeans and Native Americans.

9 For a discussion of sewant's role in Coastal Algonquian societies, see, for instance, K. J. Bragdon, *Native People of Southern New England, 1500–1650* (Norman, OK: University of Oklahoma Press, 1996) and M. Schmidt, 'Why Wampum Is More Money than Scholars Think: A New View on Seventeenth Century Coastal Algonquian Societies', *Suomen Antropologi*, 39:2 (2014), pp. 20–38.

10 J. Michaëlius, 'Letter of Reverend Jonas Michaëlius', in J. F. Jameson (ed.), *Narratives of New Netherland, 1609–1664* (New York: Charles Scribner's Sons, 1909), pp. 117–33.

11 K. J. Waterman, *'To Do Justice to Him & Myself': Evert Wendell's Account Book of the Fur Trade with Indians in Albany, New York, 1695–1726* (Philadelphia, PA: American Philosophical Society Lightning Rod Press, 2008).

12 R. G. Thwaites (ed.), *The Jesuit Relations and Allied Documents*, vol. VI (Cleveland: Burrows Brothers, 1896–1901), p. 297.

13 'Among our people, too, it is in general use for buying everything one needs.' See A. van der Donck, *A Description of New Netherland* (Lincoln, NE: University of Nebraska Press, 2008), p. 95.

14 'No money circulates in this country among the common people but zeewan, [...] and a year and a day can expire before beavers are bartered therefore.' B. Fernow (ed.), *The Records of New Amsterdam from 1653 to 1674 Anno Domini*, vol. 2 (New York: Knickerbocker Press, 1897), p. 6.

15 The main reason for this was that the production of the beads was labour-extensive and complicated. It was indeed mainly members of Coastal Algonquian societies such as the Narragansett, Massachusetts and especially members of those tribes living on Long Island like the Shinnecock and Montauk who performed most of this work. See J. R. Brodhead, E. B. O'Callaghan and B. Fernow (eds.), *Documents Relative to the Colonial History of the State of New York*, vol. 1 (New York and Albany: Weed, Parsons and Company, 1856–1887), p. 360.

16 See the Provisional Regulations for the Colonists adopted by the Assembly of the Nineteen of the West India Company, March 28, 1624, published in van Laer, *Documents Relating to New Netherland 1624–1626*, pp. 1–18.

17 On the problem of smuggling, however, see, for example, O. A. Rink, *Holland on the Hudson: An Economic and Social History of Dutch New York* (Ithaca: Cornell University Press, 1986), p. 90.

18 E. B. O'Callaghan (ed.), *Laws and Ordinances of New Netherland, 1638–1674* (Albany, NY: Weed, Parsons and Company, 1868), passim.

19 Brodhead et al, *Documents Relative to the Colonial History of the State of New York*, p. 386.

20 Fernow, *The Records of New Amsterdam from 1653 to 1674 Anno Domini*, passim.

21 W. Weeden, 'Indian Money as a Factor in New England Civilization', in *Johns Hopkins University Studies in Historical and Political Sciences*, 2nd Series, VIII – IX (Baltimore, 1884), pp. 5–51, p. 15.

22 B. Fernow (ed.), *Documents Relating to the History of the Early Colonial Settlements Principally on Long Island* (Albany, NY: Weed, Parsons and Company, 1883), p. 451; New York State Archive, New York Colonial Manuscripts 13 (NYCM), p. 56.

23 C.T. Gehring (ed.), *Fort Orange Court Minutes, 1652–1660* (Syracuse, NY: Syracuse University Press, 1990), p. 501; NYCM 16, p. 169.

24 In the ordinances of 18 April 1641 and 30 May 1650, O'Callaghan, *Laws and Ordinances of New Netherland, 1638–1674*, p. 26, p. 115; NYCM 4, p. 90, p. 352. The ordinance of 14 September 1650 tackles the problem of 'poor strung Wampum' that '[...] even for small items is rejected and refused by Shopkeepers, Brewers, Bakers, Tapsters, Tradespeople and Laboring men, to the great confusion and inconvenience of the Inhabitants.' p. 116; NYCM 16, p. 22.

25 O'Callaghan, *Laws and Ordinances of New Netherland*, pp. 119–20, p. 149; NYCM 16, p. 23, p. 38.

26 O'Callaghan, *Laws and Ordinances of New Netherland*, p. 290; NYCM 8, p. 383.

27 29 November 1657, 11 November 1658 and 28 December 1662. O'Callaghan, *Laws and Ordinances of New Netherland*, p. 289, p. 317, p. 357 and p. 433; NYCM 16, p. 98, p. 119, NYCM 8, p. 1023, NYCM 10, p. 299..

28 It is justified to juxtapose these different measurements without discussing in detail what especially triggered them, because my argument claims that the oscillation between them was a systemic problem, stemming from not acknowledging the priority of market forces and the necessity to act politically.

29 NYCM 8, pp. 1027–33, p. 1027; my translation. Dated 11 November 1658, this document was written as a reaction to the ordinance of the same date. De Deckere was also aware of the fact that after a reduction of sewant, for common goods 'now would not be paid less gulden than before it' – a further reduction of the value of sewant would hence be 'futile and without acceptance', p. 1028.

30 These were primarily expressed by Adriaen van der Donck's Vertoogh van Nieu-Neder-Land, published in 1650. See A. van der Donck, *Vertoogh van Nieu-Neder-Land, weghens de Gheleghentheydt, Vruchtbaerheydt, en soberen Staet desselfs* (De Hague: Michiel Stael, 1650). The answer of de Rasiere's successor, Cornelis van Tienhoven, to van der Donck's discussion of the sewant problem in the Vertoogh is illuminating as he acknowledges the impossibility to solve the problem: 'The reason for not prohibiting unstringed wampum was, because no money was in circulation, and mechanics, farmers and the rest of the Commonalty, having no other currency, would suffer serious loss; and had it been cried down, doubtless the Remonstrants would have booked the circumstance among the rest of their grievances.' His answer can be found in A. van der Donck, *Remonstrance of New Netherland, and the Occurences There* (Albany, NY: Weed, Parsons and Company, 1856).

31 In his famous *The Modern World-System*, Wallerstein, however, offers a different perspective on the relations between politics and economy in the Dutch Republic: 'The United Provinces were dominant, and "liberalism suits dominant economies well"; but whenever liberalism conflicts with the possibility of continued dominance, it has a way of not lasting. This is why the "liberal" decentralised structure of the Dutch state can be taken as an indicator of strength rather than of weakness.' See I. Wallerstein, *The Modern World-System II, Mercantilism and the Consolidation of the European World-Economy, 1600–1750* (New York: Academic Press, 1980), pp. 61–62.

32 M. Schmidt, 'Zur Heterologie kolonialer Ökonomien: Der Biber und sein Fell als Fetisch in den nordamerikanischen Kolonien des 17. Jahrhunderts', *Ilinx: Berliner Beiträge zur Kulturwissenschaft*, 3 (2013), pp. 25–38.

33 P. de la Court, *Interest van Holland, ofte Gronden van Hollands-Welvaren* (Amsterdam: Joan Cyprianus vander Gracht, 1662); see also A. Weststeijn, *Commercial Republicanism in the Dutch Golden Age: The Political Thought of Johan & Pieter de la Court* (Leiden: Brill, 2012).

34 O. A. Rink, 'New Netherland and the Amsterdam Merchants: Unraveling a Secret Colonialism', in N. A. McClure Zeller (ed.), *A Beautiful and Fruitful Place: Selected Rensselaerwijck Seminar Papers* (Albany, NY: New Netherland Publishing, 1991), pp. 269–82.

35 R. Williams, *Key into the Language of America* (Providence: Roger Williams Press, 1936), p. 36.

36 J. Bartlett, *The Letters of Roger Williams 1632–1682* (Providence: Printed for the Narragansett Club, 1874), p. 305.

37 R. Williams, *The Bloody Tenent Yet More Bloody: By Mr. Cotton's Endevour to Wash It White in the Blood of the Lamb* (London: J. Haddon, 1652), p. 217.

38 J. H. Trumbull, *Natick Dictionary* (Washington: Government Printing Office, 1903), p. 76.

39 Williams, *Key into the Language of America*, p. 164 [my emphasis].

40 M. Mauss, *Essai sur le don* (Paris: PUF, 2007); see also M. Bloch and J. Parry, *Money and the Morality of Exchange* (Cambridge: Cambridge University Press, 1989).

41 It is not surprising that these 'non-liquidating transactions' were enacted by embedding them in terms of generosity and friendship: 'Cowetompatimmin./We are friends. [. . .] Noonamautuckquawhe./Trust me.' See Williams, *Key into the Language of America*, pp. 166–67. The term 'non-liquidating transaction' was coined by H. P. Znoj, *Tausch und Geld in Zentralsumatra: Zur Kritik des Schuldbegriffs in der Wirtschaftsethnologie* (Berlin: Reimer, 1995).

42 Williams, *The Bloody Tenent Yet More Bloody*, p. 217.

43 Williams, *Key into the Language of America*, p. 159.

44 W. Wood, *New England's Prospect* (Amherst: University of Massachusetts Press, 1977), p. 121.

45 Trumbull, *Natick Dictionary*, p. 8.
46 Williams, *Key into the Language of America*, pp. 162–64.
47 A. J. Ray and D. B. Freeman, *'Give Us Good Measure': An Economic Analysis of Relations Between the Indians and the Hudson's Bay Company Before 1763* (Toronto: University of Toronto Press, 1978).
48 J. Bartlett (ed.), *Records of the Colony of Rhode Island and Providence Plantations*, vol. 1 (Providence, RI: A. Craword Greene and Brother, State Printers, 1856), pp. 33–34.
49 'The very concept of money was foreign to Indian ideology.' See G. S. Snyderman, 'The Functions of Wampum', *Proceedings of the American Philosophical Society*, 98 (1954), pp. 469–94, p. 471.
50 In addition to their inability to solve the problem of monetary instability that was a consequence of their loss of the control of the quantity of sewant, the political authorities were forced to deal with the problem of securing the quality of currency at least since 1641: 'We have [. . .] seen the decline and daily depreciation of the loose Wampum, among which are circulating many without holes and half finished; also some of Stone, Bone, Glass, Muscle-shells, Horn, yea even of Wood and Broken beads.' See O'Callaghan, *Laws and Ordinances of New Netherland, 1638–1674*, p. 115, also p. 80; NYCM 4, p. 352, NYCM 16, p. 21. It is highly probable that a lot of these 'sewant' came from Native Americans, who, while keeping good sewant, got rid of inferior beads, which they would not accept in return, enacting what is nowadays known as Gresham's Law. The following quote exemplifies this problem: 'The Indians abuse the English with much bad, false and unfinished peage, [. . .] the Indians, who best understand the qualities and defects of peage will not willingly take back.' See J. H. Trumbull (ed.), *Public Records of Connecticut*, vol. 1 (Hartford, CT: Brown and Parsons, 1850), p. 179.
51 Fernow, *The Records of New Amsterdam from 1653 to 1674 Anno Domini*, pp. 260–61.
52 A 'fathom' was a string of beads of 1.8 metres in length. The average fathom consisted of 360 beads.
53 See J. Guyer, *Marginal Gains: Monetary Transactions in Atlantic Africa* (Oxford: Oxford University Press, 2004).

# Part II

# Encounters with the periphery

# 3 European merchant trading firms and the export of the precious metals from the Kingdom of Bohemia during the sixteenth century

*Petr Vorel*

In foreign trade, precious metals were considered a basic commodity that, for many well-known reasons, could generate immense profits. That is why political power centres strove to control both their mining and subsequent trade. During the Late Middle Ages, the Kingdom of Bohemia (today the western part of the Czech Republic, European Union) was the main producer and exporter of newly mined silver in Central Europe. The actual silver was mined by private miners, while Italian merchants controlled the export of the precious metal to southern Europe and beyond to intercontinental markets at the turn of the thirteenth and fourteenth centuries.[1] In legal terms, the system of trade relations, which gave the King of Bohemia a steady 12 per cent share of the export price of silver, was based on the Decree of 1300 (the so-called *Ius regale montanorum*) issued by King Václav II.[2] This law prohibited and severely punished doing business using metallurgical silver in any form. The transport of silver within the country and abroad was allowed only in the form of minted silver coins (Prague groats), since the process of monetisation in a single, centralised mint, located in Kutná Hora, made it possible to allocate the king's statutory share from the newly mined silver. This system worked under the requirement that miners bring all their newly mined precious metal to the mint. In exchange, they got back 88 per cent of the silver by weight in the form of minted coins, with which they then were free to do business.

The Kingdom of Bohemia was the traditional supplier of this precious metal during the Late Middle Ages. The Kingdom owed its exceptionally strong position in the thirteenth and especially fourteenth centuries, when the kings of Bohemia of the Luxembourg house became Holy Roman emperors, primarily to its silver fortune. By virtue of the successful power politics of Emperor Charles IV of Luxembourg, the Kingdom of Bohemia was the main political, cultural and economic centre of the Holy Roman Empire during the entire second half of the fourteenth century.[3] The period during which the King of Bohemia was the ruling power in the Empire saw many decades of relative peace and prosperity, contrasting with the periods that preceded and followed it.

I briefly mention this earlier phase because medieval state laws formed the basis of exporting Bohemian silver still at the turn of the fifteenth and sixteenth centuries.[4] In the second half of the fifteenth century, prior to the discovery of the American continent, most of the newly mined silver shipped to the international markets of Europe, Africa and the Near East came from three sources in Central Europe: from the Austrian Tyrol, from German Saxony and from Bohemia.[5] But the political state of affairs in the Kingdom of Bohemia was one that stemmed diametrically from the one 100 years before. The Hussite revolution,[6] and the years of anarchy that followed it, saw a redistribution of political power as well as of the property of several important aristocratic families. With the exception of a few short pauses, the Kingdom of Bohemia was beset by war for 60 years, from 1419 to 1479. The end of hostilities led to an economic boom in the country, mostly enriching large landowners who had begun commercial activities in various branches, including fish farming, brewing, and mining precious and nonferrous metals. Prospecting activities led to the discovery of new sources of iron, copper, tin and other metals. The luckier ones also found precious metals on their domains. The discovery of special sources of high-grade silver ore during the second decade of the sixteenth century brought fame to the Ore Mountains (in Czech, Krušné Hory; in German, Erzgebirge), which formed the border between Bohemia and Saxony. Large quantities of silver had been mined on the German side of these mountains for a long time prior to that and it was easy to assume that significant veins existed on the Bohemian side as well. These expectations were fulfilled about 1512, when a major find of silver ore was discovered along the northwest edge of the kingdom near the later city of Jáchymov (Joachimsthal) in the territory that mostly belonged to the Schlick family of Pasoun (Bassano). This discovery happened at a time when the political power of the king had been greatly weakened by the Estates and several factions, consisting of the most powerful noble families, were fighting amongst themselves for decisive control. In 1515, King Vladislav Jagiello authorised one of the magnates, Hynek Berka of Dubá, to control the flow of traffic on public roads in Bohemia and to confiscate all illegally transported silver. Doing business with unminted, newly mined silver ore or silver ingots was forbidden under threat of confiscation, and exporting it abroad was simply out of the question. The Bohemian legal code classified such activity as one of the most serious offences. In 1515, Berka was allowed to keep half of the confiscated precious metal, with the other half turned over to the royal treasury to pay off the king's debts. This action should have prevented illegal export of silver from Bohemia to neighbouring Saxony carried on by the Schlicks and their foreign customers, but controversy between the Schlicks and other members of the Bohemian aristocracy had earlier roots.

The Schlicks were not typical members of the Bohemian aristocracy. One will not find them among the older families of the Bohemian aristocracy during the Middle Ages. They were originally townsmen from Cheb (Eger) who did business in fabrics and finance on the German-Bohemian border. Of particular fame in this history is Jasper (Kašpar) Schlick, who was an important diplomat in the service of Emperor Sigmund of Luxembourg (†1436). Sigmund elevated him to the ranks of the knights' order in 1416, bestowing several privileges on him in the process. Towards the end of Sigmund's life, Jasper

Schlick became imperial chancellor and, thanks to his excellent knowledge of Czech, he conducted negotiations with the Czech Hussites regarding the ascension of Emperor Sigmund to the Bohemian throne. Jasper Schlick (†1449) remained an important figure at the imperial court until his death and thanks to the many years of service that he rendered to the imperial chancellery, he received the title (but no property) of Count of Pasoun (i.e. Bassano, after a county and town of Bassano in northern Italy).

Most of the land deeded to the Schlick family was located in northwest Bohemia. These claims (including, later on, Jáchymov) mostly involved the male members of the Schlick family, and it was these 'Schlick lords' who usually represented the interests of the entire family during disputes. But several property deeds of gift held by the Schlick family were later unmasked as forgeries, probably committed by Jasper Schlick when, as imperial chancellor, he had the documents drawn up for his relatives without the knowledge of the monarch.[7]

The Bohemian aristocracy, however, did not consider the Schlicks to be sufficiently highborn on account of their well-known lay origins, despite their use of the title count (which in any case did not bestow any social privileges on the bearer of this title in the Kingdom of Bohemia). Their property claims were challenged partly because they were based on forged documents. In their dispute with the Bohemian aristocracy, the Schlicks sought an alliance with neighbouring Saxony, inasmuch as the imperial court under the weak emperor Frederick III had ceased to exert any powerful influence for them. They even attempted to secede from Bohemia and join up with Saxony. This threat to the legal framework of the kingdom, combined with the failure of the Schlicks to respect the decision of the Bohemian Estates Court, led to several military incursions into their domains. The most serious conflict to take place was the so-called Loket War of 1504–1506, when the Bohemian government army conquered Loket Castle and forced the Schlick family to yield before the law of the land.

A few years later, in 1512, a fabulous mother lode of silver was found in the domains of Ostrov nad Ohří, which, from the time of Emperor Sigmund, had been pledged to the Schlick family. The Schlicks themselves did not have enough resources to begin mining and refining the silver ore. At that time, the demand for silver in Europe was so high that it was easy to interest investors who were willing to put their money in such a business. Mining and metallurgical works, which took place in the middle of the second decade of the sixteenth century on the Bohemian side of the Ore Mountains, were organised by Saxon mining entrepreneurs. They supplied both equipment and trained personnel. The operation was therefore funded by mining magnates from nearby Saxony, who provided the technology and workforce for the 'Valley of Saint Joachim' (in Czech, Jáchymov; in German, Joachimstal), the name given to the new mining region after operations began there in 1516.[8]

A relatively dramatic struggle concerning mining and handling of silver took place in the country over the course of three decades (1516–1547) that resulted in a complete change in the conditions for the silver trade, mainly due to changes in policy. I briefly summarise the new information that we have about the matter and point out some interesting sources available to us. The individual phases of this process can be listed as follows:

## The period of 1516–1519

Until this day we still do not really know what happened to the silver mined in Jáchymov between 1516 and shortly after. It is reasonable to assume that it was exported to Saxony across the border, just a few kilometres away, in order to cover the start-up capital and as mining revenue for Saxon investors.

In terms of the law of the land, however, this practice was illegal and severely infringed on the rights of the King of Bohemia. It was difficult to enforce the law with the breakdown of royal authority that followed the death of King Vladislav II Jagiellon and the accession to the throne in 1516 of his 10-year-old son Louis (Ludvík). His interests were supposed to be defended by his principal guardian, Emperor Maximilian I of the House of Habsburg.

Although the Kingdom of Bohemia was not yet a part of the Holy Roman Empire at that time,[9] Emperor Maximilian held major influence over the domestic political scene as the guardian of the under-aged king and gave preferential treatment to the South German bankers, who were seeking a monopoly in the trade of precious metals. In the struggle for a share of the profits from the Jáchymov silver, it seems that because of his position, the Emperor was able to promote the interests of South German bankers who were his creditors. The trade in Jáchymov silver involved far too much money to escape the attention of the most influential financiers of Europe.

An investment agreement concluded by the Schlick family in 1518 with the Nuremberg bankers Hanz Nützel and Jacob Welser was meant to provide for the long-time export of silver from Bohemia.[10] The Nuremberg merchants would have a monopoly over Jáchymov silver for a period of three years and be the main guarantors of mining costs as well as of the profits of the private mining companies. The owners of the land (the Schlicks) would be entitled to only 3 per cent of the estimated market value of the traded silver (8.25 Rhenish guilders for one Erfurt talent of pure silver = 234.62 g). The rights of the King of Bohemia, who was the *de jure* owner of all precious metals hidden underground, were completely ignored. So the Emperor's creditors, from several banks in South Germany, profited from the first phase of mining silver in Jáchymov by collecting the cheaply mined silver and exporting it from the Kingdom of Bohemia in violation of the laws in force at that time. The Bohemian Estates protested against these activities and began to prepare specific punitive measures to prevent these exports from occurring.

## The period of 1519–1528

After the death of Emperor Maximilian I (†1519), the political balance in Central Europe shifted in another direction, and the Habsburgs, in their pursuit of the Roman crown for Charles V, had to compromise in some ways with their principal rival within the Empire, the Elector of Saxony. So again, a new opportunity arose for the possibility of reorganising relationships, such as in the case of Jáchymov. The expected destination of the exports, however, completely changed, as it was shifted north to Saxony, where a significant portion of the Jáchymov private mining companies and investors came from.

Significantly, the Bohemian Estates representation also entered the scene. Under the pretext of protecting the rights of the king, they also wanted to gain something out of this situation. The Bohemian Land Diet found a way to tax the exported Jáchymov silver. Since the precious metal could only be exported in the form of minted coins, production had to be carefully documented. Silver from the Bohemian side of the Ore Mountains could then be exported freely to Saxony in the future, but only in a monetised form as coins.

For that purpose, however, the domestic Prague groat coins were not appropriate because of low alloy and weight, but commercial coins needed to be used, which until then had not been produced in Bohemia at all. So the Bohemian Estates ordered the minting of new large coins in addition to the traditional Prague groats, using the metrological standards of Saxony. Heavy coins with high purity were good for export. In January 1520, the Bohemian Land Diet decided on the outer appearance of these new coins, which became later known as 'thalers'.[11]

One side of the coin showed the heraldry of the Kingdom of Bohemia (crowned double-tail lion) and name of the King Louis (who was formally declared the issuer of these coins). The other side had the coat of arms of the Schlick family and the name of Stephan Schlick of Pasoun as the representative of the entire clan. The organisation of the very profitable mining of silver ore, its metallurgical processing, producing the coins and doing business with silver,[12] were directly linked to an export centre in Leipzig, Saxony.

The highest Bohemian officials, who were themselves creditors of the underaged king, concluded their own agreement that called for them to receive nearly 4 per cent of the market price from the monetised silver, the amount to be used for the repayment of royal debts.[13]

From spring 1520 onwards, new Czech commercial coins could be regularly delivered to Leipzig, in what was then the main centre of silver trade. Here the delivered coins were regularly subjected to metrological tests and then sold on as commercial silver to exporters. For record purposes the delivered coins were usually marked by their place of origin, the new Bohemian coin was named 'The Silver groat from the Valley of Saint Joachim' (in German: Sant-Joachimsthalerguldengrosch), abbreviated as 'tolský' (in Czech) or 'thaler' (in German).[14]

Practically all the silver mined during these years was monetised, with the vast majority of it exported in the form of tolars to the market for precious metals in Leipzig, and then further on to the markets of North Germany, Scandinavia and Eastern Europe in particular. Detailed documentation on the export of Czech silver tolars from the years 1520–1528 has been preserved from the major trading centre in precious metals in Leipzig, Saxony.[15] Figure 3.1 outlines the net earnings of the mining companies during this period.

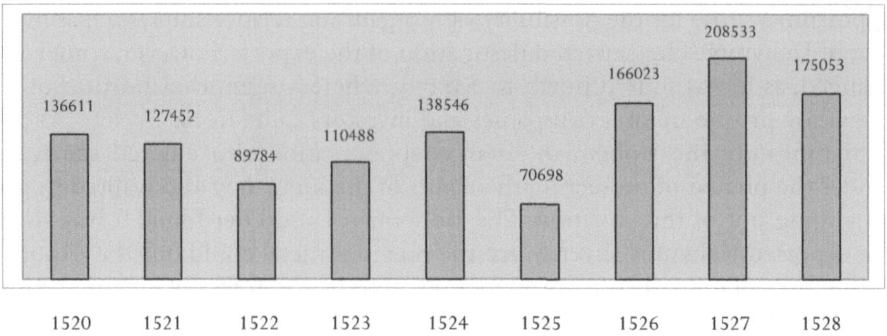


*Figure 3.1* Net earnings of mining companies in Joachimstal from 1520 to 1528 (in thalers).

At the beginning of the 1520s, it was not possible to export silver from Bohemia other than in the form of minted coins. That is why the Schlicks probably monetised the vast majority of the extracted precious metal into thalers (or ½-thalers and ¼-thalers of the same purity of silver and the relevant weight), which in the early '20s of the sixteenth century became a highly desired form of commercial silver thanks to their large quantities, their high silver content and heavy weight. This is why large commercial silver coins became known in central and north-west Europe as 'thaler' (according to their place of origin in Joachimstal) or in eastern Europe as 'jefimok' (as a representation of St. Joachim), because they were the first coins of this type that began to be used for trade in such vast quantities.

The commercial success of the thalers from Jáchymov in the early 1520s was also due to the success of the Saxon trade policy for precious metals. Metrological parameters of the Saxon silver groat (thereafter referred to by its Bohemian version 'thaler') were quickly adapted by other major central European producers of silver, with the exception of the Habsburgs in Austria. This was displayed in the negotiations for the adoption of the Imperial Minting Order in 1524, where the influence of the Saxons prevailed during its preparation.[16] However, after the death of the Elector of Saxony Frederick (†1525), Saxony changed its attitude towards Imperial monetary integration, and individual coin producers from the large family of Saxony princes began to assert more of their own economic interests. Even the original Saxon thaler coins began to gradually lose their metrological stability. Seemingly paradoxically, in the end, the only major commercial silver coin minted according to the Imperial Minting Order of 1524 became the Jáchymov thaler and was made in Bohemia, which was outside of the Empire.

## The period of 1528–1545

After the death of Louis Jagiello (†1526), King Ferdinand I of Habsburg was elected to the Bohemian throne. Shortly after his accession, already in 1528, he managed to transfer ownership of the Jáchymov Mint to the sovereign, but even here he had to compromise. Though the Bohemian Land Diet, in 1528, had annulled its decision of 1520, which authorised the Schlicks to establish new mints under their direction, King Ferdinand still did not have full influence over the Jáchymov coin business in 1528. The Schlicks were still operating the mining of local silver and continued to rent the Royal Mint until 1545. All miners were required to bring their mined silver to the mint; the mint administration was to remain under the control of the Schlicks, who were to receive almost 1.5 per cent of the price of the monetised metal for a limited period of ten years. This peculiar situation, of course, gave rise to legal problems and disputes, as well as tensions between the royal and Schlicks officials, who were responsible for the operation of the mint and its administration. The Schlicks could, for example, significantly influence the structure of denominations produced (the commercial coins were still preferred instead of common ones of lower weight and value).

But the economic interest of the sovereign had a noticeable impact on the major change that occurred in the commercialisation of mined silver.[17] The new king from the Habsburg family again yielded to the interests of his creditors in South Germany (mainly the Fuggers of Augsburg) and allowed Bohemian silver to be exported to the Fugger business network under the direction of newly established administrative institutions.[18]

Even after the formal change of the outer appearance of the Jáchymov coins minted from 1528 as royal currency, the growth in silver mining and supply of commercial thaler coins from Jáchymov to the European market continued. The change that resulted after 1528 involved only the external appearance of the Jáchymov thalers, which began to be produced according to the Tyrolean model of minting, with only the symbols of the sovereign: their obverse was to display a portrait and their reverse an emblem.

But the thaler coins from Jáchymov retained their original metrological characteristics. The king could not change those on his own without the consent of the Bohemian Land Diet. So even twenty years after the Imperial Minting Order of 1524, Bohemian thalers were still being produced in Jáchymov, basically corresponding to the parameters of this provision, although the Kingdom of Bohemia was not a part of the Empire. In addition, they were being issued in the name of King Ferdinand, who himself had never respected the Imperial Minting Order in his hereditary Austrian territories inside the Empire. Jáchymov ultimately remained the only mint in Europe that made thalers with their original higher content of silver. That was still true in the second half of the 1540s. Therefore, even the business world until the 1540s distinguished between 'real Jáchymov thalers' (with higher silver content) and only 'ordinary' thalers.[19]

In Jáchymov itself, however, distinctions were being made in the ratio between the contents of newly mined silver on the one hand and processed silver coins (monetised) on the other. Before the year 1528, it is most likely that the vast majority of Jáchymov silver was monetised into silver commercial coins (thalers), because otherwise it would not have been possible to legally export them from Bohemia. Today we have evidence of the total volume of silver mined as well as of the quantity of coins produced after 1528.[20] In the 1530s and the first half of the 1540s, only 20–30 per cent of newly mined metal was used for minting coins, as the Jáchymov silver trade was taken under the control of royal officials. Moreover, for the royal chamber, it was more profitable to export silver in the form of silver bars, which bypassed the cost of monetisation. About 70–80 per cent of the silver mined at the time was directed to the commercial network of South Germany.

At the same time, however, a significant quantity of mined silver was apparently exported to Saxony outside of royal control (see Figure 3.2), as evidenced by several court trials involving officials from the mint and mining authority.[21] Naturally, the Schlicks also took part in these transactions as the tenants of the mint and holders of the mining rights.

## The period of 1545–1547

King Ferdinand I ended the disputes over the revenue from mining and mint operations in 1545. Following a decision by the Bohemian Estates Court, he stripped the Schlicks of all their rights to the mines and the mint, and cut off the illegal export of the precious metals to Saxony. This action had wider political implications with regard to the ongoing struggle between the Habsburgs and the Wettins of Saxony for political power in the Empire. In the war fought in 1546–1547, the Schlicks took the Saxon side and, in the wake of the victory of the Lutheran opposition in the realm, they expected a renewal of their activities in the silver trade. However, after the defeat of the Elector of Saxony at the battle of Mühlberg in April 1547, Schlicks' and Saxon interests in the Bohemian silver trade were completely eliminated.[22] One result of the compromise between the Bohemian Estates and the king after the disintegration of the Estates' resistance in 1547 was a new agreement about the metrological parameters of Bohemian coins. As of 1547 the silver content of thalers minted

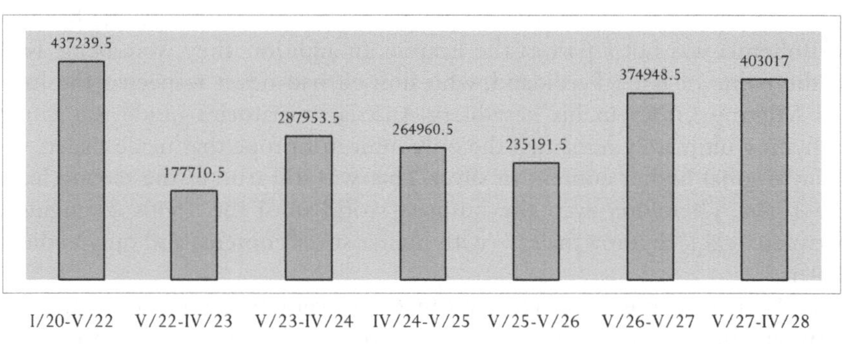


*Figure 3.2* The export of silver from Joachimsthal to Saxony (pieces of thalers) from January 1520 to April 1528.

in Jáchymov was harmonised with Austrian coinage. As a result of Habsburg indebtedness to the bankers of South Germany, the export of Bohemian silver again became part of the commercial network of the Fuggers of Augsburg.[23]

From 1547 onwards, the Jáchymov Mint functioned as a normal government mint. Its former special status, based on extremely rich local resources of newly mined silver, gradually began to change. This was due to a significant decrease in actual mining of Jáchymov silver from the mid-sixteenth century. The most abundant resources had already been exhausted. There was also a profound change in the European market in precious metals, which from the '40s of the sixteenth century began to be supplied with large quantities of commercial silver from the Spanish colonies in Central and South America. The rapid growth of operating costs for mining and smelting activities, accompanied by a decline in the market price of silver, caused a significant decline in profitability of the entire Jáchymov business.[24] (See Figure 3.3.)

The characteristics of Bohemia were significant for the outcome of the struggle for Jáchymov silver in the first half of the sixteenth century. At a time when rich and large royal cities (Prague, Vratislav, Brno, Olomouc, Pilsen, etc.) were being founded, which would have extraordinary political influence on the structure of the Estates, no large commercial or financial companies were established in Bohemia that could have entered into the silver trade. Instead, this role was assumed by the landed magnates from among the wealthiest nobility, who were actively involved in commercial and lending transactions on an international scale. The ever-changing outcome of the long-term political struggle for power in this country between the monarch and the Estates had a fundamental effect on the commercial, and especially export, potential of the region.[25] This was subsequently the case in the exports of food, alcohol and other commodities such as linen, hemp, iron, nonferrous metals, etc.[26] Hence, when Central Europe was enjoying an economic boom in the last third of the sixteenth century thanks to war in the Netherlands, it in turn handicapped competitors and opened markets for producers in Bohemia.

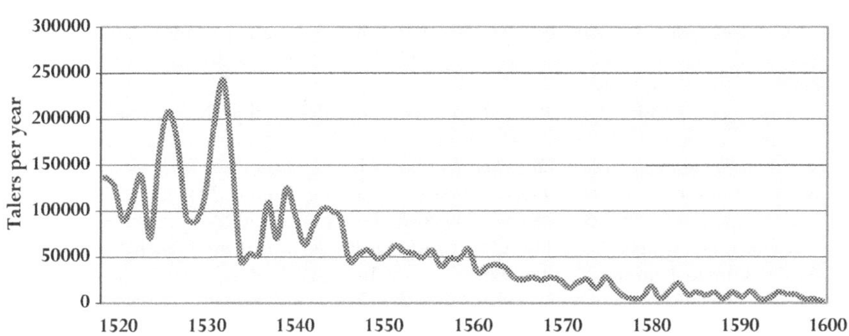


*Figure 3.3* Long-term net earnings of mining companies in Joachimstal from 1520 to 1600 (in thalers).

## Notes

1 P. Spufford, *Money and Its Use in Medieval Europe* (Cambridge: Cambridge University Press, 1988), pp. 137–39; H. Samsonowicz, 'European Economic Zones in the Middle Ages and Early Modern Times: An Attempt to Make a Comparative Analysis', in J. Kłoczowski (ed.), *East-Central Europe's Position Within Europe: Between East and West* (Lublin: Instytut Europy Środkowo-Wschodniej, 2004), pp. 135–53. On the extent of Bohemian silver production in the Late Middle Ages, see J. H. Munro, 'The Central European Silver Mining Boom, Mint Ouputs and Prices in the Low Countries and England 1450–1550', in E. Cauwenberghe (ed.), *Money, Coins and Commerce* (Leuven: Leuven University Press, 1991), pp. 119–83; M. North, *Das Geld und seine Geschichte: Vom Mittelalter bis zur Gegenwart* (München: C. H. Beck, 1994), pp. 41–43 ('Europäische Münzproduktion im Spätmittelalter (in kg)'); E. P. Hunt and J. M. Murray, *A History of Business in Medieval Europe 1200–1550* (Cambridge: Cambridge University Press, 1999), pp. 130–31 ('Trading, Tourism and Silver-mining Centers of Late Medieval Western Europe') and pp. 172–74.

2 H. Jireček (ed.), *Codex juris municipalis Regni Bohemiae*, Tomus I (Prague, 1867), pp. 265–435.

3 K. Krofta, 'Bohemia in the Fourteenth Century', in C. W. Previté-Orton and Z. N. Brooke (eds.), *Cambridge Medieval History, vol. VII: Decline of Empire and Papacy* (Cambridge: Cambridge University Press, 1932), pp. 155–82.

4 J. U. Nef, 'Silver Production in Central Europe 1450–1618', in D. O. Flynn and A. Giráldez (eds.), *Metals and Monies in an Emerging Global Economy* (Aldershot:Variorum, 1997), pp. 1–17.

5 J. W. Thompson, *Economic and Social History of Europe in the Later Middle Ages* (New York and London: Century Co, 1931), pp. 218–23, pp. 481–507; F. Braudel, *Civilisation and Capitalism, 15th – 18th Century*, vol. 2, trans. S. Reynolds (London: Harper and Row, 1982), p. 197; Hunt and Murray, *A History of Business in Medieval Europe, 1200–1550*, pp. 172–74; P. Vorel, 'European Silver and Coins at the Turn of the 15th and 16th Centuries', in *From the Silver Czech Tolar to a Worldwide Dollar: The Birth of the Dollar and Its Journey of Monetary Circulation in Europe and the World from the 16th to the 20th Century* (New York: Columbia University Press, 2013), pp. 1–26.

6 J. Klassen, 'Hus, the Hussites and Bohemia', in C. Allmand (ed.), *The New Cambridge Medieval History, vol. VII: c. 1415–1500* (Cambridge: Cambridge University Press, 1998), pp. 367–91.

7 M. Dvořák, 'Die Fälschungen des Reichskanzklers Kaspar Schlick', *Mitteilungen des Instituts für Österreichische Geschichtsforschung*, 22:1 (1901), pp. 51–107.

8 W. Weizsäcker, *Sächsisches Bergrecht in Böhmen: Das Joachimsthaler Bergrecht des 16: Jahrhunderts* (Reichenberg: Stiepel, 1929); P. Vorel, 'History of the Jáchymov Mint and Catalogue of Coinage from the Years 1519/1520–1619', in L. Nemeškal and P. Vorel (eds.), *Dějiny jáchymovské mincovny a katalog ražeb, I. 1519/1520–1619* (Pardubice: Univerzita Pardubice, 2010), pp. 261–68.

9 P. Vorel, 'Die Länder der böhmischen Krone und das Heilige Römische Reich in der Frühen Neuzeit', in J. Pešek and P. Vorel (eds.), *Neue tschechische Interpretationen der Fragen des tschechisch-deutschen Zusammenlebens: die Vortragenden der tschechischen Gastsektion / 47: Deutscher Historikertag, Dresden 2008* (Magdeburg: Meine, 2011), pp. 21–32; P. Vorel, 'Státoprávní vyčlenění českých zemí ze Svaté říše římské: Důsledky říšské reformy Maxmiliána I. Habsburského' ['The Constitutional Exclusion of the Czech Lands from the Holy Roman Empire: Consequences of the Imperial Reform of Maximilian I of the House of Hapsburg'], *Český časopis historický [The Czech Historical Review]*, 111 (2013), pp. 743–804.

10 Nemeškal and Vorel, *Dějiny jáchymovské mincovny*, pp. 10–11.

11 P. Vorel, 'The Political Context of the Origin and the Exportation of Thaler-Coins from Jáchymov (Joachimsthal) in the First Half of the Sixteenth Century', in N. Holmes (ed.),

*Proceedings of the XIVth International Numismatic Congress Glasgow 2009, II* (Glasgow and London: Spink, 2011), pp. 1778–82.

12 See diagram no. 1, 'Net Earnings of Mining Companies in Joachimstal from 1520 to 1528 (in Thalers)'; for records, see Nemeškal and Vorel, *Dějiny jáchymovské mincovny*, table 5, p. 40.

13 P. Vorel, *Od pražského groše ke koruně české: Průvodce dějinami peněz v českých zemích [From the Prague Groat to the Czech Crown: History of Money in the Czech Lands]*, 2nd edition (Prague: Rybka, 2004), pp. 101–11.

14 P. Vorel, 'Czech Roots of the American Dollar', *Kosmas*, 23:2 (2010), pp. 32–42.

15 See diagram no. 2, 'The Export of Silver from Joachimsthal to Saxony (Pieces of Thalers) from January 1520 to April 1528'; for records, see Nemeškal and Vorel, *Dějiny jáchymovské mincovny*, tables 3–4, p. 39.

16 P. Vorel, 'First Imperial Minting Order of 1524', in *Monetary Circulation in Central Europe at the Beginning of the Early Modern Age: Attempts to Establish a Shared Currency as an Aspect of the Political Culture of the 16th Century (1524–1573)* (Pardubice: Univerzita Pardubice, 2006), pp. 43–60.

17 P. Vorel, '"Gold era" of Central European Silver (1519–1545)', in *Stříbro v evropském peněžním oběhu 16.-17: století (1472–1717) [Silver in the European Monetary Circulation of the 16th and 17th Centuries (1472–1717)]* (Prague: Rybka, 2009), pp. 123–56.

18 P. Vorel, 'Landesfinanzen und Währung in Böhmen (Finanz- und Münzpolitik im Spannungsfeld von Ständen und Königtum während der Regierung Ferdinands I. und Maximilians II.)', in F. Edelmayer, M. Lanzinner, and P. Rauscher (eds.), *Finanzen und Herrschaft (Zu den materiellen Grundlagen fürstlicher Politik in den habsburgischen Ländern und im Heiligen Römischer Reich im 16. Jahrhundert), Veröffentlichungen des Instituts für österreichische Geschichtsforschung*, vol. 38 (Munich and Vienna: Institut für österreichische Geschichtsforschung, 2003), pp. 186–214.

19 P. Vorel, 'Směnné kursy jako nástroj mocenské politiky v Římsko-německé říši počátkem čtyřicátých let 16. Století' ['Exchange Rates as a Tool of Power Politics in the Holy Roman Empire at the Beginning of the 1540s'], *Český časopis historický [The Czech Historical Review]*, 112:3 (2014), pp. 379–401.

20 Nemeškal and Vorel, *Dějiny jáchymovské mincovny*, pp. 47–76.

21 P. Vorel, 'Jáchymovský mincmistr Mikuláš (Klaus) Kraus a jeho působení v obchodě s českým stříbrem v letech 1530–1535' ['Jáchymov's Münzmeister Nicolaus (Klaus) Kraus and His Activities in the Trade with Bohemian Silver Between 1530–1535'], *Theatrum historiae*, 1 (2006), pp. 69–81; P. Vorel, 'Jáchymovské tolary z roku 1527 se jménem Jeronýma Šlika a jejich význam pro stanovení chronologie jáchymovských ražeb' ['Thalers Struck in Joachimsthal in 1527 with the Name of Jerome Schlick and Their Importance for Chronology of the Coins from Joachimsthal'], *Numismatické listy*, 68 (2013), pp. 56–69.

22 P. Vorel, *The War of the Princes: The Bohemian Lands and the Holy Roman Empire 1546–1555* (Saint Helena, CA: Helena History Press, 2015), pp. 137–41, 169–74.

23 J. Janáček, 'Die Fugger und Joachimstal', *Historica*, 6 (1963), pp. 109–44; P. Vorel, 'Money in the Political Culture of 16th Century Central Europe', in H. Manikowska, J. Pánek, M. Hułas, M. Holý, and R. Baron (eds.), *Political Culture in Central Europe (10th – 20th Century), Part I: Middle Ages and Early Modern Era* (Prague: Historický ústav Akademie věd, 2005), pp. 179–201.

24 See diagram no. 3, 'Long-term Net Earnings of Mining Companies in Joachimstal from 1520 to 1600 (in Thalers)'; for records, see Nemeškal and Vorel, *Dějiny jáchymovské mincovny*, table 5, p. 40; table 15, p. 75; table 18, p. 91; table 22, p. 111; table 26, p. 130.

25 P. Vorel, 'Frühkapitalismus und Steuerwesen in Böhmen (1526–1648)', *Anzeiger der philosophisch-historischen Klasse, Österreichische Akademie der Wissenschaften*, 137:1 (2002), pp. 167–82; P. Vorel, *Monetary Circulation in Central Europe at the Beginning of the Early Modern Age: Attempts to Establish a Shared Currency as an Aspect of the Political Culture of the 16th Century (1524–1573)* (Pardubice: Univerzita Pardubice, 2006), pp. 103–9.

26 J. Janáček, 'Export of Agricultural Products from the Czech Lands and Transportation Expenses in the 16th Century', in *Hospodářské dějiny [Economic History]*, 1 (Published on the occasion of the VIIth International Economic History Congress in Edinburgh 1978) (Prague: Institute of Czechoslovak and World History of the Czechoslovak Academy of Sciences, 1978), pp. 169–91; E. Maur, 'Der böhmische und mährische Adel vom 16. bis zum 18. Jahrhundert', in H. Feigl and W. Rosner (eds.), *Adel im Wandel (Vorträge und Diskussionen des elften Symposions des Niederösterreichischen Instituts für Landeskunde, Horn, 2.-5. Juli 1990), Studien und Forschungen aus dem Niederösterreichischen Institut für Landeskunde*, vol. 15 (Wien: Niederösterreichisches Institut für Landeskunde, 1991), pp. 17–38.

# 4 Trade, truck, custom and barter – glimpses from slave-trade cargoes

*Cheryl Susan McWatters and Yannick Lemarchand*

> *In effect, this commerce is not only precious for the gold and ivory; it is infinitely more so for the Blacks that it procures, the only ones capable of supporting the painful work in the colonies that the cultivation and the refineries require, where the heat of the climate is an overwhelming weight [ . . . ] What commerce could be compared to this one, the result of which is to obtain men in exchange for merchandise! It must truly be regarded as the foundation of the colonies, and consequently, as the principal return of our maritime trade.*[1]

Men for merchandise – such was the view expressed by the *Chambre de Commerce* of Nantes in September 1762. Written as the Seven Years' War drew to a close and the slave trade demonstrated signs of resurgence in French ports, this declaration can be analysed and interpreted from any number of competing perspectives, much like the examination of the Atlantic slave trade itself. We do not review this extensive slave-trade literature. Our objective is more modest and focuses on this '*exchange for merchandise*'. Much less attention has been paid to these cargoes in terms of their content, the change in their composition over time and how these goods were integrated into local market patterns of the African continent.[2]

Richardson, amongst others, argues that the role of African traders in their capacity as consumers of the Atlantic slave-trade goods raises important questions of Western bias: African traders were 'unsophisticated and gullible'.[3] Both pejorative and patronising myths have coloured the historiography. As noted by Alpern, arguments that nothing was provided to the African market which was not already available – given African self-sufficiency, that the market was motivated by prestige and novelty-seeking behaviour or further that it consisted of 'geegaws' – are misleading at best. Citing Hopkins, the market instead is described as a 'floating supermarket' with a wide variety of trade goods on offer by the end of the seventeenth century with an expansion in market offerings over the next century.[4]

The examination of the eighteenth-century trade has provided important insights into its market structure, the provenance of trade goods, the judgements and calculations required by traders to prepare cargoes to meet market demand, and the need for multi-skilled captains to handle the operations once the vessel left port. In an era of imperfect information and communication lags, the preparation of cargoes fell victim to demand shifts and also the need to adjust them based on availability and prices on the supply side, not only before departure, but *à l'improviste* when on the African coast. In the French case, which we have examined elsewhere and our focal point in this instance, the situation was similar to that investigated more extensively for the English context, apart from the greater disruption of the trade during wartime periods. The trade was entwined in a global and networked marketplace as goods were sourced to meet the market preferences, quality and cost concerns of both *armateurs* and their African counterparts, along with respecting state restrictions. Thus we see, for example, fabrics from India, Brazilian tobacco via Portugal, arms from England and cowries from the Maldives making their own trade circuit before being included as merchandise in a trade voyage.[5] As noted with respect to the 'Age of Commerce', the slave-trade economy was integrated into a global market with its own social and structural dynamics and what duPlessis terms its own 'distinctive economic ecology'.[6]

Kouamé emphasises the Euro-centric bias of research into slave-trade cargoes – the merchandise left rather un-examined, apart from its exchange value.[7] The classification in the literature of cargoes in terms of the type of good, their function, use, prestige and so forth has reflected this bias. Kouamé proposes an alternative classification from the African point of view: goods related to physical and social wellbeing; goods harmful to health and which promoted deviant behaviour; and goods that nurtured war and insecurity.[8] However, few records exist of these goods in terms of their diffusion and exchange once initially traded for captives on the African coast. While Kouamé judges oral histories of these events to be less than reliable chronologically, they do provide clues to 'discern the mental attitude towards European trade merchandise available at coastal forts' and also to comprehend traditional economic activities.[9] We do know that the choice of merchandise by all participants was not random, the composition of these cargoes changed over time and space, and importantly their cost relative to the overall expenses of preparing a vessel to leave port was not inconsequential. One important source of detail (informative albeit scarce) is the accounting and shipping records of these voyages, which outline in granular detail the goods shipped, their costs and their exchange. Drilling down into these records and related correspondence provides further information into the choices made in terms of suppliers, sources, substitutions of different goods for others, cross-border sourcing and so on. Vessel logs and firm correspondence contribute to painting a more complete picture of how both African and European traders reacted to this market setting. This market was integrated into and supported by a global exchange economy, which had created trade circuits for the movement of goods, people and knowledge. The records of those engaged in the slave trade provide glimpses into the juggling act and decisions of participants. What we can piece together remains fragmentary and the motivation to generalise a dangerous one. We explore, thus on this basis, cargoes from the eighteenth-century slave trade emanating from France.

## The French eighteenth-century slave trade

Evidence has shown and the case made that the slave trade operated akin to a lottery where rich gains could be made yet were frequently offset by losses.[10] Thus the nature of the risks involved in each individual voyage renders cross-sectional generalisations and 'averages' less valuable. Our focus is the French slave trade (*la traite negrière*),[11] specifically the interval from the Seven Years' War to the French Revolutionary period. This latter point was one in which the trade was at a high peak after its almost complete disruption during the war period and its significant drop during the revolutionary period (abolition of the trade, illegal trade, re-instatement during the Napoleonic period, then a further period of illegal trade after 1814). More specifically, we analyse the trade originating in the port city of Nantes, as the leading trade centre, only to cede this rank to Bordeaux in the latter stages. The position of Nantes is revealed via figures for departure points for voyages leaving the five major ports: trade from Nantes represents slightly more than 57 per cent of the voyages (see Table 4.1).

From 1763 to 1792, the total number of ships 'outfitted' at Nantes rose from 127 to 230 per year and the average increase in tonnage from 182.28 to 235.97 tonnes. The corresponding averages for slave-trade vessels (*négriers*) for departures are 29 in 1763 and 21 in 1792 and average tonnage rose from 117.52 to 233.7 tonnes.[12] After the Seven Years' War, trade increased and returned to pre-war levels and also increased participation by *armateurs* in other cities, particularly La Rochelle and Bordeaux. Table 4.2 outlines the percentage of captives carried on vessels originating in Nantes declined from approximately 50 per cent before 1759 to less than 40 per cent after 1763.

The outfitting for the slave trade differed very little from other areas of maritime commercial shipping.[13] The *armateur* engaged in seeking partners who would associate with him to finance the purchase of the vessel, the cargo destined for the trade, and the advances paid to the ship officers and crew. As lead partner, he took care of these expenses and then launched a call for funds from the other interested partners by delivering to each of them a copy of the *compte d'armement* of the vessel. After leaving port, the ship captain – sometimes himself a partner in the operation – took charge of the common interests.

*Table 4.1* Departure point of the voyages examined.

| *Port of Registry* | *Number of voyages (1713–1792)* |
|---|---|
| Nantes | 1,402 |
| La Rochelle | 423 |
| Bordeaux | 393 |
| Saint Malo | 214 |
| Vannes | 12 |
| Total | 2,444 |

Source: Jean Mettas, *Répertoire des expéditions négrières françaises au XVIIIe siècle* (Paris: Société française d'histoire d'Outre-mer, 1984)

*Table 4.2* Percentage of captives transported by *les négriers nantais*.

| *Period* | *Percentage* |
|---|---|
| 1710–1719 | 65 |
| 1720–1729 | 45 |
| 1730–1739 | 53 |
| 1740–1749 | 49 |
| 1750–1759 | 56 |
| 1760–1769 | 44 |
| 1770–1779 | 35 |
| 1780–1789 | 30 |
| 1790–1793 | 36 |

Source: McWatters (2008)

His mission was to proceed with the purchase of captives, in exchange for the trade merchandise, then sell them to plantation owners and other buyers upon arrival in the Antilles. He then selected and prepared return cargoes with the merchandise received in exchange for captives, purchased for hard currency or exchanged for bills of exchange or other forms of credit.

Upon return of the vessel, the *armateur* was responsible for settling with the officers and crew, after the captain had given his formal account of his management of the voyage. Subsequently, he worked to obtain proceeds realised from the sale of the return cargoes of merchandise (*les retours*) and finally distribute the net proceeds amongst the investors, by delivering to each one of them a statement of all sales and proceeds via the *compte de désarmement*. While described succinctly, it is important to recognise that this process was long-term in nature with returns and sales from an individual voyage tracked for months and often years.

Thus we have what is familiarly called the 'triangular trade', recognised as such by the *Chambre de commerce* of Nantes well before named such by historians. Importantly, this triangular trade underscored that profit was long-term in nature and subject to market dynamics and trends:

> Profit is not determined solely by the sale of Blacks, some fairly good sales of them often take place; but the lack of exactitude in their payments by buyers, along with the debts on the return sales, that the buyer himself notes, have removed all appearance of profit. Its groundwork is laid by the economical purchase of merchandise in Europe and by the provisioning of the vessel, by the luck of a good trade on the Coast [of Africa], by a good sale in America, but it really resides only in the liquidation of returns in France.[14]

Frequently misinterpreted and misunderstood by those not delving into the accounts and their 'accounting' for the trade, profits arose from the ultimate sale of colonial commodities in the markets of Europe and not a calculation of the net difference between the cost of captives and their selling prices in the colonies. It is perhaps the tendency to perceive 'profit' in this manner that has contributed to the lack of interest in the merchandise itself. Yet the citation highlights the need for *armateurs* to select and purchase merchandise carefully subject to availability, price and quality.

From one *armateur* to another and from one port to another, the *comptes d'armement* and *désarmement* (outfitting and lay-out) were prepared and presented in a relatively standardised format, a sort of accounting standardisation before the term existed – a standardisation that resulted notably from the fact that each merchant trader could find himself alternatively in the position of *armateur* and an investor in shares of a number of voyages, moreover frequently with the same partners. These relations demonstrated the shared norms and co-operative competition that resulted from relations of reciprocity and co-operation, along with market competition, in terms of the undertaking of commercial activities that led to what was early 'normalisation' of private accounting.

However, only the *compte d'armement*, or also the '*compte d'achat, armement et entière mise-hors du navire Untel*' ('the purchases account, outfitting and entire cargo of vessel X') is of interest here. One finds therein the following categories:

- the cost of the vessel if it deals with a purchase or of the expenses to renew the vessel in the case of a used vessel, along with various equipment needed for its navigation;
- foodstuffs and utensils;
- advances to the crew;
- the purchase cost of the (merchandise) cargo;
- miscellaneous expenses: towage, carrier fees, duties, etc.;
- insurance on the vessel and cargo; and
- the commission by the *armateur*, generally 1–2 per cent on the total.

The global total of these costs was shared amongst the co-proprietors on the basis of this recapitulation. Each one of them received a copy of the summary in full detail.

In the case of the slave trade, the category of 'cargo' represented a very significant share of the total cost of the vessel's outfitting. In the case of Nantes, a calculation that we have undertaken based on the *comptes d'armements* of 38 vessels, outfitted by several *armateurs* of the city and studied by Meyer, gives an average proportion of 61 per cent of the total cost of the *armement*. This percentage is analogous to that which one finds in several archives studied by Deveau for La Rochelle, in effect, 58 per cent on average for seven vessels.[15] For Bordeaux, Saugera indicates that he examined only a very small sample and even if the percentages that he obtained are slightly lower than those of Meyer, the differences are hardly significant.[16] For three voyages of vessels from Bordeaux, returned to later (*Le Joujou*, 1785 and 1788; *La Manette*, 1788),[17] and whose *comptes d'armements* were not used by Saugera, we obtain an average of 63 per cent.

An indication of the importance of the merchandise cargo can be seen by sampling the activities of one *armateur nantais*, François Deguer. Deguer had begun his trading activities in collaboration with extended family in Cadiz, under the Assiento Contract of Spain. After the loss of this contract, he continued this line of trade and remained involved until the French Revolution when many traders lost their livelihood and fortunes from both the war and the subsequent revolution in Saint Domingue (present-day Haiti). While he outfitted and held diversified investments in many voyages and types of trade, an examination of the voyages of one vessel, le *Saint Jean-Baptiste*, provides insights into the value of merchandise cargoes. The three voyages of interest took place from June 1771 to June 1776. The cargoes represented 67, 71 and 80 per cent respectively of the total investment in each voyage. While Deguer expressed satisfaction with the first voyage (although he later dismissed the vessel captain Bodin des Plantes for ineffective management in the Antilles), he noted with concern that the value of merchandise for the second voyage had increased considerably. While the value of the entire *armement* had increased by 21 per cent, that of the merchandise alone was 28 per cent. In his view, based on correspondence to others in his trading network, these extra expenses resulted from market challenges and competition, which he had no option but to confront.[18]

## Merchandise cargo

A number of authors have addressed the question of slave-trade cargoes. Besides the synthesis works of Renault and Daget,[19] then Daget,[20] there are important studies of what were the slave-trade ports of Nantes,[21] La Rochelle,[22] Bordeaux[23] and Saint-Malo[24] and other work tracing the career of one captain[25] or one specific trade location.[26] In our opinion, the most complete examination of these cargoes remains the thesis of Aka Kouamé, which shifts the focus onto the merchandise itself beyond its exchange value but to investigate it much more deeply within a broader social and institutional context, particularly its impacts on those who did not benefit directly from the trade.

According to Kouamé, it was at the beginning of the second half of the seventeenth century that the assortment of slave-trade merchandise began to stabilise, after a phase during which slave traders (*négriers*) were initially inspired by the tradition of trans-Saharan trade exchanges between 'black Africa' (the part of Africa south of the Sahara Desert) and the Maghreb.[27] For Daget, who provides a list of 195 products, the assortment became almost invariable ('*à peu près invariable*') slightly later, from the end of the seventeenth. In effect, one can consider that the range of products that came to compose the cargoes was thus fixed (and Daget provides a list of 11 categories), but each category could only include a more limited number of items.[28] Regardless of their composition, the process to account for them became standardised over time, reflecting the communities of practice within the trade at the level of investors and traders, as well as ship captains.

### *Accounting for cargoes*

The merchandise cargoes can be studied on the basis of two types of different documents: the *compte d'armement*, already noted, and the ship's *journal de traite* (slave-trade journal). The *compte d'armement* included a detailed list of the merchandise, along with indication of their purchase costs and suppliers. In the slave-trade journal – not to be confused with the ship log (*journal de bord*) related to events concerning navigation – the accounting inscriptions of cargo operations were to be preceded with a '*facture*', effectively an invoice statement that detailed the specifics of the merchandise cargo without mention of the suppliers. In one or the other case, the document must be understood within the context of the money of account that presided during trade exchanges. It was in this manner, for example, that the *comptes d'armement* of *la Musette* and of *le Saturne* were concluded by a table presenting the conversion of the cargo into trade ounces (*réduction de la cargaison en onces de traite*) or that of *l'Aimable Aline* where we find the invoice statement of the cargo converted into bars (*facture de la cargaison réduite en barres*).[29] A copy of this invoice also had to be included in the vessel captain's *journal de traite*.

Thus, this 'invoice' should be analysed in terms of a contractual document linking the captain to the *armateur*, operating at the same level as the formal instructions that had been delivered to him.[30] Having as his mission to procure a given number of captives in exchange for the various elements of this cargo, he had to take account of and bear responsibility for its use. He met these obligations, in part, through the elaboration of a recapitulative table whose columns corresponded to the various merchandise of the cargo and the rows detailed one by one the different purchases of captives along with the specific merchandise given in exchange. This *tableau de traite*, of which Gaignat[31] provided a model that he had intended to commercialise, also would reveal the stock of merchandise remaining once trade operations concluded. Ship captains frequently were given specific instructions in their letters of instruction about the handling of this excess merchandise.

### *The model cargo*

Various authors provide the ideal type in terms of cargoes. We have, for example, the case of Savary, as well as his son Savary des Bruslons,[32] in the article '*commerce d'Afrique*' in the *Dictionnaire du commerce*. The latter work includes a multitude of quantitative and qualitative information drawn from the experience of the Compagnie de Guinée at the beginning of the eighteenth century, along with a variety of diverse *mémoires* such as the stories of the Chevalier des Marchais.[33] The article is organised in function of the diverse points of trade situated all along the coasts of Africa, from Sénégal to Mozambique, and provides several assortments of merchandise relative to local preferences. He pinpoints as well the *coutumes* (customs) and fees to pay, as well as the gifts when it was customary to present them. Later, Chambon[34] offers an overview of the merchandise for the trade along the Angolan coast, suggesting that the latter was much less well known by the French. Even later still, at a time when the trade relaunched after having been prohibited from February 1794 to May 1802,[35] Labarthe outlines equally 'model assortments', based on information collected in a set of reports prepared by officers of the marine who had sailed the coasts of Africa in the 1780s. Chambon insists on the necessity of diversifying the merchandise cargo:

> It is certain that if the trade could be undertaken with only one type of merchandise [*les 'rassades'* that is glassware], the profit would be immense; but as I have already observed, it is imperative that the cargo be varied, the payment for each slave being made with the most different types of merchandise possible. It is up to the captains, on a second voyage, to change the assortment according to the present tastes of the Angolans, and the abundance or the rarity of the merchandise mentioned above.[36]

The *armateur* Francois Deguer was well aware of the need for diversification and the risks from not doing so, expressing the view as early as the 1760s that certain voyages ended up as losses in that the merchandise sent to the African coast did not include an adequate variety of merchandise. Besides variety, he also deemed it important to be aware of the different market tastes and preferences at the various trade locations.[37] Certain *armateurs* including Deguer established a distinction between '*grandes marchandises*' and '*petites marchandises*'. The first incorporated the majority of fabrics, in particular Indian weaves, considered to be more expensive but necessary in some locations, specifically Angola, in terms of market preferences.[38]

As confirmed by any number of *comptes d'armement*, the primary merchandise category affecting the overall cost of these cargoes was fabrics, particularly those from India. The result was that cargoes destined for Angola, in which Indian merchandise was favoured, were more expensive than those prepared for the Côte de l'Or where we note a greater preference for *eau de vie* and *cauris*.[39] Similarly, in a proposal for a slave-trade expedition to the Angolan coast prepared in 1784 (*Projet d'une expédition de 350 nègres pour la côte d'Angole*) and examined by Labarthe, the composition of the cargo adopted merchandise distinctions.[40] Yet Labarthe also interjects an evaluation in terms of their necessity, declaring that there were '*grandes et petites marchandises*', yet deems the second as simply accessory.[41] However, this point would contradict what *armateurs* seemed to know in terms of the necessity of having the right assortment of goods in the right location. The cargo of *l'Africain*, a vessel outfitted at Nantes by Portier de Lantimo *frères* and destined for the trade on the Angolan coast, was divided into three categories: large, small and gift merchandise (*grandes marchandises, petites marchandises et marchandises de présent*).[42] As noted earlier, instructions given to captains included details on how to manage the cargo. For example, George David, captain of *la Bonne Société* from La Rochelle, was instructed to manage his '*grandes marchandises*' as much as possible in order to facilitate the end of his trade and also to use first as much of his '*petites marchandises*' as possible.

Further, it was underscored that if David did not use all of his merchandise, including that designated as *coutumes* and gifts (examined later), it would be noted favourably in terms of his performance.[43] Similar instructions were given to Philippe Hamon de Courchamp, captain of *la Reine des Anges,* who left the port of Nantes in 1741[44] and to Pierre-Ignace-Liévin Van Alstein by Portier frères for the voyage of *le Pompée* to the Coast of Angola. These instructions also included an article (XIII) that set out what should be done with merchandise that remained once trade had been completed.[45]

### Merchandise quality

The quality of the merchandise was recognised and evaluated by all parties involved. *Armateurs*, *négriers*, ship captains, supplier, agents and clearly those with whom they traded were well aware of the quality of the goods provided and of their estimation. Preferences were remarked upon, be it fabrics from India or arms from England versus what were perceived to be lower-quality substitutes. Moreover, traders were well aware that those with whom they exchanged goods were sophisticated in terms of their tastes and their bargaining:

> I could never recommend often enough that one bring good merchandise if one does not wish to be interrupted during their sale. Good faith even demands that one not sell anything for more than what the item is really worth. One could succeed once in trickery, but fraud once discovered will reflect on the Nation of those who undertook it. One must choose silk fabrics and colours that are genuine. I have seen assortments sent from Lyon for Guinea consisting of painted and gilded paper; all remained unsaleable. What idea do we have of these people? And what do we wish to make them think of the French?[46]

With respect to quality, it is well documented that French traders sourced guns from England, deeming those from France of lesser quality and subject to more defects. Fabrics were evaluated for their colour, weight and design. While fabrics sourced in France translated into lower costs, they were judged not to hold up equally to those from India and frequently discounted in terms of value by African traders. Deguer's correspondence to members of his merchant network, including amongst others suppliers, colonial agents, investors, other *armateurs* and ship captains, never failed to mention these elements: the need to meet the demands of courtiers in Africa, merchandise prices, terms of exchange and, of course, the prices of colonial goods on the European market. His correspondence conveys richly the multi-faceted business and global world in which he and his counterparts operated.[47] Deguer was meticulous and demanding in his orders – orders which he placed across Europe with comparison prices, payment details and market intelligence shared with others in his network. While *armateurs* competed, they also co-operated, as did ship captains either by choice or necessity (for example, refashioning and trading with other vessel captains their merchandise in Africa to meet demand). Correspondence to and from ship captains and agents relayed market information across the network enabling those engaged in the trade to adapt as best they could, given time lags and imperfect information, to changing market circumstances. *Armateurs* balanced market preferences with cost factors, along with issues of quality and timeliness of delivery. The composition of a cargo was a lengthy operation with orders sent to agents across France and Europe. The quality factor was critical, be it for fabrics, guns and gunpowder (often sought from London where credit and insurance markets deemed more attractive).

### *Merchandise exchange*

If we deem quality and cost as the basis of exchange, the exchange of captives for merchandise did not result from simple barter since buyers and slave merchants utilised a money of account to express the price of *les captifs*. Along the length of what was called the Coast of Guinea (*la côte de Guinée*), this unit of account was the trade ounce (*l'once de traite;* subdivided into *l'écu*, one-sixteenth of an ounce), and as a multiplier, *le marc*, eight ounces. In Senegal, as well as in Calabar in the Niger Delta, it was *la barre* (bar of iron). Finally, along the Coast of Angola, it was *la pièce*[48] (a piece of fabric) subdivided into *le pagne*, one quarter of a piece. Chambon explains this system as follows:

> The Angolese never make use of cash species. They have imagined an ideal value, based on their most urgent needs. They have established it for the price of a small piece of fabric the size of one of our handkerchiefs, which they attach to their belt like an apron to appear without shame in public. [. . .] These pieces of fabric are called '*pagnes*', four of which comprise *la pièce* which serves as a measure or the price of all of our merchandise. Thus, if one of our pieces of fabric is evaluated at 18 *pagnes*, it is the same thing as saying four and ½ pieces and vice versa.[49]

During each purchase of a lot of captives, once the price in ounces, bars or pieces had been established as a result of a first encounter, it was necessary to convert the latter into merchandise; moreover, each item of merchandise carried by the slave vessels had equally a price expressed according to the unit of account specific to the area. As confirmed by Chambon, this price resulted from local preferences:

> One can conceive readily that the real value of our merchandise, relative to what it cost in France, depends on the capriciousness of the Angolans, who value sometimes at six *pièces*, an item sold in France for 60 *livres*, and value at ten *pièces* another item that would have been purchased for only 30 *livres*. The desire to have a few pieces of our merchandise, or the utility that they

> believed that they could gain from it, can lead to an increase or decrease in their prices. However, since this trade would become arbitrary if the fantasies of the Angolans were to be the unique rule and the amount of cargo adequate for the purchase of 400 negroes were sufficient sometimes for only 200; if we were obligated to conform to their whims, it was necessary to fix the evaluation, both of our merchandise as well as for slaves, according to their sex and their age. It is up to our captains to display firmness to maintain the price of their merchandise.[50]

Chambon sets out two essential questions: that of the prices relative to merchandise, prices which differed depending on whether it was the purchase price for the *armateurs* or that which had been attributed to merchandise by their African courtiers; then next, that of the stability of these same prices. We first explore the second question before returning to examine the former.

### *Price stability*

The prevailing prices are known to us thanks to the tables for the conversion of cargoes into ounces, bars or pieces, which we noted earlier, and which appear in the *comptes d'armement* and more commonly in the (slave) trade journals. Moreover, one also finds these prices in the detail provided of each transaction, as recorded in the trade journal, such as the transaction in Figure 4.1 for an entry of 4 July 1741 from the trade journal of *la Reine des Anges*, a vessel originating in Nantes:[51]

4 juillet 1741. Au Petit Popo, traité ce jourd'huy à terre avec les nègres marchands du dit lieu deux hommes, un à huit onces et l'autre à sept onces, et deux femmes, l'une à six onces et l'autre à cinq, et une négritte à quatre onces et demi et quatre écus, pour le compte de la cargaison du navire en les marchandises suivantes :

| | | onces | | écus |
|---|---|---|---|---|
| 7 | Ancre d'eau de vie | 7 | | |
| 11 | Once de bouges (cauris) | 11 | 1/2 | |
| 48 | Pièce de platilles | 6 | | |
| 3 | Baril de poudre de 18 livres | 1 | 1/2 | 4 |
| 4 | Pièce de salempouris bleus | 2 | | |
| 1 | Pièce de guingans | | 1/2 | |
| 3 | Pièce de caftas | 1 | 1/2 | |
| 4 | Barre de fer | | 1/2 | |
| | | 30 | 1/2 | 4 |

*Figure 4.1 La Reine des Anges* (July 1741).

Source: ADLA Fonds Chaurand 16 J 9

*Table 4.3* Examples of prices in *onces de traite*.

| | *La Reine des Anges* | *Le Roi Dahomey* | *La Suzanne Marguerite* | *Le Pactole* Rinchon, pp. 348–350 | *La Musette* | *Le Saturne* | Labarthe (Juda, pp. 261–262) |
|---|---|---|---|---|---|---|---|
| | 1741–1742 | 1773 | 1775 | 1777 | 1786 | 1789 | 1788 |
| Pièce d'indienne | 1/2 | 1/2 | 1/2 | 1/2 | 1/2 | 1/2 | 1/2 |
| Pièce de platilles | 1/8 | 1/8 | 1/8 | 1/8 | 1/8 | 1/8 | 1/8 |
| Pièce de salempouris bleus | 1/2 | – | 1/2 | – | – | – | – |
| Pièce de guingans | 1/2 | 1/2 | – | 1/4 | – | – | 1/4 |
| Pièce de batujapeaux | – | 1/2 | – | 1/2 | – | 1/2 | 1 |
| Pièce de guinée | – | 1/2 | – | 1/2 | – | 1/2 | 1/2 |
| Pièce de mouchoirs de Cholet | – | 1/2 | 1/2 | 1/2 | 1/2 | – | – |
| Pièce de coutil | – | 1 | – | 1/2 | – | 1 | – |
| Pièce de mouchoirs de Rouen | – | 1/2 | – | | – | 1/2 | – |
| Pièce de siamoise | – | 1 | 1 | 1 | 1 | 1 | 1 |
| Chapeau bordé | – | – | 1/8 | 1 1/4 | 1 | 1 | 1 |
| Chapeau | – | 1/8 | 1/8 | 1/25 | 1/8 | 1/8 | 1/4 |
| Ancre d'eau de vie | 1 | 1 | 1 | 1 | 1 | 1 | 1 |
| Fusil | 1/4 | 1/4 | 1/4 | 1/4 | 1/4 | 1/4 | 1/4 |
| Pierre à fusils (le 100) | – | 1/30 | 1/40 | – | – | – | – |
| Baril de poudre de 30 livres | 1 | 1 | 1 | 1 | 1 | 1 | 1 |
| Once de bouges (cauris) | 1 | 1 1/10 | – | – | 1 | 1 | 1 |
| Coffre de pipes | 4 1/2 | 3 | – | 1 | 2 | 2 | 2 |
| Barre de fer | 1/8 | 1/4 | 1/4 | 1/4 | 1/4 | 1/4 | 1/4 |
| Rolle de tabac du Brésil | 1 1/2 | 1 | – | 1 | 1 | 1 | 1 |

*Table 4.4* Trade prices in *barres*.

| | *La Marie Aline* | *Le Guerrier*[1] | *La Bonne Mère* |
|---|---|---|---|
| | 1787 | 1790 | 1815 |
| Pièces de Guinées de l'Inde | 4 1/2 | 4 1/2 | 4 1/2 |
| Pièces de Chasselas de l'Inde | 4 1/2 | 4 1/2 | 4 1/2 |
| Pièces de limeneas idem | 4 1/2 | 4 1/2 | 4 1/2 |
| Pièces d'indiennes d'Orillard | 4 1/2 | 4 1/2 | 4 1/2 |
| Pièces de Nicaneas de l'Inde | 3 1/2 | 3 1/2 | 3 1/2 |
| Pièces de phautes de Rouen | 3 1/2 | 3 1/2 | – |
| Pièces de romals de l'Inde | 3 | 3 | 3 |
| Pièces mouchoirs de Cholet | – | 3 | 3 |
| Barres de fer | 1 | 1 | 1 |
| Fusils français | – | 4 | 4 |
| Neptunes de cuivre | – | 3 | 3 |
| Masses rassades | 1 | 1 | 1 |
| Douzaines de couteaux flamands | 20 couteaux/barre | 20 couteaux/barre | 20 couteaux/barre |
| Douzaines de miroirs | 6 barres la dzne | 6 barres la dzne | – |
| Douzaines de cadenas | 3 barres la dzne | 3 barres la dzne | – |
| Sacs de plomb à giboyer | 6 sacs/barre | 2 sacs la barre | 2 sacs la barre |

1 ADLA. 1 J 679, Facture des marchandises qui composent la cargaison du navire le Guerrier, capitaine Vincent Magouët, armateur René Odiette, allant à Banny rivière du Kalbar pour y faire la traite des nègres.

Thus if the price of captives evolved – for example, it was necessary to pay at least the equivalent of 50 ounces in Juda in 1788 to procure an analogous group of captives, according to the information given by Labarthe[52] – merchandise prices demonstrated a relative fixity. Tables 4.3, 4.4 and 4.5 present the accounting documents related to a sample of vessels, along with the details provided by a number of contemporary authors. We include in these tables only the merchandise that figured in at least two different cargoes, and some items have been eliminated given the inability to determine their prices in a precise manner based on the data at our disposal. The first table is based on ounces (*l'once*), the second on the bar (*la barre*) and the third is per piece (*la pièce*).

Contrary to the arguments of Kouamé,[53] the use of the ounce (*l'once*) as a unit of account dates well before the 1770s, given that it appears in the trade journal (*le journal de traite*) of *la Reine des Anges*, which arrived on the coast of Africa in 1741. Its use is likely much older, as reported by Johnson;[54] nevertheless we find no mention in either Savary des Bruslons or the Chevalier

*Table 4.5* Trade prices in *pièces*.

| | Van Alstein, pp. 49–50 | | *Le Pompée* | Proyart[1] | Chambon | Labarthe | Labarthe | *Le Joujou* |
|---|---|---|---|---|---|---|---|---|
| | 1754 | 1754 | 1769 | 1776 | 1783 | 1784 | 1784 | 1788 |
| | Loango | Malimba Cabinda | Côte d'Angole | Loango pp. 152–155 | Côte d'Angole | Loango pp. 294–296 | Malimba Cabinda pp. 291–293 | Ambris |
| Pièce de guinées | 2 1/2 | 3 | 3 | 2 1/2 | 3 | 2 1/2 | 3 | 3 |
| Pièce d'indiennes | 2 1/2 | 3 | 3 | 2 1/2 | 3 | 2 1/2 | 3 | 3 |
| Pièce de limeneas | 2 1/2 | 3 | 3 | – | – | 2 1/2 | 3 | 3 |
| Pièce de chasselas | 2 | 2 1/2 | 2 1/2 | 2 | – | 2 | 2 1/2 | 2 1/2 |
| Pièce batujapeaux | 2 | 2 1/2 | 2 1/2 | 2 | – | 2 | 2 1/2 | 2 1/2 |
| Pièce néganepeaux | 2 | 2 1/2 | 2 1/2 | 2 | – | 2 | 2 1/2 | 2 1/2 |
| Pièce grands Nicaneas | 1 1/2 | 2 | 2 | 1 1/2 | – | 1 1/2 | 2 | 2 |
| Pièce tapsels | 1 1/2 | 2 | 2 | – | 1 1/2 | 1 1/2 | 2 | 2 |
| Pièce nicanéas de l'Inde | 1 1/4 | 1 1/2 | | – | 1 1/2 | 1 1/4 | 1 1/2 | 1 1/2 |
| Pièce mouchoirs Cholet | – | – | 1 1/2 | 1 1/2 | – | 1 1/2 | | 1 1/2 |
| Bayettes | – | – | 1/2 | – | – | | 1 | 2/3 |
| Caves d'eau de vie | 1 | 1 | – | – | 1 | | | – |
| Fusils | 1 | 1 | 1 | 1 | 1 | 1 | 1 | 1 |
| Sabres | – | – | 1/4 | 1/4 | 1/2 | | | 1/4 |
| Barres de fer | 1/2 | 1/2 | 1/2 | 1/2 | – | 1/2 | 1/2 | 1/2 |
| Sacs de plomb | 1/4 | 1/4 | 1/4 | 1/2 | – | | | 1/5 |
| Douzaines de couteaux | 1/4 | 1/4 | 1/4 | 1/4 | 1/4 | | | 1/4 |
| Barril de poudre | 1 | 1 | – | 1 | 1 | 1 | 1 | 1/3 |
| Masse rasade | – | – | 1 | – | 1 | 1/2 | | 1/4 |
| Douzaines de cadenas | – | – | – | – | – | | | 5/8 |
| Cannettes de grés | 1/10 | 1/10 | 1/10 | – | 1/8 | 1/10 | | – |

1 M. l'Abbé Proyart, *Histoire de Loango, Kakongo et autres royaumes d'Afrique* (Paris and Lyon: Berton, Crapart, Bruyset-Ponthus, 1776).

des Marchais. While the number of data points for comparison is limited, one notices nevertheless a remarkable stability in prices for almost fifty years for *les platilles*, *les indiennes*, *l'eau de vie*, *les fusils* and also *les barils de poudre*.

Beyond the question of their relative stability, the three tables demonstrate that these prices were well known by vessel captains. The trade journals constitute precious sources of information in this regard, information collected and manifestly shared across the communities of practice of both *armateurs* and their captains.[55] These journals also indicate that the process of converting units of account into currency was well known, formalised and regularised.

## Conversion of units of account into currency

In previous research based on an example of a trade journal from the vessel, *Le Senaut*, developed by Gaignat in his *Guide du commerce*,[56] we established the value of an ounce to be 40 *livres*, 5 *sols* and 10 *deniers*. By recapitulating the details of the slave purchases in their entirety and then adding up on one side, the price of captives in ounces and, on the other, the price of their equivalent merchandise in *livres, sols* and *deniers*, we then demonstrated that this result was very close to the value that appears in a document reproduced in Renault and Daget[57] that presents the conversion of trade merchandise from *La Musette*, a *négrier* from Nantes which departed 6 September 1788 for Juda. This '*réduction de la cargaison en onces de traite*'[58] enabled the vessel captain to determine the equivalence of 1 gold ounce as being 41 *livres*, 16 *sols* and 3 *deniers*. While we have not been able to date with exact precision the voyage or voyages that served as the source of inspiration for Gaignat, we have shown that it (or they) must have taken place prior to 1756. At almost thirty years distant, it suggests a remarkable stability in the price of trade merchandise and in the preference scales of African courtiers.

In effect, a sort of average equivalence seems to have been communally accepted for these units of account. While indicating the price of a Negro at Axim (Ghana) in 1788 to be 14 ounces in merchandise, Labarthe becomes more precise by noting, 'In this area of the coast, an ounce in merchandise is worth 40 *livres*.'[59] In the same manner, according to Rinchon, 'In 1750, a piece of the cargo is worth on average ten *livres tournois*.'[60] Moreover, subsequent to this initial research, we have assembled further data that demonstrate that the conversion of trade cargoes into ounces or pieces could result in the emergence of significant variations in the value attributed to this unit of account (see Table 4.6).

In our estimation, these differences are the consequence of two phenomena: first, the co-existence of two systems of relative prices – that of the *armateurs* and that of the Africans – the first subject to the variations linked to the market situation in Europe, whereas the second seems to have remained relatively fixed, as noted earlier; and second, the variation in the composition of cargoes. The comparison of conversion of the contents of two successive cargoes of *le Joujou*, outfitted within a three-year interval for the same destination by the trading house of Castaing of Bordeaux illustrates this point perfectly (Table 4.7).

The two cargoes of *le Joujou* each comprised forty-seven types of merchandise, thirty of which they shared in common. Yet in three years, the average value of a *pièce*, that is the purchase cost of a group of merchandise that was the equivalent of one *pièce* at the time of the outfitting, had gone from 8£ 8s, 16d to 5£ 18s, effectively a reduction of 31 per cent. In the end, with a one-third increase in the number of *pièces* in the 1788 cargo compared to that of 1785, the cargo of the 1788 voyage had nonetheless a cost which was approximately

*Table 4.6* Value in *livres* (money of account).

| | £ | *s* | *d* | Armateur | Destination | Source |
|---|---|---|---|---|---|---|
| *Onces* | | | | | | |
| *Le Senaut* | 40 | 5 | 10 | | | Gaignat (1773) |
| *Le Pactole*, 1777 | 34 | 4 | 11 | Nairac (Bx) | Guinée | Rinchon (1964, p. 350) |
| *La Musette*, 1786 | 34 | 17 | – | Lincoln (Nts) | Côte d'Or | ADLA 1 J 681 |
| *La Jeanne Thérèse*, 1785 | 30 | 6 | 8 | Chaurand (Nts) | Côte d'Or | ADLA 101 J 27 |
| *La Musette*, 1788 | 41 | 16 | 3 | Lincoln (Nts) | Juda | Renault et Daget (1985) |
| *Le Saturne*, 1789 | 32 | 5 | – | Lincoln (Nts) | Côte d'Or | ADLA 1 J 681 |
| *Pièces* | | | | | | |
| *Le Joujou*, 1785 | 8 | 12 | 9 | Castaing (Bx) | Angola | A.M. Bordeaux 1 S 1 |
| *Le Pompée*, 1786 | 8 | 14 | 7 | Portier (Nts) | Angola | Rinchon (1964, p. 236) |
| *La Manette*, 1787 | 7 | 1 | 5 | Castaing (Bx) | Angola | A.M. Bordeaux 1 S 1 |
| *Le Joujou*, 1788 | 5 | 18 | – | Castaing (Bx) | Angola | A.M. Bordeaux 1 S 1 |
| *Barres* | | | | | | |
| *L'Aimable Aline*, 1787 | 4 | 2 | 11 | Chaurand (Nts) | Calabar | ADLA 101 J 27 |
| *La Bonne Mère*, 1815 | 4,20 francs | | | Trottier (Nts) | Calabar | Saugera (1995) |

*Table 4.7* Comparison of cargoes – *Le Joujou*.

| | *Le Joujou* 1785 | | | *Le Joujou* 1788 | | |
|---|---|---|---|---|---|---|
| | Number of *pièces* | Total amount | Value of a *pièce* | Number of *pièces* | Total amount | Value of a *pièce* |
| | 10 129 | 87 948 | 8.12.9 | 13 728 | 81 051 | 5.18.0 |
| *Grandes marchandises* | 6 111 | 67 386 | 11. 0.7 | 7 130 | 56 309 | 7.18.0 |
| Cargo percentage | 60% | 77% | | 52% | 69% | |
| *Petites marchandises* | 4 018 | 20 562 | 5. 2.4 | 6 598 | 24 742 | 3.15.0 |
| Cargo percentage | 40% | 23% | | 48% | 31% | |

10 per cent lower overall. This difference can be explained by both the fact that small merchandise represented the most important share of the cargo and by the decrease in the purchase cost of the merchandise overall.

Thus one had to strike the right balance in constituting a cargo in order to result in one that was the least costly as possible, all the while enabling the maximisation of purchases. This same point has been made by Labarthe.[61] This balancing act demonstrated that traders were well aware of these cost trade-offs, as noted earlier in the case of Deguer. As we next discuss, it was also necessary to navigate the trade customs and negotiating norms.

## Coutumes, les palabres – *trade preliminaries and negotiations*

### *Obtaining the right to begin trade*

Amongst other usages, the word '*coutume*' had been used in France to denote the dues or tolls (*péages*) paid by the common carriers (*voituriers*) at the entry to cities, for the maintenance of bridges and roads, or also the duties paid for the entry or outflow of merchandise from certain ports such as Bordeaux and Bayonne. In terms of trade along the African coast, *les coutumes*

> were the duties that are paid on the coast of Guinee [...] to obtain permission from the Negro kings to trade on their lands. These *coutumes* are not uniform everywhere, some are heavy and others less so. There are some that reach as high as 2000 *livres*, French currency, but which are paid in terms of merchandise specific to the country; such as iron, *eau-de-vie*, fabrics, glassware, knives, etc.[62]

In the examples provided by Savary, certain *coutumes* are very similar to those that one finds in the work of Gaignat, for example, as indicated in Figure 4.2, the equivalent of eight captives offered in this respect to the king at Juda.[63]

We have a detailed description of these preliminaries from the trade journal of the vessel, *le Roi Dahomet*:

> One has the habit of acting a bit politically in the contact that one undertakes with these Negro *canotiers and patrons* (boaters and bosses), given the indispensable need that one has of them as it should be observed that every cargo passes through their hands and that they can make you huge losses which cannot be remedied, being even free from the least reproach, it being very easy for them to fill their pirogues at will and even capsize on the bar, if they had absolutely resolved to see the loss of a captain who had molested, beaten or struck them; one has examples of all types of things, moreover, they are their own boss. One has seen those who, for minor annoyances, have abandoned the ship in the middle of the trade and have retreated, their pirogue in tow, let one judge for himself the humiliation that it has brought to those to whom this happened...

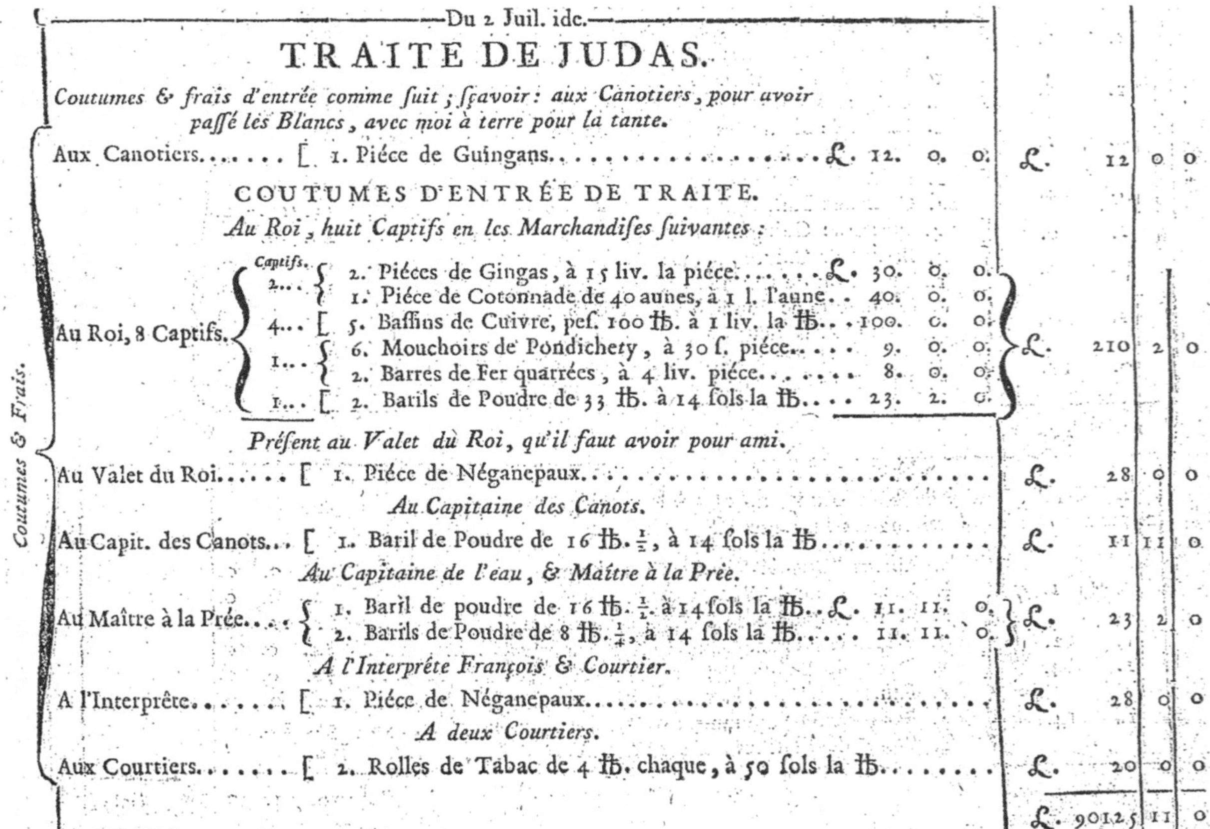

Du 2 Juil. idc.

TRAITE DE JUDAS.

*Coutumes & frais d'entrée comme ſuit ; ſçavoir : aux Canotiers, pour avoir paſſé les Blancs, avec moi à terre pour la tante.*

| | | | | | | | | |
|---|---|---|---|---|---|---|---|---|
| Aux Canotiers....... | [ 1. Piéce de Guingans.................... £. | 12. | 0. | 0. | £. | 12 | 0 | 0 |

COUTUMES D'ENTRÉE DE TRAITE.

*Au Roi, huit Captifs en les Marchandiſes ſuivantes :*

| | Captifs. | | | | | | | | |
|---|---|---|---|---|---|---|---|---|---|
| Au Roi, 8 Captifs. | 2... | 2. Piéces de Gingas, à 15 liv. la piéce....... £. | 30. | 0. | 0. | £. | 210 | 2 | 0 |
| | | 1. Piéce de Cotonnade de 40 aunes, à 1 l. l'aune.. | 40. | 0. | 0. | | | | |
| | 4... | 5. Baſſins de Cuivre, peſ. 100 ℔. à 1 liv. la ℔... | 100. | 0. | 0. | | | | |
| | 1... | 6. Mouchoirs de Pondichery, à 30 ſ. piéce..... | 9. | 0. | 0. | | | | |
| | | 2. Barres de Fer quarrées, à 4 liv. piéce........ | 8. | 0. | 0. | | | | |
| | 1... | 2. Barils de Poudre de 33 ℔. à 14 ſols la ℔.... | 23. | 2. | 0. | | | | |

*Préſent au Valet du Roi, qu'il faut avoir pour ami.*

| | | | | | |
|---|---|---|---|---|---|
| Au Valet du Roi...... | [ 1. Piéce de Néganepaux........................ | £. | 28 | 0 | 0 |

*Au Capitaine des Canots.*

| | | | | | |
|---|---|---|---|---|---|
| Au Capit. des Canots... | [ 1. Baril de Poudre de 16 ℔. ½, à 14 ſols la ℔........... | £. | 11 | 11 | 0 |

*Au Capitaine de l'eau, & Maître à la Prée.*

| | | | | | | | | | |
|---|---|---|---|---|---|---|---|---|---|
| Au Maître à la Prée..... | 1. Baril de poudre de 16 ℔. ½. à 14 ſols la ℔.. £. | 11. | 11. | 0. | £. | 23 | 2 | 0 |
| | 2. Barils de Poudre de 8 ℔. ¼, à 14 ſols la ℔..... | 11. | 11. | 0. | | | | |

*A l'Interprête François & Courtier.*

| | | | | | |
|---|---|---|---|---|---|
| A l'Interprête....... | [ 1. Piéce de Néganepaux........................ | £. | 28 | 0 | 0 |

*A deux Courtiers.*

| | | | | | |
|---|---|---|---|---|---|
| Aux Courtiers....... | [ 2. Rolles de Tabac de 4 ℔. chaque, à 50 ſols la ℔....... | £. | 20 | 0 | 0 |
| | | £. | 90125 | 11 | 0 |

*Coutumes & Frais.*

*Figure 4.2 Coutumes* and fees (July 1761).

> Finally, it is to be noted to show complaisance towards them and a few appropriate preliminaries will put them at the ready, such as a bonnet or hat to the two bosses, a handful of small merchandise, a drink of *eau-de-vie* when the bosses arrive in the evening to make their report to the captain to determine what one will have to do the next day, above all essential and to note clearly, give them what has been promised, better to offer nothing than to later refuse and to give them their exact payments every Sunday.[64]

These preliminaries can be readily characterised as a normal cost of doing business – both to open and close the trade. There is no deep sense that these exchanges were deemed cultural in nature. Letters by *armateurs* to their captains, agents and market colleagues note that the amounts to pay were well known including differences in these amounts in terms of competition and also location. For example, records of *La Reine des Anges*, noted earlier, indicate the *coutumes* paid to the King at Grand Popo in 1741, which with other records, suggest that the amounts paid were not random but represented a relatively fixed scale contingent on the number of captives traded. The *Guide du commerce*, in which Gaignat outlines slave-trade operations and their accounting, offers the reader the minute details of these transactions – at the beginning and the end of the trade in 1761 – at a series of locations. These payments to the king, courtiers and to others for various services rendered are entered into the accounts in granular detail, noting what was given, to whom and the value of these items in *livres*. Along with a variety of fabrics, hats and utensils, one notes the trade in guns, *eau-de-vie* and tobacco. Indeed, Kouamé would go further and emphasise the prevalence of such noxious and harmful items. However, it would be difficult to generalise this point given the relative paucity of the evidence. We also do not know what actually was done with these items – whether they were then traded, gifted or kept for personal use. The correspondence of Deguer also notes these payments and impact of competition on the amount of *coutumes* required. For example, correspondence of July and August 1774 to various partners and agents indicates his concerns about the excessive cost of the trade, including the increased amount of *coutumes* required, the equivalent of 10 *pièces*. These costs led Deguer to speculate that it would be necessary to give up this trade altogether in that it would never result in the returns anticipated.[65]

### *Presents*

Savary des Bruslons expresses perfectly the difference between *coutumes* and presents. 'Besides *les coutumes*, which are established rights, one also offers presents to the kings, Negro princes on the Coast, to secure an audience with them; moreover, it is clear that one does not appear before them without giving them something.'[66] It was not possible to escape the former yet the latter were no less unavoidable given that the need to obtain the good graces of the sovereign and further of a host of other individuals who would intervene in the trade operations and of whose services it would be necessary to be assured.

This point is evident in reading correspondence of *armateurs* such as Deguer who frequently commented via his correspondence with his trading partners and vessel captains on the state of competition and the ability to obtain preference relative to other slave-trade vessels. This preference was essential whether vessels were French or not.

Chambon speaks in similar terms with respect to the presents to be given to the sovereign of Cabinda on the Angolan Coast: 'Customary gifts that one should consider of necessity since not one captain can dispense with them'.[67] However, our archival research to date does not find these merchandise items frequently distinguished or isolated. For example, Gaignat includes these presents seemingly within entries for other *coutumes* and fees or *dachy* – a term adopted from the Portuguese *daçao* for various commissions.[68] In the case of the *armateur* Chaurand, we see these presents indicated for one vessel, *l'Aimable Aline*, which left for the coast of Galbar in February 1787. The accounting entries for these presents include a variety of items similar to those noted by Chambon: festooned hats, silk fabrics, mahogany bowls and containers, armchairs, scarlet fabrics (frequently noted also by Savary), dress clothes and so on. The cost of this merchandise was not minor, in this case, the reported cost being over 3,800 livres.[69] We would agree with Kouamé that while other parts of the expedition might be planned and estimated – and over time with some precision given the communities of practice and knowledge transfer within the trade – these gifts were not as readily quantified or regularised. Moreover, gifts frequently were given to others to lubricate the trading mechanisms. Finally, the use to which all of this merchandise was put is not certain, apart from what might be assumed to have been delivered for personal consumption based on conveyed preferences.

## Concluding remarks

Beyond detailed lists of merchandise in what might appear to the uninitiated as excruciating detail, what does the examination of slave-trade cargoes offer in terms of understanding the complex mercantilist relations of this period? Our initial glimpses into their composition and evolution over time confirm that these archival sources indeed deserve more examination and analysis, given the details on offer whose surface we have only scratched. These accounting documents display a sheer labour intensity in their preparation, compilation and reconciliation, which was analogous to the actual work to compose these cargoes. While we subscribe to the view that each slave-trade voyage was unique, each one also shared practices and techniques across these merchant communities. These shared understandings were reflected in the goods selected, standards of trade, the adoption of common practices related to *coutumes*, fees and presents, along with the evolution of goods provided in light of market preferences.

At this juncture, we would suggest areas for future work, especially to bring together the details from these cargoes with more macro-level analyses of global changes in trade and colonisation. The accounting for these cargoes and related correspondence of merchant traders confirm that these cargoes were no set of randomly assembled goods. Rather, *armateurs* and traders reacted to market signals, quality, cost factors and agent reliability, amongst other factors. They made informed choices to acquire goods in one market or another contingent on these multiple factors and market intelligence. For example, the composition of cargoes reveals frequent decisions to source goods domestically or to import them, including the weighing of preferences in the African market for goods that relied upon global supply networks. The decision to import often had a political dimension, particularly in wartime when traders would develop mechanisms to work around political barriers judged to be short-term or transient in nature. Importing goods – for example, arms and related supplies from England – conflicted with the view that domestic production should be given preference. Time also factored into decisions as the non-arrival of goods could lead to delays from port.

The cargoes suggest changing consumption patterns and an informed and perceptive African market player in terms of merchandise, its quality and cost. Yet we know little of the markets for these goods once traded. Bathily notes the economic and social impacts of this merchandise trade and its disruption of local African production especially that of food-stuffs that were exchanged for goods and shifted from domestic consumption to slave-trade input.[70]

Our analysis of slave-trade merchandise underscores yet again that the slave-trade was not an isolated industry but captured within a complex global project. Goods were circulating well beyond the Europe-African axis, and consumption patterns in Africa reflected this global 'supermarket'. Parallels are obvious with the fur trade in North America where similar impacts on consumption patterns and dependency have been revealed.[71] As Gervais and McWatters have argued, this globalisation differs from one frequently noted in the literature:

> Yet more recently, historians of earlier periods have called attention to the considerable enlargement of the sphere of merchant activity from the Lower Middle Ages on. For many specialists in 'Atlantic' history, and its successor 'global' history, globalisation actually started in the thirteenth or fourteenth century, with the development of European trade networks and their subsequent taking over of vast swaths of other continents.[72]

In their view, this global world of commodities, bank notes and commercial paper was well established by the end of the eighteenth century.

Our analysis would suggest that African traders were sophisticated consumers in their demands for particular items sourced from particular locales. We know from the correspondence of Deguer that he worried incessantly about issues of quality, cost and timeliness. For instance, fabrics from India were more expensive than others yet were preferred in the Angolan market – domestic fabrics being deemed inadequate substitutes. Deguer was also well aware that African markets were not all alike with the evolution of merchandise cargoes in response to trade location – yet within an overarching need to control costs.[73]

Moreover, merchant correspondence and accounting records underline that while trade had both an economic and social dimension, these merchandise cargoes (including goods allocated to *coutumes* and fees) were a cost of doing business. Presents, especially on repeat trade expeditions, might have been more customised. Nevertheless, they were not in the nature of items offered as mere gifts but rather as a requisite and routine element to facilitate trade.

The richness of these archival sources motivates deeper analysis in terms of the goods provided, how they were sourced and the series of market transactions and transaction costs that brought goods from around the globe to be introduced into the African slave-trade markets. Tracing goods for a particular cargo or several cargoes potentially would reveal, in concrete ways, the sinews of trade in which these markets and merchants operated. While not generalisable, patterns of action might be discernible for certain times and contexts, given what we know already of merchant practices and the willingness of these communities to both co-operate and compete. Critical to this mercantilist world was the accounting that recreated and re-presented it, notably accounting's ability to provide mechanisms to cross time and space. More than numbers and entries, these records established accountability and agency relations in a world of time lags and distance. Nonetheless, while this trade was unique in some respects, it should remind us too that merchants were adopting and adapting systems and techniques already well established in a world of global commodities.

## Notes

1 Archives départementales de Loire-Atlantique (hereafter ADLA). C881, f° 202, le 30 septembre 1762: « [. . .] En effet, ce commerce n'est pas seulement précieux par l'or et l'ivoire; il l'est infiniment plus par les Noirs qu'il procure, seuls capables de supporter les travaux pénibles que la culture et les raffineries exigent dans les colonies, où la chaleur du climat est un poids accablant [. . .] Quel commerce pourrait être comparé à celui dont le résultat est d'obtenir des hommes en échange des marchandises! On doit réellement le regarder comme la base des colonies, et par conséquent comme le principal ressort de notre commerce maritime ».

2 S. D. Behrendt, 'The Journal of an African Slaver, 1789–1792, and the Gold Coast Slave Trade of William Collow', *History in Africa*, 22 (1995), pp. 61–71. Behrendt provides insights into 'financial transactions for slaves between European and African traders on the coast of Africa during the late eighteenth century' for the English trade. Collow was one of the largest traders on the Gold Coast. The details from what is actually an 'account book' offer some comparative and confirmatory evidence, particularly as Callow engaged in the French trade and withdrew due to the financial impacts of the French revolution and the revolution in Saint Domingue.

3 D. Richardson, 'West African Consumption Patterns and Their Influence on the Eighteenth-Century Slave Trade', in H. A. Gemery and J. S. Hogendorn (eds.), *The Uncommon Market: Essays in the Economic History of the Atlantic Slave Trade* (New York and London: Academic Press, 1979), p. 304. A comparison with the modalities of the fur trade in North America seems obvious.

4 S. B. Alpern, 'What Africans Got for Their Slaves: A Master List of European Trade Goods', *History in Africa*, 22 (1995), pp. 5–43. See also P. D. Curtin, *Economic Change in Precolonial Africa: Senegambia in the Era of the Slave Trade* (Madison: University of Wisconsin Press, 1975); D. Richardson, 'West African Consumption Patterns and Their Influence

on the Eighteenth-Century Slave Trade', in J. T. Lindblad and R. Ross (eds.), *Gemery and Hogendorn (eds.), The Uncommon Market, and M. Johnson, Anglo-African Trade in the Eighteenth Century: English Statistics on African Trade 1699–1808* (Leiden: Centre for the History of European Expansion, 1990). For French exports, see S. Berbain, *Le comptoir français de Juda (Ouidah) au XVIIIe siècle* (Larose: Paris, 1942) [Mémoires de l'IFAN – 03], pp. 82–88. For the analogy to a supermarket, see A. G. Hopkins, *An Economic History of West Africa* (Longman: London, 1973), p. 111.

5 S. Daget, *La traite des noirs: Bastilles négrières et velléités abolitionnistes* (Rennes: Ouest-France université, 1990).

6 R. DuPlessis, 'Reorienting Early Modern Economic History: Merchant Economy, Merchant Capitalism and the Age of Commerce', in P. Gervais, Y. Lemarchand, and D. Margairaz (eds.), *Merchants and Profit in the Age of Commerce, 1680–1830* (Pickering and Chatto: London, 2014), pp. 171–80.

7 A. Kouamé, 'Les cargaisons de traite nantaises au XVIIIe siècle: Une contribution à l'étude de la traite négrière française' (Thèse de doctorat d'histoire, Université de Nantes, 2005).

8 Kouamé, 'Les cargaisons de traite nantaises au XVIIIe siècle', pp. 386–93.

9 Kouamé, 'Les cargaisons de traite nantaises au XVIIIe siècle', p. 111: « d'imaginer leur attitude mentale à l'égard des marchandises de traite européennes disponibles dans les forts côtiers ». See also E.-G. Kwaku, *Bono Manso: An Archaeological Investigation into Early Akan Urbanism* (Calgary: Department of Archaeology, University of Calgary Press, 1985).

10 C. S. McWatters, 'Investment Returns and la traite négrière: Evidence from Eighteenth Century France', *Accounting, Business and Financial History*, 18:2 (2008), pp. 161–85. O. Pétré-Grenouilleau, *Les traites negrieres: Essai d'histoire globale* (Paris: Gallimard, 2004).

11 As we have done elsewhere, to maintain the integrity of the French terms and to avoid complex translations, we adopt the following French terms, which do not have simple English equivalents: *l'armateur* – a ship owner, specifically a diversified entrepreneur engaged in maritime trade. The scope of the latter included vessel selection, the acquisition of investment capital, engagement of experienced captains and officers, and overall management, frequently with significant amounts of personal capital at risk; *le négociant* – merchant, but legally distinct in being engaged in wholesale trade yet prohibited from operating a retail establishment; *un négrier* – a vessel engaged in the trade, hence *la traite negrière* – the slave trade. See further O. Pétré-Grenouilleau, *Les négoces maritimes français XVIIe – XXe siècle* (Paris: Éditions Belin, 1997), pp. 35–101 for the emergence and evolution of the first two terms.

12 Averages are based on Meyer; J. Meyer, *L'armement nantais dans la deuxième moitié du XVIIe siècle, tome I et II* (Paris: Éditions de l'École des Hautes Études en Sciences Sociales, 1999). Tonnage figures contain over- and under-estimation; a tendency to understate initially to avoid taxes and duties, a tendency to over-estimate, especially after 1784 given state incentives, based on vessel tonnage, to encourage trade. See also G. Martin, *L'ère des négriers (1714–1774): Nantes au XVIIIe siècle* (Paris: Editions Karthala, 1993), p. 23. The percentage of the trade undertaken by *les armateurs nantais* declined after 1762, but Nantes continued to dominate the trade, while its percentage share increased significantly after the Restoration and during the period of illegal trade, Nantes' percentage share increased significantly. The year 1792 saw a significant drop in the trade due to insurrections in the colonies. The number of departures was 43 in 1789, 43 in 1790, and 40 in 1791, respectively.

13 Y. Lemarchand, 'Les comptes d'armement revisités: Les particularités comptables des sociétés quirataires à Nantes au XVIIIe siècle', *Revue d'histoire moderne et contemporaine*, 42:3 (1995), pp. 435–53; McWatters, 'Investment Returns and la traite négrière', pp. 161–85. These articles offer a more extensive presentation of the *compte d'armement* and of the triangular trade process.

14 ADLA. C881, f° 281, le 21 mars 1763: « Le profit n'est pas déterminé seulement par la vente des Noirs, il s'en fait souvent d'assez belles ventes; mais le défaut d'exactitude des

acheteurs dans les payements, joint aux dettes sur les retours, que l'acheteur remarque lui-même, ont ôté toute apparence de profit. Il est préparé par l'économie dans l'achat des marchandises en Europe et dans l'armement du vaisseau; par l'avantage d'une bonne traite à la Côte, par une bonne vente à l'Amérique, mais il ne réside réellement que dans la liquidation des retours en France. »

15 Meyer, *L'armement nantais dans la deuxième moitié du XVIIe siècle*, pp. 275–82; J.-M. Deveau, *La traite rochelaise* (Paris: Karthala, 1990), pp. 70–71.

16 É. Saugera, *Bordeaux port négrier, XVII^e-XIX^e siècles* (Biarritz-Paris: J et D éditions, Karthala, 1995), p. 245.

17 Archives municipales de Bordeaux, 1 S 1, Livre des comptes d'armement et désarmement de différents navires partis du port de Bordeaux, 1782–1802.

18 ADLA. Fonds Delaville-Deguer 8 J 20, 8 J 21, 8 J 23, 8 J 24, 8 J 5–8, 8 J 7–8, cf. C. S. McWatters 2008.

19 F. Renault and S. Daget, *Les traites négrières en Afrique* (Paris: Karthala, 1985), pp. 87–91.

20 Daget, *La traite des noirs*, pp. 85–99 and pp. 113–16.

21 D. Rinchon, *Les armements négriers au XVIII^e siècle d'après la correspondance et la comptabilité des armateurs et des capitaines nantais* (Bruxelles: Académie Royale des Sciences coloniales, 1956).

22 Deveau, *La traite rochelaise*, pp. 69–88.

23 Saugera, *Bordeaux port négrier, XVII^e-XIX^e siècles*, pp. 245–47.

24 A. Roman, *Saint-Malo au temps des négriers* (Paris: Karthala, 2001), pp. 77–82.

25 D. Rinchon, *Le trafic négrier d'après les livres de commerce du capitaine gantois Pierre-Ignace-Liévin Van Alstein* (Bruxelles: Éditions Atlas, 1938); D. Rinchon, *Pierre-Ignace-Liévin Van Alstein capitaine négrier: Gand 1733 – Nantes 1793* (Dakar: Institut Français d'Afrique Noire, 1964); A. Yacou, *Journaux de bord et de traite de Joseph Crassous de Médeuil de la Rochelle à la côte de Guinée et aux Antilles (1772–1776)* (Paris: Karthala – CERC, 2001).

26 S. Berbain, *Le comptoir français de Juda (Ouidah) au XVIII^e siècle* (Paris: Larose, 1942), pp. 77–88.

27 Kouamé, 'Les cargaisons de traite nantaises au XVIIIe siècle', p. 344.

28 Daget, *La traite des noirs*, p. 88.

29 ADLA. Fonds Chaurand, 101 J 27 Livre d'armements et désarmements 1784–1787.

30 For a cross-sectional analysis of these instructions, their contractual basis and the elaboration of the terms and conditions over time, see C. S. McWatters and Y. Lemarchand, 'Accounting for Triangular Trade', *Accounting, Business and Financial History*, 19:2 (2009), pp. 189–212.

31 C. Gaignat de l'Aulnais, *Guide du commerce* (Paris: Despilly, Durande, et Valade, 1773).

32 J. Savary des Bruslons, *Dictionnaire universel de Commerce* (Genève: Kramer et Philibert, 1742), tome I, partie II, pp. 613–672.

33 R. Père Labat, *Voyage du chevalier Des Marchais en Guinée, isles voisines, et à Cayenne: fait en 1725, 1726 et 1727* (Paris: Saugrain, 1730).

34 M. Chambon, *Traité général du commerce de l'Amérique* (Amsterdam-Marseille: Marc-Michel Rey, Jean Mossy, 1783), tome II, pp. 381–95.

35 Cf. É. Saugera, *La Bonne-Mère, navire négrier nantais – 1802–1815* (Nantes: Association Les Anneaux de la mémoire, 2012), pp. 45–50.

36 Chambon, *Traité général du commerce de l'Amérique*, p. 394: « Il est certain que si la traite pouvait se faire avec cette seule espèce de marchandise [les ‹ rassades › c'est-à-dire la verroterie], le profit serait immense ; mais, comme je l'ai déjà observé, il faut qu'une cargaison soit variée, le paiement de chaque esclave se faisant avec le plus de différentes marchandises qu'il est possible. C'est aux capitaines, dans un second voyage, de changer l'assortiment sur le goût actuel des Angolois, et l'abondance ou la rareté des marchandises ci-dessus mentionnées ».

37 ADLA. Fonds Delaville-Deguer, 8 J 4. Livre et Copie de lettres commencé le 3 décembre 1766 et fini le 1^e 8^bre 1768. F^o 5. Deguer à Verduc Vincent et Cie et Delaville frères

à Cadix, as cited also in Kouamé, 'Les cargaisons de traite nantaises au XVIIIe siècle', p. 343.

38 See R. S. DuPlessis, *The Material Atlantic: Clothing, Commerce, and Colonization in the Atlantic World, 1650–1800* (Cambridge: Cambridge University Press, 2015) for the examination of the market networks of the Atlantic basin with respect to fabrics and textiles.

39 Kouamé, 'Les cargaisons de traite nantaises au XVIIIe siècle', pp. 551–52.

40 P. Labarthe, *Voyage à la Côte de Guinée, ou description des côtes d'Afrique depuis le cap Tagrin jusqu'au cap de Lopez-Gonzalves* (Paris: Debray, 1803), pp. 294–97.

41 Labarthe, *Voyage à la Côte de Guinée*, p. 292.

42 Rinchon, *Pierre-Ignace-Liévin Van Alstein capitaine négrier*, p. 147.

43 Ordres et instructions pour servir à Monsieur George David, capitaine du navire la Bonne Société de la Rochelle, expédié pour aller à la Côte d'Angole traiter des noirs. 5 juillet 1783, Bibliothèque municipale de La Rochelle, Ms 2291. « Ménagez vos grandes marchandises autant que vous pourrez afin de faciliter la fin de votre traite et faites passer le plus qu'il vous sera possible de petites si vous réussissez à compléter votre traite sans employer toute la cargaison et vos présents, nous en serons extrêmement flattés. » 'Manage your large merchandise as much as you can in order to facilitate the end of your trade and exchange as much of the small merchandise as possible; if you are able to complete your trade without using all of your cargo and your presents, we will be extremely satisfied.'

44 ADLA. Fonds Berthrand de Cœuvres 16 J 9: « fera en sorte de se défaire dans le haut de la côte des marchandises qu'il prévoira n'être pas bonnes dans le bas » 'ensure that you rid yourself on the upper coast of the merchandise that you foresee not to be good in the lower'.

45 « Vous aurez soin de passer ce que vous aurez de plus commun dans votre cargaison au commencement de votre traite, pour n'avoir que du beau en terminant. » cited in Rinchon, *Voyage à la Côte de Guinée*, p. 240. 'You will need to take care to place that which is the most common in your cargo at the start of your trading, in order not to have only what is fine when ending it.' On these instructions, see also L.-M.-J. Ohier de Grandpré, *Voyage à la côte occidentale d'Afrique, fait dans les années 1786 et 1787: contenant la description des moeurs, usages, lois, gouvernement et commerce des Etats du Congo, fréquentés par les Européens, et un précis de la traite des noirs, ainsi qu'elle avait lieu avant la Révolution française* (Paris: Dentu, 1801), tome II, p. 59.

46 « Je ne saurais assez recommander de porter de bonnes marchandises, si on veut n'être point arrêté dans la vente. La bonne foi même exige de ne vendre quoi que ce soit, que pour ce que la chose vaut réellement. On peut réussir une première fois à tromper ; mais la fraude une fois découverte, retombe sur la Nation de ceux qui l'ont faite. Il faut choisir les étoffes de soie bien travaillées et que les couleurs soient vraies. J'ai vu des assortiments envoyés de Lyon pour la Guinée, consistant en papiers peints et dorés ; tout revint invendu. Quelle idée avait-on de ces peuples ? Et que voulait-on leur donner à penser des Français ? » Chambon, *Traité général du commerce de l'Amérique*, p. 89.

47 See Kouamé, 'Les cargaisons de traite nantaises au XVIIIe siècle', p. 177 and also ADLA. Fonds Delaville-Deguer 8 J 3 to 8 J 9 varia.

48 The expression '*pièce d'Inde*', signifying at its origin a piece of Indian fabric, was used equally in certain countries to represent a sort of standard measure of '*un captif*', namely a black of 15 to 30 years of age, healthy, robust, well-built, and with all his teeth ('*un noir de 15 à 30 ans, sain, robuste, bien fait et qui a toutes ses dents*'). See Chambon, *Traité général du commerce de l'Amérique*, p. 399. « On appelle pièce d'Inde, tout nègre sans défaut notable, depuis 15 jusqu'à 35 ou 36 ans, de même que les négresses ayant des enfants à la mamelle, ou non. » Savary des Bruslons, *Dictionnaire universel de Commerce*, p. 646.

49 « Les Angolais ne se servent point d'espèces courantes ; ils ont imaginé une valeur idéale, fondée sur leurs plus pressants besoins. Ils l'ont établie sur le prix d'une petite pièce de

toile, de la grandeur de nos mouchoirs, qu'ils attachent à la ceinture comme un tablier, pour paraître sans honte en public. . . . Ces morceaux de toile sont appelés pagnes, et quatre composent la pièce qui sert de mesure ou de prix de toutes nos marchandises. Ainsi, si une de nos pièces de drap est évaluée 18 pagnes, c'est la même chose que si on disait quatre pièces et demi et réciproquement. » Chambon, *Traité général du commerce de l'Amérique*, p. 382.

50 « On conçoit aisément que la valeur réelle de nos marchandises, relativement à ce qu'elles ont coûté en France, dépend du caprice des Angolais, qui estimeront quelquefois six pièces, un effet vendu en France 60 livres, et estimeront dix pièces un autre effet qui n'aura été acheté que 30 livres. Le désir d'avoir quelques espèces de nos marchandises, ou l'utilité qu'ils croiront en retirer, peuvent faire hausser ou baisser leur prix. Cependant, comme ce commerce deviendrait arbitraire si la fantaisie des Angolais en faisait l'unique règle, et que le montant d'une cargaison pour l'achat de 400 nègres ne suffirait pas quelquefois pour 200, si nous étions obligés de nous conformer à leur caprice, il a été nécessaire de fixer l'évaluation, tant de nos marchandises que des esclaves, suivant leur sexe et leur âge. C'est à nos capitaines à montrer de la fermeté pour maintenir le prix de leurs marchandises. » Chambon, *Traité général du commerce de l'Amérique*, p. 382.

51 ADLA. Fonds Berthrand de Cœuvres 16 J 9.

52 Labarthe, *Voyage à la Côte de Guinée*, p. 264.

53 Kouamé, 'Les cargaisons de traite nantaises au XVIIIe siècle', p. 289.

54 M. Johnson, 'The Ounce in Eighteenth-Century West African Trade', *The Journal of African History*, 7:2 (1966), pp. 197–214.

55 McWatters and Lemarchand, 'Accounting for Triangular Trade', pp. 189–212.

56 C. S. McWatters and Y. Lemarchand, 'Accounting Representation and the Slave Trade: the Guide du commerce of Gaignat de l'Aulnais', *The Accounting Historians Journal*, 33:2 (2006), pp. 1–37.

57 Renault and Daget, *Les traites négrières en Afrique*, p. 88.

58 'reduction of the trade cargo into ounces'.

59 Labarthe, *Voyage à la Côte de Guinée*, p. 57: « dans cette partie de la côte, l'once en marchandises vaut 40 livres ».

60 Rinchon, *Pierre-Ignace-Liévin Van Alstein capitaine négrier*, p. 51: « en 1750, la pièce de cargaison vaut en moyenne dix livres tournois ».

61 Labarthe, *Voyage à la Côte de Guinée*, pp. 141–42.

62 Savary des Bruslons, *Dictionnaire universel du Commerce*, p. 1181: « sont les droits qui se payent sur les côtes de Guinée [. . .] pour obtenir des rois nègres la permission de faire commerce sur leurs terres. Ces coutumes ne sont pas partout uniformes, les unes étant plus fortes, et les autres moins. Il y en a qui vont jusqu'à 2000 livres, monnaie de France, mais qui ne se payent qu'en marchandises propres au pays comme du fer, de l'eau de vie, des toiles, de la verroterie, des couteaux, etc. » According to Rinchon (1938, p. 183), coutumes were also known as 'welcome duties' (droits de bienvenue), an expression used on the Coast of Angola.

63 Gaignat de l'Aulnais, F° 327; Savary des Bruslons, *Dictionnaire universel de Commerce*, p. 659.

64 « On a coutume d'agir un peu politiquement dans la conduite qu'on tient avec ces nègres canotiers et patrons, vu le besoin indispensable qu'on en a car il est à observer que toute la cargaison passe par leurs mains et qu'ils peuvent vous faire souffrir de grandes pertes auxquelles on ne peut remédier, étant même à l'abri du moindre reproche, leur étant très facile de faire remplir leurs pirogues à volonté et même de faire gribou sur la barre, s'ils avaient absolument résolu la perte d'un capitaine qui les aurait molestés, battus ou frappés on a des exemples de toutes ces choses, d'ailleurs, ils ne dépendent que d'eux-mêmes.

On en a vu qui, pour de légers mécontentements, ont abandonné le navire au milieu de sa traite et se sont retirés amenant avec eux la pirogue qu'on juge de l'embarrais de ceux à qui cela est arrivé . . .

Enfin, il est à remarquer d'avoir de la complaisance pour eux et quelques amorces à propos leur mettent le cœur au vent, comme un bonnet ou chapeau aux deux patrons, une poignée de menues marchandises, un coup à boire d'eau de vie quand les patrons viennent le soir au comptoir faire leur rapport au capitaine pour savoir ce que l'on aura à faire le lendemain, surtout choses essentielle à remarquer, de bien leur donner ce que l'on promet, mieux ne rien offrir que de refuser ensuite et leur faire tous les dimanches leur payement exacts. » Extrait du Journal de navigation du navire Le Roi Dahomet, Archives Municipales de La Rochelle, Ms E 282, cited by R. Damon, *Joseph Crassous de Médeuil, 1741–1793: marchand, officier de la Marine royale et négrier* (Paris: Karthala, 2004), pp. 111–12.

65 ADLA. Fonds Delaville-Deguer, 8 J 8, f° 170 to 182. Deguer did not give up this trade, despite these oft-cited misgivings, until much later in his career. See also Rinchon, *Pierre-Ignace-Liévin Van Alstein capitaine négrier*, which details these expenditures in relation to the voyage of Le Roy Guinguin in 1763.

66 Savary des Bruslons, *Dictionnaire universel de Commerce*, p. 67: « Outre les coutumes, qui sont des droits convenus, on fait aussi des présents aux rois, ou princes nègres de la Côte, pour en avoir audience et il est établi de ne pas paraître devant eux sans leur présenter quelque chose ».

67 Chambon, *Traité général du commerce de l'Amérique*, pp. 395–96: « présents d'usage et qu'on devrait appeler de nécessité puisqu'aucun capitaine ne peut s'en dispenser ». « Ces présents consistent, pour le Roi, en un collier de corail, ou un miroir de moyenne grandeur, ou un manteau d'écarlate, ou une robe de chambre de damas ou de satin doublée d'un taffetas à flammes, d'une couleur bizarre, avec une cave de liqueurs ou d'eau-de-vie. Les présents pour le Mafouque et le Manbouq, sont une cave d'eau-de-vie, et en étoffes, la valeur de quatre à cinq piéces pour chacun. Ces présents peuvent valoir ensemble environ 35 pièces ».

68 N. L. Gayibor, 'La traite négrière sur la côte occidentale des esclaves', *Cahiers des Anneaux de la mémoire*, 1 (1999), pp. 219–48.

69 ADLA. Fonds Chaurand, 101 J 27 f° 256–257.

70 A. Bathily, 'La Traite Atlantique des Esclaves et ses Effets Économiques et Sociaux en Afrique: La Cas du Galam, Royaume de l'Hinterland Sénégambien au Dix-Huitième Siècle', *The Journal of African History*, 27:2 (1986), pp. 269–293.

71 See further, F. Tough, 'Native Labour and Imperial Consumption on the Periphery of Empire as Revealed by the York Factory Account Books of the Hudson's Bay Company, c. 1869–1870' in this volume.

72 P. Gervais and C. S. McWatters, 'Globalisation', in A. de Jong, S. Toms, J. Wilson, and E. Buchnea (eds.), *The Routledge Companion to Business History* (London: Routledge/Taylor and Francis, 2017), p. 317.

73 ADLA. Fonds Delaville-Deguer 8 J 3 Folio 373. See also Kouamé, 'Les cargaisons de traite nantaises au XVIIIe siècle', pp. 370–380, for an analysis of trade patterns.

Part III

# Production, consumption and management of the colonial economy

# 5 Glimpses of an Indigenous economy

## Patterns of consumption and production of Indigenous peoples in the nineteenth-century fur trade and whaling industry

*Leanna Parker*

Despite numerous attempts to document and examine the social interactions between Indigenous peoples and the merchants and traders who arrived on their lands in the nineteenth century, significantly fewer scholars have attempted to understand the economic relationships that developed between these two disparate groups. This limited analysis has resulted in part from a hesitation by some historians to delve into the accounting records kept by merchants and traders. While these accounting records are complex and can be challenging to analyse, the level of detail in the records can be useful for identifying consumption and production patterns of Indigenous peoples involved in trade and other mercantile industries. These patterns can provide another way to understand both the complex relationships between the Indigenous peoples and the mercantilists, and the economic activities of the Indigenous peoples once they began to engage with these commercial industries.[1]

An examination of the consumption and production patterns of Indigenous peoples actively engaged in the fur trade in Canada and the whaling industry in New Zealand demonstrates the modifications to the Indigenous economies that allowed the Indigenous peoples to incorporate new opportunities and adapt to changing circumstances introduced by these commercial industries. The Hudson's Bay Company (HBC) in Canada kept extensive accounting records, including detailed inventories of trade items, skins and pelts, goods provided to employees and their families, goods purchased by the employees and their families, profit and loss statements and goods purchased by Indians not formally employed by the post.[2] This chapter is based in part on analysis of the so-called 'Indian ledgers' that were used to record the basic purchases of the Indigenous peoples coming in to trade at Ile a la Crosse (Île-à-la-Crosse) and at least some of the items brought in by Indigenous peoples to pay off their debts. These ledgers provide a rich and detailed data set, although possibly fragmentary or incomplete, that reveals some of the basic consumption and production patterns of Indigenous peoples in northern Saskatchewan over time.[3]

Similarly, Octavius Harwood kept various accounting records for his store at the Otakou whaling station in southern New Zealand. Although not nearly as complete or diversified as the HBC accounting records, Harwood's ledgers and notebooks also provide a detailed data set of the consumption and production patterns of Maori living in or travelling through the Otago region. Although Harwood did not keep separate ledgers for Maori costumers, he frequently recorded their Maori names and/or identified them as 'Native' in the ledgers and notebooks. Thus, it is possible to single out the Maori in these accounting records and to develop an understanding of the consumption and production patterns of the Maori in the Otago region over time.

These consumption and production patterns provide an understanding of some of the adaptations to the Indigenous peoples' economies as a result of changing circumstances introduced by engaging in commercial industries, as well as the long-term consequences of such adaptations and changes to their economies. These modifications were not temporary or minimal as demonstrated by continual adaptations by the Indigenous peoples to adjust to changes in the broader colonial economies to maintain access to the goods to which they had become accustomed and, in some cases, on which they may have come to rely as natural resources in their territories dwindled and changed over time. Nonetheless, the resiliency of the Indigenous economies allowed the Indigenous peoples to maintain key aspects of their economies and their cultures in the face of significant changes occurring on their lands.

## Production and consumption by Dene, Cree and Métis at the Ile a la Crosse Post, 1832–1879[4]

The Indian ledgers maintained by the HBC at Ile a la Crosse reveal the basic patterns of consumption and production by the Indigenous peoples (mostly Dene, Cree and Métis) who lived in the region and who were engaged in trapping, hunting, fishing and gathering activities as part of the larger fur trade. This study analyses a selection of Indian ledgers spanning the years 1832 to 1879 to demonstrate some of the consumption and production trends of some of the Indigenous peoples in the English River District.

The time period of this analysis covers an interesting period for the Ile a la Crosse post. It starts during a period roughly ten years after the merger of the HBC and the Northwest Company at a time when competition from outside sources was limited. Over the next several decades, however, more free traders and other companies began to move into the region.[5] Fur trade operations had also expanded into the Athabasca and Mackenzie regions, changing some of the trade dynamics for Ile a la Crosse.[6] By the 1870s, Rupertsland had formally been sold to the Dominion of Canada, resulting in some further reorganisation of the company's operations.[7] Still, Ile a la Crosse itself remained relatively remote from the larger agricultural and industrial centres further south and east and the fur trade remained the dominant industry throughout the entire time period. Thus, the consumption and production patterns revealed by these

Indian ledgers reflect activities that had been well established in the decades prior and continued through a period of active, although changing, trade.

Table 5.1 presents the number and price of items purchased by Indians at the Ile a la Crosse post from 1832 to 1876 and includes a total for the entire period. The figures are for outfit years, which ran from 1832–1833 to 1875–1876.[8] Although in most cases the Indian ledgers recorded the specific items purchased at the post, I have grouped these items into 13 basic categories for ease of analysis – ammunition, guns and rifles, trapping technology, fishing technology, hunting technology, tools and other technology, household items, clothing, sewing materials, food, tobacco, personal hygiene and miscellaneous. While the clerk at Ile a la Crosse generally recorded the dates of transactions, sometimes it was not always clear when certain purchases were made. These transactions were recorded under the column heading 'Unknown years'. Some outfit years, particularly 1836–1837 and 1860–1861, had only a few transactions recorded in the ledgers (perhaps because many of the Indian ledgers spanned several outfit years and thus the years at the beginning and end of the ledgers were often incomplete compared to the years in the middle). These small numbers can affect the patterns and trends in the data; thus, care has been taken to note when data in these years appear to influence some of the trends disproportionately. If these beginning and ending years are ignored, the trade remains fairly stable over time, with a possible increase in the total number of transactions in the 1860s and 1870s.

The types of items purchased by Indians each year at the Ile a la Crosse post show an interesting shift in purchasing preferences over time. In the 1830s, ammunition was the most frequently purchased item at Ile a la Crosse. By the 1860s, however, clothing or sewing materials had replaced ammunition as the most commonly purchased item. Finally, by 1875–1876, household items had become the most commonly purchased item.[9] Given the importance of hunting in the Cree, Dene and Métis economy, it is not surprising that ammunition was a key item of trade, and even in the years when it was not the most commonly traded item, it was still purchased frequently. However, the shift in purchasing preferences to sewing materials, clothing and household items over the years suggests the influence the fur trade had on the lifestyle of the Indigenous peoples in the region. It would seem that by the 1860s at least, an increasing number of European-style items were being incorporated into the Indigenous peoples' lifestyle, either by choice or by necessity as the game and populations of fur-bearing animals in the region began to decline.[10]

The cost of items purchased shows similar trends over time as the number of items purchased. As with the number of transactions, the cost of items purchased remained relatively stable over time if one takes into consideration the limited number of transactions recorded for outfit years that fell at the beginning or end of a particular ledger. Again, much like the number of transactions, the cost of items purchased seems to increase in the 1860s and 1870s.

The cost of transactions follows a similar pattern as the number of transactions, with one exception. In the 1830s, the items Indians spent the most on

*Table 5.1* Number and cost of items purchased by Indians, Ile a la Crosse Post, 1832–1876.

| *Category of item* | *1832–1833* | | | | *1833–1834* | | | | *1834–1835* | | | |
|---|---|---|---|---|---|---|---|---|---|---|---|---|
| | *Number of items purchased* | *Percent of total* | *Cost of items purchased (£/s/d)* | *Percent of total* | *Number of items purchased* | *Percent of total* | *Cost of items purchased (£/s/d)* | *Percent of total* | *Number of items purchased* | *Percent of total* | *Cost of items purchased (£/s/d)* | *Percent of Total* |
| Ammunition | 362 | 40.3% | 47/16/8 | 16.7% | 589 | 35.1% | 82/3/4 | 22.3% | 395 | 39.9% | 58/5/0 | 15.2% |
| Guns and rifles | 7 | 0.8% | 3/6/8 | 1.2% | 13 | 0.8% | 8/11/1 | 2.3% | 4 | 0.4% | 1/5/7 | 0.3% |
| Trapping technology | 8 | 0.9% | 1/16/8 | 0.6% | 35 | 2.1% | 6/3/4 | 1.7% | 10 | 1.0% | 1/13/4 | 0.4% |
| Fishing technology | – | – | – | – | 12 | 0.7% | 2/9/5 | 0.7% | 7 | 0.7% | 1/3/4 | 0.3% |
| Hunting technology | 12 | 1.3% | 0/8/4 | 0.1% | 70 | 4.2% | 2/8/4 | 0.7% | 18 | 1.8% | 0/11/1 | 0.1% |
| Tools and other technology | 15 | 1.7% | 0/15/0 | 0.3% | 175 | 10.4% | 10/2/9 | 2.8% | 50 | 5.0% | 4/4/5 | 1.1% |
| Household items | 23 | 2.6% | 7/7/3 | 2.6% | 86 | 5.1% | 28/2/9 | 7.6% | 18 | 1.8% | 4/16/8 | 1.3% |
| Clothing, total | 76 | 8.5% | 10/7/9 | 3.6% | 191 | 11.4% | 33/3/4 | 9.0% | 75 | 7.6% | 12/0/0 | 3.1% |
| Clothing, unspecified | 76 | 8.5% | 10/7/9 | 3.6% | 183 | 10.9% | 31/12/3 | 8.6% | 72 | 7.3% | 10/6/8 | 2.7% |
| Clothing, men's | – | – | – | – | 3 | 0.2% | 1/0/0 | 0.3% | 3 | 0.3% | 1/13/4 | 0.4% |
| Clothing, women's | – | – | – | – | 5 | 0.3% | 0/11/1 | 0.2% | – | – | – | – |
| Clothing, children's | – | – | – | – | – | – | – | – | – | – | – | – |
| Sewing materials | 48 | 5.3% | 8/3/4 | 2.9% | 106 | 6.3% | 28/4/5 | 7.7% | 71 | 7.2% | 8/3/11 | 2.1% |
| Food, total | 25 | 2.8% | 11/10/0 | 4.0% | 13 | 0.8% | 8/1/1 | 2.2% | 27 | 2.7% | 18/4/5 | 4.8% |
| Food, imported | 2 | 0.2% | 0/4/5 | 0.1% | 1 | 0.1% | 0/1/1/ | 0.01% | – | – | – | – |
| Food, country produce | 23 | 2.6% | 11/5/7 | 3.9% | 12 | 0.7% | 8/0/0 | 2.2% | 27 | 2.7% | 18/4/5 | 4.8% |
| Tobacco | 109 | 12.1% | 11/10/7 | 4.0% | 178 | 10.6% | 23/12/9 | 6.4% | 101 | 10.2% | 12/4/5 | 3.2% |
| Personal hygiene | 4 | 0.4% | 0/8/4 | 0.1% | 25 | 1.5% | 0/18/4 | 0.2% | 2 | 0.2% | 0/1/8 | 0.02% |
| Miscellaneous | 209 | 23.3% | 182/2/9 | 63.8% | 184 | 11.0% | 134/3/4 | 36.4% | 213 | 21.5% | 260/6/1 | 68.0% |
| **Total** | **898** | | **285/13/4** | | **1,677** | | **368/4/3** | | **991** | | **382/19/1** | |

| *Category of item* | *1835–1836* | | | | *1836–1837* | | | | *1860–1861* | | | |
|---|---|---|---|---|---|---|---|---|---|---|---|---|
| | *Number of items purchased* | *Percent of total* | *Cost of items purchased (£/s/d)* | *Percent of total* | *Number of items purchased* | *Percent of total* | *Cost of items purchased (£/s/d)* | *Percent of total* | *Number of items purchased* | *Percent of total* | *Cost of items purchased (£/s/d)* | *Percent of total* |
| Ammunition | 399 | 32.7% | 98/18/2 | 29.6% | 52 | 36.4% | 8/6/6 | 28.4% | 10 | 17.5% | 2/5/5 | 26.2% |
| Guns and rifles | 21 | 1.7% | 15/0/0 | 6.2% | – | – | – | – | – | – | – | – |
| Trapping technology | 7 | 0.6% | 1/13/9 | 0.7% | 2 | 1.4% | 0/9/0 | 1.5% | – | – | – | – |
| Fishing technology | 5 | 0.4% | 1/5/0 | 0.5% | 1 | 0.7% | 0/4/0 | 0.7% | 5 | 8.8% | 0/11/10 | 6.8% |
| Hunting technology | 61 | 5.0% | 2/11/3 | 1.1% | 4 | 2.8% | 0/3/0 | 0.5% | 4 | 7.0% | 0/3/2 | 1.8% |
| Tools and other technology | 218 | 17.9% | 14/4/5 | 5.9% | 6 | 4.2% | 0/6/6 | 1.1% | 5 | 8.8% | 0/4/7 | 2.6% |
| Household items | 76 | 6.2% | 31/16/3 | 13.1% | 2 | 1.4% | 0/5/0 | 0.9% | 1 | 1.8% | 0/6/4 | 3.7% |
| Clothing, total | 198 | 16.2% | 34/19/5 | 14.4% | 6 | 4.2% | 0/16/0 | 2.7% | 8 | 14.0% | 1/0/0 | 11.5% |
| Clothing, unspecified | 193 | 15.8% | 34/6/11 | 14.1% | 6 | 4.2% | 0/16/0 | 2.7% | 8 | 14.0% | 1/0/0 | 11.5% |
| Clothing, men's | – | – | – | – | – | – | – | – | – | – | – | – |
| Clothing, women's | 5 | 0.4% | 0/12/6 | 0.3% | – | – | – | – | – | – | – | – |
| Clothing, children's | – | – | – | – | – | – | – | – | – | – | – | – |
| Sewing materials | 85 | 7.0% | 23/7/6 | 9.6% | 16 | 11.2% | 1/4/0 | 4.1% | 14 | 24.6% | 2/17/3 | 33.1% |
| Food, total | 20 | 1.6% | 7/18/9 | 3.3% | 12 | 8.4% | 6/8/0 | 21.9% | 5 | 8.8% | 0/11/10 | 6.8% |
| Food, imported | – | – | – | – | – | – | – | – | 5 | 8.8% | 0/11/10 | 6.8% |
| Food, country produce | 20 | 1.6% | 7/18/9 | 3.3% | 12 | 8.4% | 6/8/0 | 21.9% | – | – | – | – |
| Tobacco | 68 | 5.6% | 9/7/6 | 3.9% | 16 | 11.2% | 2/5/6 | 7.8% | 2 | 3.5% | 0/4/7 | 2.6% |
| Personal hygiene | 9 | 0.7% | 0/8/9 | 0.2% | 2 | 1.4% | 0/1/6 | 0.3% | – | – | – | – |
| Miscellaneous | 54 | 4.4% | 28/10/0 | 11.7% | 24 | 16.8% | 8/16/6 | 30.1% | 3 | 5.3% | 0/8/2 | 4.7% |
| **Total** | **1,221** | | **243/0/8** | | **143** | | **29/5/6** | | **57** | | **8/13/2** | |

(*Continued*)

*Table 5.1* (Continued)

| *Category of item* | *1862–1863* | | | | *1863–1864* | | | | *1865–1866* | | | |
|---|---|---|---|---|---|---|---|---|---|---|---|---|
| | *Number of items purchased* | *Percent of total* | *Cost of items purchased (£/s/d)* | *Percent of total* | *Number of items purchased* | *Percent of total* | *Cost of items purchased (£/s/d)* | *Percent of total* | *Number of items purchased* | *Percent of total* | *Cost of items purchased (£/s/d)* | *Percent of total* |
| Ammunition | 592 | 16.9% | 116/16/6 | 16.4% | 94 | 17.8% | 15/17/6 | 18.7% | 30 | 7.4% | 4/4/6 | 3.7% |
| Guns and rifles | 50 | 1.4% | 43/0/0 | 6.0% | 7 | 1.3% | 4/3/4 | 4.9% | 2 | 0.5% | 0/17/0 | 0.7% |
| Trapping technology | 67 | 1.9% | 11/18/6 | 1.7% | 9 | 1.7% | 1/5/0 | 1.5% | 5 | 1.2% | 0/17/6 | 0.8% |
| Fishing technology | 199 | 5.7% | 26/0/0 | 3.6% | 30 | 5.7% | 3/9/7 | 4.1% | 4 | 1.0% | 3/11/8 | 3.1% |
| Hunting technology | 112 | 3.2% | 5/6/0 | 0.7% | 15 | 2.8% | 0/10/5 | 0.6% | 2 | 0.5% | 0/1/0 | 0.04% |
| Tools and other technology | 248 | 7.1% | 18/11/4 | 2.6% | 36 | 6.8% | 2/16/3 | 3.3% | 4 | 1.0% | 0/10/0 | 0.4% |
| Household items | 336 | 9.6% | 83/13/0 | 11.7% | 47 | 8.9% | 8/9/7 | 10.0% | 22 | 5.4% | 20/10/6 | 17.8% |
| Clothing, total | 692 | 19.8% | 134/4/0 | 18.8% | 109 | 20.7% | 18/3/4 | 21.4% | 74 | 18.3% | 17/13/0 | 15.3% |
| Clothing, unspecified | 563 | 16.1% | 108/5/6 | 15.2% | 84 | 15.9% | 12/4/2 | 15.0% | 55 | 13.6% | 12/16/0 | 2.4% |
| Clothing, men's | 73 | 2.1% | 13/11/6 | 1.9% | 17 | 3.2% | 4/4/2 | 5.0% | 11 | 2.7% | 2/1/0 | 1.8% |
| Clothing, women's | 51 | 1.5% | 11/19/0 | 1.7% | 8 | 1.5% | 1/5/2 | 1.5% | 8 | 2.0% | 2/16/0 | 2.4% |
| Clothing, children's | 5 | 0.1% | 0/9/0 | 0.1% | – | – | – | – | – | – | – | – |
| Sewing materials | 646 | 18.5% | 122/0/6 | 17.1% | 90 | 17.1% | 14/10/5 | 17.1% | 142 | 35.1% | 50/18/1 | 44.1% |
| Food, total | 130 | 3.7% | 37/7/0 | 5.2% | 30 | 5.7% | 6/16/8 | 8.1% | 52 | 12.9% | 6/18/0 | 6.0% |
| Food, imported | 115 | 3.3% | 26/3/0 | 3.7% | 27 | 5.1% | 4/6/8 | 5.1% | 50 | 12.4% | 6/9/8 | 5.6% |
| Food, country produce | 15 | 0.4% | 11/4/0 | 1.6% | 3 | 0.6% | 2/10/0 | 3.0% | 2 | 0.5% | 0/8/4 | 0.4% |
| Tobacco | 124 | 3.5% | 18/4/0 | 2.6% | 19 | 3.6% | 3/3/4 | 3.7% | 54 | 13.4% | 8/3/6 | 7.1% |
| Personal hygiene | 43 | 1.2% | 2/6/0 | 0.3% | 2 | 0.4% | 0/1/8 | 0.1% | 11 | 2.7% | 0/12/6 | 0.5% |
| Miscellaneous | 258 | 7.4% | 93/12/4 | 13.1% | 39 | 7.4% | 5/7/6 | 6.3% | 2 | 0.5% | 0/11/0 | 0.5% |
| **Total** | **3,497** | | **713/0/7** | | **527** | | **84/15/0** | | **404** | | **115/8/4** | |

| *Category of item* | *1875–1876* | | | | *Unknown years* | | | | *Total of all years* | | | |
|---|---|---|---|---|---|---|---|---|---|---|---|---|
| | *Number of items purchased* | *Percent of total* | *Cost of items purchased (£/s/d)* | *Percent of total* | *Number of items purchased* | *Percent of total* | *Cost of items purchased (£/s/d)* | *Percent of total* | *Number of items purchased* | *Percent of total* | *Cost of items purchased (£/s/d)* | *Percent of total* |
| Ammunition | 292 | 9.1% | 110/15/6 | 7.5% | 151 | 16.7% | 25/6/8 | 12.5% | 2,966 | 21.9% | 568/15/9 | 14.5% |
| Guns and rifles | 4 | 0.1% | 26/10/0 | 1.8% | 14 | 1.5% | 12/10/0 | 6.2% | 122 | 0.9% | 115/3/8 | 2.9% |
| Trapping technology | 101 | 3.2% | 42/10/0 | 2.9% | 15 | 1.7% | 4/5/7 | 2.1% | 259 | 1.9% | 72/12/8 | 2.9% |
| Fishing technology | 95 | 3.0% | 42/17/11 | 2.9% | 11 | 1.2% | 1/9/5 | 0.7% | 369 | 2.7% | 83/2/2 | 2.1% |
| Hunting technology | 46 | 1.4% | 7/15/1 | 0.5% | 45 | 5.0% | 2/4/5 | 1.1% | 389 | 2.9% | 22/2/1 | 0.6% |
| Tools and other technology | 182 | 5.7% | 71/2/2 | 4.8% | 80 | 8.8% | 7/12/3 | 3.8% | 1,019 | 7.5% | 130/9/8 | 3.3% |
| Household items | 1,057 | 33.0% | 168/9/7 | 11.4% | 114 | 12.6% | 29/13/4 | 14.6% | 1,782 | 13.2% | 361/0/3 | 9.2% |
| Clothing, total | 466 | 14.5% | 240/5/0 | 16.4% | 191 | 21.1% | 38/12/3 | 19.9% | 2,086 | 15.4% | 543/14/1 | 13.9% |
| Clothing, unspecified | 293 | 9.1% | 126/17/6 | 8.6% | 163 | 18.0% | 31/3/4 | 15.4% | 1,696 | 12.5% | 380/5/1 | 9.7% |
| Clothing, men's | 92 | 2.9% | 67/1/0 | 4.5% | 18 | 2.0% | 5/10/0 | 2.7% | 217 | 1.6% | 95/1/0 | 2.4% |
| Clothing, women's | 53 | 1.7% | 39/17/0 | 2.7% | 10 | 1.1% | 1/18/11 | 1.0% | 140 | 1.0% | 58/19/6 | 1.5% |
| Clothing, children's | 28 | 0.9% | 8/19/6 | 0.6% | – | – | – | – | 33 | 0.2% | 9/8/6 | 0.2% |
| Sewing materials | 430 | 13.4% | 292/9/4 | 19.8% | 192 | 21.2% | 40/0/0 | 19.7% | 1,840 | 13.6% | 591/18/9 | 15.1% |
| Food, total | 366 | 11.4% | 340/14/10 | 23.1% | 32 | 3.5% | 14/7/9 | 7.1% | 712 | 5.3% | 458/18/4 | 11.7% |
| Food, imported | 313 | 9.8% | 295/6/4 | 20.0% | 21 | 2.3% | 3/7/9 | 1.7% | 534 | 3.9% | 336/10/9 | 8.6% |
| Food, country produce | 53 | 1.7% | 45/8/6 | 3.1% | 11 | 1.2% | 11/0/0 | 5.4% | 178 | 1.3% | 122/7/7 | 3.1% |
| Tobacco | 63 | 2.0% | 40/15/2 | 2.8% | 26 | 2.9% | 4/3/11 | 2.1% | 760 | 5.6% | 133/16/9 | 3.4% |
| Personal hygiene | 79 | 2.5% | 8/9/9 | 0.6% | 8 | 0.9% | 0/6/8 | 0.2% | 185 | 1.4% | 13/15/2 | 0.4% |
| Miscellaneous | 24 | 0.7% | 82/13/10 | 5.6% | 26 | 2.9% | 22/4/5 | 11.0% | 1,036 | 7.7% | 818/15/11 | 20.9% |
| **Total** | **3,205** | | **1,477/18/2** | | **905** | | | | **13,525** | | **3,911/15/7** | |

were classified as miscellaneous, except in 1835–1836 when they spent the most on ammunition. In these years, many of the entries were simply listed as 'sundries', and thus it was not possible to determine exactly what the Indians were purchasing. In other cases, the items were detailed, but a total cost was provided for an entire list and not each item. Thus, it was not possible to determine how much was being spent on any particular item in these cases. Less often, Indians were paying for the blacksmith and other post employees to repair various types of equipment for them (particularly traps, axes and other metal items). All of these items were classified as miscellaneous. However, in each case that miscellaneous items were the highest cost of transactions, ammunition was the second highest cost.

Much like the figures for the number of transactions, by the 1860s Indians were spending the most on sewing materials or clothing items. By 1875–1876, however, Indians were spending the most on food, even though the most frequent item purchased was household items. In fact, in this outfit year, Indians spent more on food, sewing materials and clothing than on household items. Thus, even though household items were more commonly purchased, these items had a much lower cost than other trade goods. The food that was purchased for that outfit year can also be divided into country produce (items that were grown or made in the region) or imported food (items that were grown or made outside of the region).[11] Indians spent considerably more on imported foods in this outfit year rather than on country produce, even though this was reversed in the 1830s. Again, it would seem that over time, certain European items (mainly clothing, sewing materials and food) were well incorporated into the Indigenous peoples' lifestyles by the mid-nineteenth century.

A number of individual categories of items show some interesting trends over the period as well. For example, the number of times that Indians purchased ammunition at the Ile a la Crosse post declined over time. The cost of ammunition purchased by Indians shows a similar trend, although the high proportion of miscellaneous items in the 1830s likely explains why the costs do not fluctuate in exactly the same manner as the number of transactions. As game and fur-bearing animal populations declined in the region over time, the Ile a la Crosse post provided more ammunition as gifts to encourage the Indians to continue hunting and trapping further away from the post and their main camps.[12] Considering that the volume and cost of trade seemed to increase in the 1870s, it would seem unlikely that the Indians were hunting and trapping less; thus, it would seem plausible that the provision of more ammunition to the Indians by the post might explain why they were purchasing it less often over time. However, at the same time that there was a decline in the volume and cost of the trade in ammunition, there was an increase in the volume and cost of trade in fishing technology, particularly twine and net thread. Thus, it is also possible that a decline in game and fur-bearing animals caused the local Indigenous peoples to depend more on fish, at least in the 1860s. The post journals also noted unusual weather patterns that kept the local lakes open much later than usual in the 1860–1861 outfit year and noted that the buffalo were a long way from Ile a la Crosse in December 1862, the years in which fishing technology was purchased more frequently than other years.[13] These conditions might also have encouraged the Indigenous peoples to rely on fishing at that time more than in previous years.

The number and cost of clothing items purchased by Indians generally increased over time, although there may have been a small decline in the mid-1870s. Even more noticeable is the increase in the number and cost of sewing materials purchased by Indians over time, although again there seems to be a decline in the mid-1870s. It would seem that by the mid-1860s, the local Indigenous peoples had incorporated European-style clothing into their lifestyles, or were at least making regular use of European fabrics.

Finally, the volume and cost of food items purchased by Indians at the Ile a la Crosse post generally increased over time as well. There was also a shift from purchasing predominantly country produce to predominantly imported foods. The reasons for these shifts in purchasing patterns are discussed more fully in the analysis section below.

In addition to recording the detailed items purchased by Indians at the Ile a la Crosse post, the Indian ledgers also recorded the items brought in by Indians to pay off their accounts and debts at the post. Table 5.2 presents the number and value (i.e. the amount paid to Indians) of items traded by Indians at Ile a la Crosse by outfit year from 1832–1833 to 1875–1876.[14] While the Indian ledgers recorded some level of detail of the items brought in for trade, I have grouped these items into seven main categories – furs and skins, country produce, country manufactured goods, skins with meat, labour/employment, cash and miscellaneous.[15] Overall, fewer items brought in for trade were recorded in the Indian ledgers than items purchased; however, the overall numbers may be misleading as often the ledgers simply indicated that 'furs' were brought in with no indication of the number or type of furs, only the amount paid. Perhaps because the number and type of furs were counted carefully and provided in detail in the fur returns and packing lists that were sent to the head office each year, the clerks found it unnecessary to be precise in this type of detail in the Indian ledgers.

The number of trade transactions each year shows a similar trend as the total number of items purchased by Indians, except that there were fewer overall items brought in for trade. It is likely that the small numbers reflect the tendency to list simply 'furs' as a trade item without any indication of number, whereas the items purchased were often listed in more detail. However, in the late 1870s, the number of items brought in for trade by Indians increased considerably. This increase would seem to have been from more detailed descriptions in the ledgers (i.e. listing the particular type of pelt or skin rather than simply stating 'furs') rather than an actual increase in the number of items brought in for trade.[16]

When examining the categories of items brought in for trade, it is not surprising that in all years furs and skins accounted for the largest number of trade items. Country produce was the second most common trade item in all years except 1875–1876 when miscellaneous items, labour/employment and

*Table 5.2* Number and value of items traded by Indians, Ile a la Crosse Post, 1832–1876.

| *Category of item* | *1832–1833* | | | | *1833–1834* | | | | *1834–1835* | | | |
|---|---|---|---|---|---|---|---|---|---|---|---|---|
| | *Number of transactions* | *Percent of total* | *Value of items traded (£/s/d)* | *Percent of total* | *Number of transactions* | *Percent of total* | *Value of items traded (£/s/d)* | *Percent of total* | *Number of transactions* | *Percent of total* | *Value of items traded (£/s/d)* | *Percent of Total* |
| Furs and skins | 252 | 92.6% | 1,841/16/8 | 94.4% | 374 | 88.0% | 3,192/18/0 | 92.3% | 384 | 86.7% | 2,560/0/0 | 92.2% |
| Country produce | 15 | 5.5% | 41/10/0 | 2.2% | 48 | 11.3% | 258/0/0 | 7.5% | 52 | 11.7% | 195/15/0 | 7.1% |
| Country manufactured goods | – | – | – | – | 1 | 0.2% | 2/10/0 | 0.1% | – | – | – | – |
| Skins with meat | – | – | – | – | – | – | – | – | – | – | – | – |
| Labour/ employment | – | – | – | – | – | – | – | – | – | – | – | – |
| Cash | – | – | – | – | – | – | – | – | – | – | – | – |
| Miscellaneous | 5 | 1.8% | 62/10/0 | 3.4% | 2 | 0.5% | 5/0/0 | 0.1% | 7 | 1.6% | 20/5/0 | 0.7% |
| **Total** | **272** | | **1,862/10/0** | | **425** | | **3,458/8/0** | | **443** | | **2,776/0/0** | |

| *Category of item* | *1835–1836* | | | | *1836–1837* | | | | *1862–1863* | | | |
|---|---|---|---|---|---|---|---|---|---|---|---|---|
| | *Number of transactions* | *Percent of total* | *Value of items traded (£/s/d)* | *Percent of total* | *Number of transactions* | *Percent of total* | *Value of items traded (£/s/d)* | *Percent of total* | *Number of transactions* | *Percent of total* | *Value of items traded (£/s/d)* | *Percent of total* |
| Furs and skins | 310 | 85.2% | 1,669/5/0 | 84.8% | 128 | 75.7% | 521/5/0 | 72.5% | 299 | 88.7% | 745/13/0 | 91.2% |
| Country produce | 46 | 12.6% | 270/0/0 | 13.7% | 41 | 24.3% | 197/10/0 | 27.5% | 30 | 8.9% | 52/16/3 | 6.5% |
| Country manufactured goods | 2 | 0.5% | 4/0/0 | 0.2% | – | – | – | – | – | – | – | – |
| Skins with meat | 2 | 0.5% | 2/10/0 | 0.1% | – | – | – | – | 1 | 0.3% | 0/12/6 | 0.1% |
| Labour/ employment | – | – | – | – | – | – | – | – | – | – | – | – |
| Cash | – | – | – | – | – | – | – | – | – | – | – | – |
| Miscellaneous | 4 | 1.1% | 22/10/0 | 1.1% | – | – | – | – | 7 | 2.1% | 18/10/0 | 2.3% |
| **Total** | **364** | | **1,968/5/0** | | **169** | | **718/15/0** | | **337** | | **817/11/9** | |

(*Continued*)

*Table 5.2* (Continued)

| *Category of item* | *1863–1864* | | | | *1865–1866* | | | | *1875–1876* | | | |
|---|---|---|---|---|---|---|---|---|---|---|---|---|
| | *Number of transactions* | *Percent of total* | *Value of items traded (£/s/d)* | *Percent of total* | *Number of transactions* | *Percent of total* | *Value of items traded (£/s/d)* | *Percent of total* | *Number of transactions* | *Percent of total* | *Value of items traded (£/s/d)* | *Percent of total* |
| Furs and skins | 15 | 65.2% | 24/18/9 | 69.9% | 85 | 97.7% | 48/1/3 | 95.5% | 353 | 90.1% | 1,220/1/0 | 86.8% |
| Country produce | 6 | 26.1% | 7/15/0 | 21.7% | 2 | 2.3% | 2/5/0 | 4.5% | 4 | 1.0% | 5/0/0 | 0.4% |
| Country manufactured goods | 2 | 8.7% | 3/0/0 | 8.4% | – | – | – | – | 6 | 1.5% | 1/8/2 | 0.1% |
| Skins with meat | – | – | – | – | – | – | – | – | – | – | – | – |
| Labour/ employment | – | – | – | – | – | – | – | – | 9 | 2.3% | 18/6/3 | 1.3% |
| Cash | – | – | – | – | – | – | – | – | 1 | 0.3% | 0/10/10 | 0.04% |
| Miscellaneous | – | – | – | – | – | – | – | – | 19 | 4.8% | 159/17/0 | 11.4% |
| **Total** | **23** | | **35/13/9** | | **87** | | **50/6/3** | | **392** | | **1,406/5/9** | |

| *Category of item* | *Unknown years* | | | | *Total of all years* | | | |
|---|---|---|---|---|---|---|---|---|
| | *Number of transactions* | *Percent of total* | *Value of items traded (£/s/d)* | *Percent of total* | *Number of transactions* | *Percent of total* | *Value of items purchased (£/s/d)* | *Percent of total* |
| Furs and skins | 42 | 66.7% | 104/10/0 | 64.3% | 2,242 | 87.1% | 11,845/2/0 | 89.4% |
| Country produce | 17 | 27.0% | 49/0/0 | 30.2% | 261 | 10.1% | 1,079/11/3 | 8.1% |
| Country manufactured goods | 1 | 1.6% | 0/4/0 | 0.1% | 12 | 0.5% | 11/2/2 | 0.1% |
| Skins with meat | – | – | – | – | 3 | 0.1% | 3/2/6 | 0.02% |
| Labour/employment | – | – | – | – | 9 | 0.3% | 18/6/3 | 0.10% |
| Cash | – | – | – | – | 1 | 0.04% | 0/10/10 | 0.004% |
| Miscellaneous | 3 | 4.8% | 8/16/0 | 5.4% | 47 | 1.8% | 298/10/6 | 2.30% |
| **Total** | **63** | | **162/10/0** | | **2,575** | | **13,256/5/6** | |

country manufactured goods all were used to pay off debts more frequently than country produce.

The value of items traded shows a similar trend as the number of items traded, except in the late 1870s. While the number of items traded increased considerably between 1875–1876 and 1877–1878 and then decreased considerably between 1877–1878 and 1878–1879, the value of items traded steadily declined from 1875–1876 to 1878–1879. The increase in the number of items traded is likely a reflection of more detailed accounting in the ledgers; however, it is not clear if the value of items traded shows an actual decline in trade. When comparing the value of items traded as reported in the Indian ledgers (which includes more than simply furs) to the value of the fur returns reported in the district accounts,[17] it would seem that some declines shown in the Indian ledgers represent incomplete data rather than actual declines in trade (particularly in the outfit years 1836–1837, 1843–1844, 1854–1855 and throughout the 1860s). However, the district accounts do show a decline in the value of the fur returns in the 1870s. The value of furs was lower in the 1870s than earlier in the nineteenth century; however, values rebounded from the 1860s on.[18] Thus, it would seem that the 1870s was a period of diminished trade at Ile a la Crosse.

As with the number of items traded, furs and skins were the trade items of highest value brought in by the Indians in every outfit year, which is to be expected given that furs and skins were the purpose of trade for the company. In all years except 1875–1876, country produce was the second highest valued trade item brought in by Indians. In the 1875–1876 outfit year, miscellaneous items and labour/employment accounted for a higher value of trade items than country produce.

Figure 5.1 presents the proportion of items purchased by Indians at the Ile a la Crosse post from 1832 to 1876 combined. During this time, ammunition was the most commonly purchased item (nearly 22 per cent). However, if items of clothing and sewing materials are combined, then these items represent 29 per cent of the items purchased by Indians. Food represented only 5 per cent of the total purchases during this time period. Thus, while it would seem that hunting and trapping remained an important element of the Indigenous economy in this region, European-style clothing and fabric had been well incorporated into their lifestyle by the mid-nineteenth century.

Figure 5.2 presents the proportion of the cost of items purchased by Indians at Ile a la Crosse from 1832 to 1876 combined.[19] Unlike the number of items purchased, sewing materials accounted for the greatest cost of items purchased by Indians (just over 15 per cent). However, ammunition accounted for the second greatest cost of items purchased (14.5 per cent). When sewing material is combined with clothing, these items account for 29 per cent of the total cost of items purchased. Food also accounted for nearly 12 per cent of the total cost of items purchased, a greater proportion than the number of food items purchased. Miscellaneous items also accounted for just over one-fifth of the total cost of items purchased. Nonetheless, the basic proportion of number of items purchased is similar to the proportion of the cost of items purchased.[20]

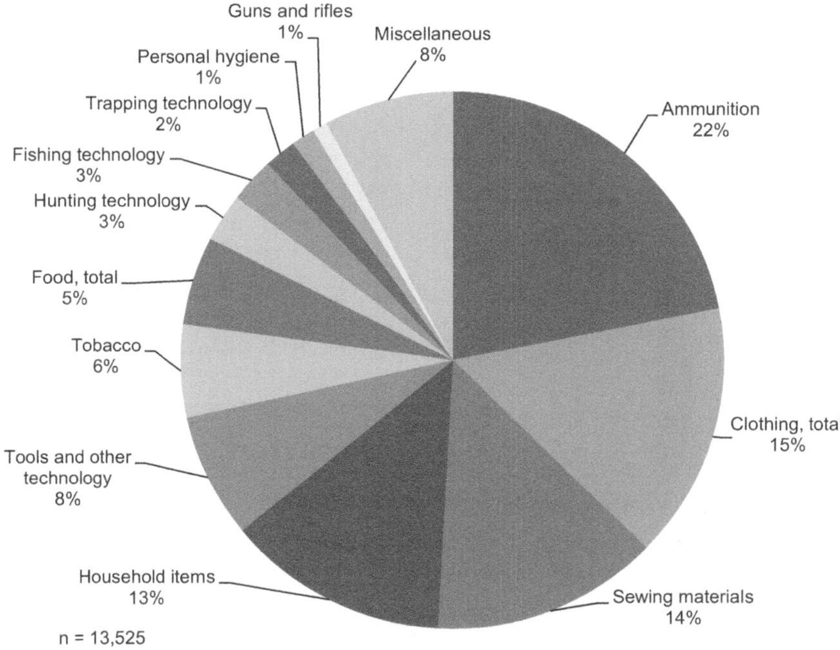


*Figure 5.1* Proportion of the number of items purchased by Indians, Ile a la Crosse, 1832–1876.

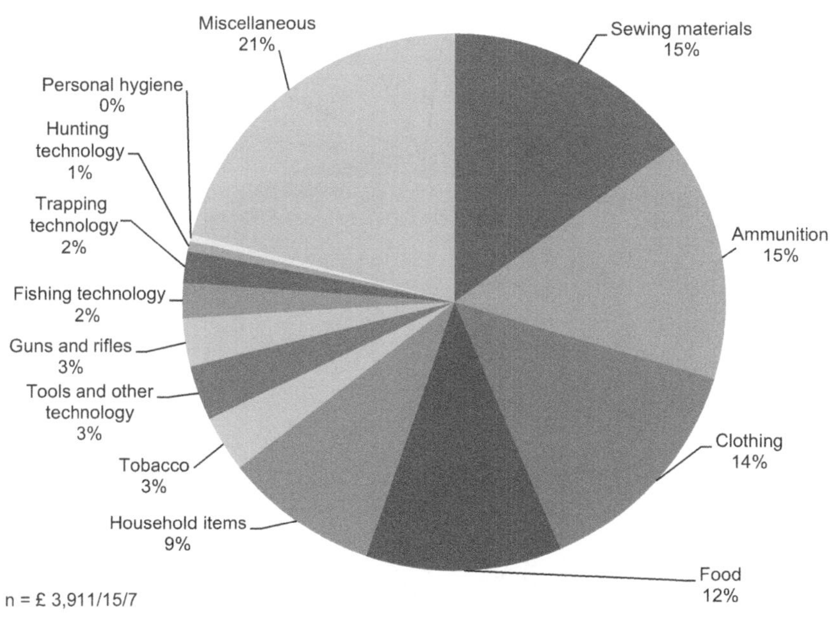


*Figure 5.2* Proportion of the cost of items purchased by Indians, Ile a la Crosse, 1832–1876.

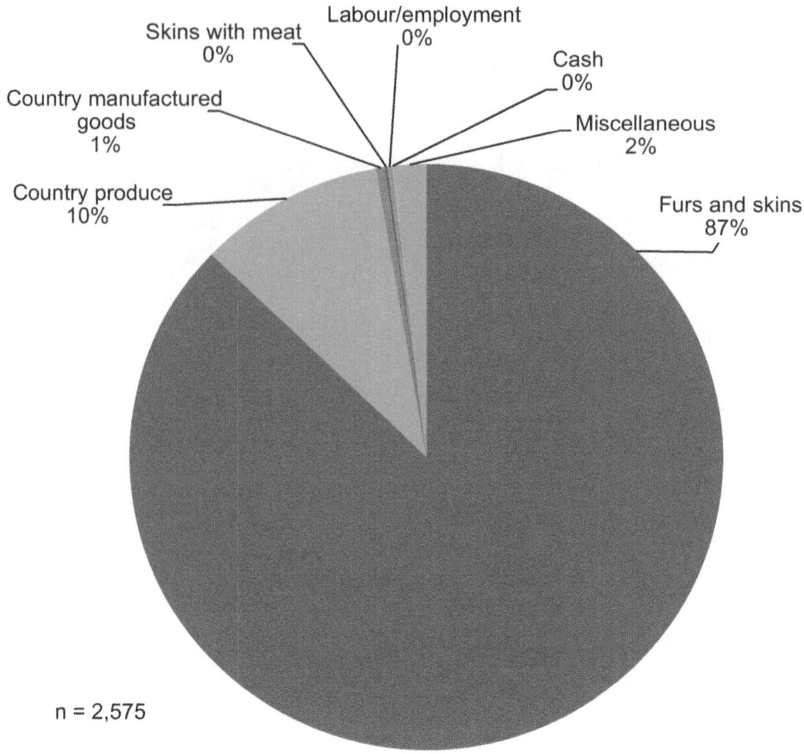


*Figure 5.3* Proportion of the number of items traded by Indians, Ile a la Crosse, 1832–1876.

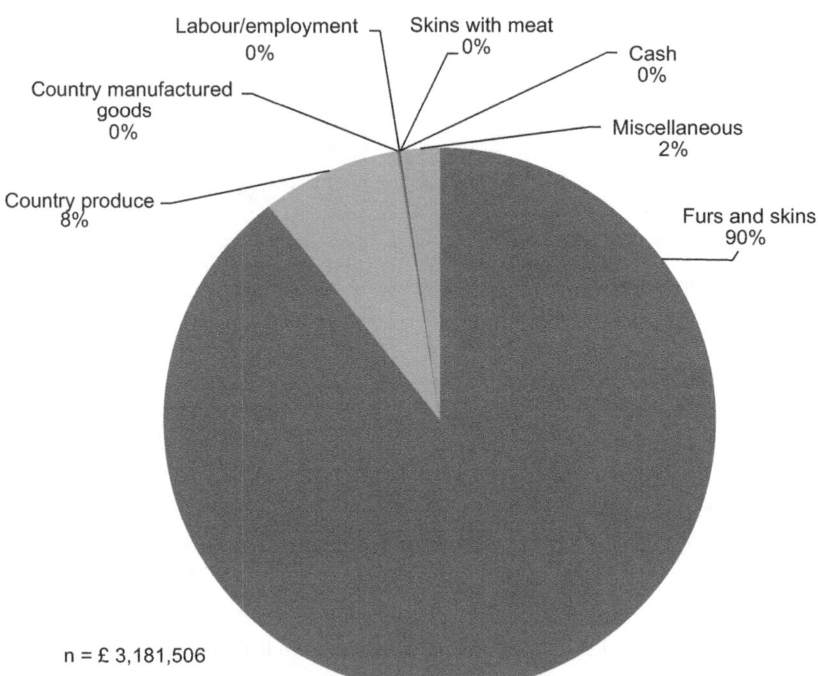


*Figure 5.4* Proportion of the value of items traded by Indians, Ile a la Crosse, 1832–1876.

Figure 5.3 presents the proportion of all items traded by Indians at the Ile a la Crosse post over the entire time period of 1832–1876 combined. As is to be expected, just over 87 per cent of the items traded by Indians were furs and skins. Country produce accounted for an additional 10 per cent of the items traded. Similarly, Figure 5.4 presents the proportion of the value of items traded by Indians at Ile a la Crosse for the entire time period combined. The importance of furs and skins is even more evident in these data, as furs and skins represented almost 90 per cent of the total value of items traded by Indians. Country produce accounted for roughly 8 per cent of the total value of items traded. Given the importance of furs, skins and provisions to the trade, these proportions are entirely expected.

## Production and consumption by Maori at the Otakou Whaling Station, 1841–1848[21]

Similar to the Indian ledgers kept by HBC, the accounting ledgers and notebooks maintained by Octavius Harwood for his store at the Otakou whaling station reveal the basic patterns of consumption and production by Maori living and traveling in the region. The surviving accounting records from the shore whaling station and Harwood's store run from 1837 until 1857. However, transactions made by Maori can only be identified in the years from 1841 to 1848.

The Weller brothers first opened the whaling station at Otakou in October 1831. They expanded their operations to include a station at nearby Purakanui in 1837. Harwood did not begin to operate his store until early in 1838. Three years later, the Wellers went bankrupt, J. Hoare continued whaling operations at the site (although on a much smaller scale) and Harwood and Charles Schultz agreed to continue operating the store at Otakou. Agricultural pursuits started to overshadow the whaling operations at Otakou by the early 1840s, but Harwood's store continued operating as a regular trading base for deep-sea whalers coming into Otago Harbour, for shore whalers still operating at Waikouaiti and Moeraki and for local Maori.[22] The production and consumption patterns revealed by Harwood's accounting records must be understood in this context of having been established over the previous decade and as operating in a period of declining whaling operations for the eight years covered by the ledgers and notebooks.

Table 5.3 presents the number and cost of items purchased by Maori at Harwood's store at the Otakou whaling station from 1841 to 1848. Although the ledgers record the specific and detailed items purchased by Maori, I have grouped those items into 12 basic categories for ease of analysis – ammunition, hunting technology, whaling technology, tools and other technology, household items, clothing, sewing materials, food, alcohol, tobacco, personal hygiene and miscellaneous.[23] While Harwood usually made note of the date of transactions, sometimes it was not clear when certain purchases were made. These items have been listed under the column heading 'Unknown years'. There were also some years when only a small number of transactions by Maori could be identified.

*Table 5.3* Number and cost of items purchased by Maori, Otakou Whaling Station, 1841–1848.

| *Category of item* | *1841* | | | | *1842* | | | | *1843* | | | |
|---|---|---|---|---|---|---|---|---|---|---|---|---|
| | *Number of items purchased* | *Percent of total* | *Cost of items purchased (£/s/d)* | *Percent of total* | *Number of items purchased* | *Percent of total* | *Cost of Items Purchased (£/s/d)* | *Percent of total* | *Number of Items Purchased* | *Percent of total* | *Cost of Items Purchased (£/s/d)* | *Percent of total* |
| Ammunition | 1 | 0.4% | 0/3/0 | 0.1% | 4 | 5.3% | 0/7/6 | 0.4% | – | – | – | – |
| Whaling technology | – | – | 0/3/0 | 0.1% | 5 | 6.6% | 69/2/8 | 77.4% | – | – | – | – |
| Hunting technology | 1 | 0.4% | – | – | – | – | – | – | – | – | – | – |
| Tools and other technology | 12 | 4.4% | 20/11/0 | 11.2% | 10 | 13.2% | 3/15/0 | 4.2% | 6 | 2.8% | 2/4/0 | 5.2% |
| Household items | 14 | 5.1% | 35172 | 2.7% | 1 | 1.3% | 0/2/6 | 0.1% | 118 | 55.4% | 5/7/9 | 12.8% |
| Clothing, total | 152 | 55.5% | 49/1/0 | 26.7% | 16 | 21.1% | 6/7/0 | 7.1% | 13 | 6.1% | 3/19/6 | 9.4% |
| Clothing, unspecified | 97 | 35.4% | 30/4/0 | 16.4% | 1 | 1.3% | 0/10/0 | 0.6% | 6 | 2.8% | 1/4/0 | 2.8% |
| Clothing, men's | 52 | 19.0% | 18/0/0 | 9.8% | 13 | 17.1% | 4/12/0 | 5.2% | 5 | 2.3% | 1/3/6 | 2.8% |
| Clothing, women's | 1 | 0.4% | 0/9/0 | 0.2% | 2 | 2.6% | 1/5/0 | 1.4% | 2 | 0.9% | 1/12/0 | 3.8% |
| Clothing, child's | 2 | 0.7% | 0/8/0 | 0.2% | – | – | – | – | – | – | – | – |
| Sewing materials | 46 | 16.8% | 6/16/6 | 3.7% | – | – | – | – | 3 | 1.4% | 3/8/0 | 8.1% |
| Food, total | – | – | – | – | 1 | 1.3% | 2/0/0 | 2.2% | 4 | 1.9% | 8/12/7 | 20.5% |
| Food, imported | – | – | – | – | 1 | 1.3% | 2/0/0 | 2.2% | 4 | 1.9% | 8/12/7 | 20.5% |
| Food, country produce | – | – | – | – | – | – | – | – | – | – | – | – |
| Alcohol | 34 | 12.4% | 97/12/6 | 53.2% | 32 | 42.1% | 5/2/6 | 5.7% | 59 | 27.7% | 10/15/9 | 25.6% |
| Tobacco | 2 | 0.7% | 1/10/5 | 0.8% | 2 | 2.6% | 1/3/0 | 1.3% | 6 | 2.8% | 7/6/3 | 17.3% |
| Personal hygiene | 2 | 0.7% | 0/4/0 | 0.1% | 1 | 1.3% | 0/0/6 | 0.03% | 4 | 1.9% | 0/10/0 | 1.2% |
| Miscellaneous | 10 | 3.6% | 2/14/6 | 1.5% | 4 | 5.3% | 1/6/0 | 1.5% | – | – | – | – |
| **Total** | **274** | | **183/17/11** | | **76** | | **89/6/8** | | **213** | | **42/3/10** | |

| *Category of item* | *1844* | | | | *1845* | | | | *1847* | | | |
|---|---|---|---|---|---|---|---|---|---|---|---|---|
| | *Number of items purchased* | *Percent of total* | *Cost of items purchased (£/s/d)* | *Percent of total* | *Number of items purchased* | *Percent of total* | *Cost of items purchased (£/s/d)* | *Percent of total* | *Number of items purchased* | *Percent of total* | *Cost of items purchased (£/s/d)* | *Percent of total* |
| Ammunition | – | – | – | – | – | – | – | – | – | – | – | – |
| Whaling technology | – | – | – | – | 2 | 2.5% | 0/2/0 | 0.3% | 1 | 8.3% | 0/1/0 | 2.0% |
| Hunting technology | – | – | – | – | – | – | – | – | – | – | – | – |
| Tools and other technology | 2 | 13.3% | 0/5/0 | 3.1% | 1 | 1.3% | 0/3/6 | 0.5% | – | – | – | – |
| Household items | 2 | 13.3% | 0/6/0 | 3.7% | 23 | 28.8% | 12/16/3 | 35.1% | 5 | 41.7% | 0/9/6 | 19.5% |
| Clothing, total | 5 | 33.3% | 2/17/0 | 34.9% | 15 | 18.8% | 4/19/6 | 13.6% | 3 | 25.0% | 1/10/0 | 61.4% |
| Clothing, unspecified | – | – | – | – | 8 | 10.0% | 1/17/6 | 5.1% | 2 | 16.7% | 0/18/0 | 36.9% |
| Clothing, men's | 5 | 33.3% | 2/17/0 | 34.9% | 7 | 8.8% | 3/2/0 | 8.5% | 1 | 8.3% | 0/12/0 | 24.6% |
| Clothing, women's | – | – | – | – | – | – | – | – | – | – | – | – |
| Clothing, child's | – | – | – | – | – | – | – | – | – | – | – | – |
| Sewing materials | 2 | 13.3% | 1/16/0 | 22.0% | 18 | 22.5% | 8/2/6 | 35.3% | – | – | – | – |
| Food, total | – | – | – | – | 5 | 6.3% | 3/4/6 | 8.8% | 1 | 8.3% | 0/4/4 | 8.9% |
| Food, imported | – | – | – | – | 1 | 1.3% | 0/12/6 | 1.7% | 1 | 8.3% | 0/4/4 | 8.9% |
| Food, country produce | – | – | – | – | 4 | 5.0% | 2/12/0 | 7.1% | – | – | – | – |
| Alcohol | – | – | – | – | 3 | 3.8% | 0/5/0 | 0.7% | 1 | 8.3% | 0/3/0 | 6.1% |
| Tobacco | 2 | 13.3% | 1/17/6 | 22.9% | 4 | 5.0% | 0/15/6 | 2.1% | 1 | 8.3% | 0/1/0 | 2.0% |
| Personal hygiene | – | – | – | – | 7 | 8.8% | 0/13/0 | 1.8% | – | – | – | – |
| Miscellaneous | 2 | 13.3% | 1/2/0 | 13.5% | 2 | 2.5% | 0/13/0 | 1.8% | – | – | – | – |
| **Total** | **15** | | **8/3/6** | | **80** | | **36/10/5** | | **12** | | **2/8/10** | |

(*Continued*)

*Table 5.3* (Continued)

| *Category of item* | *1848* | | | | *Unknown years* | | | | *Total of all years* | | | |
|---|---|---|---|---|---|---|---|---|---|---|---|---|
| | *Number of items purchased* | *Percent of total* | *Cost of items purchased (£/s/d)* | *Percent of total* | *Number of items purchased* | *Percent of total* | *Cost of items purchased (£/s/d)* | *Percent of total* | *Number of items purchased* | *Percent of total* | *Cost of items purchased (£/s/d)* | *Percent of total* |
| Ammunition | – | – | – | – | – | – | – | – | 5 | 0.7% | 0/10/6 | 0.1% |
| Whaling technology | – | – | – | – | 1 | 1.5% | 0/2/6 | 0.1% | 9 | 1.2% | 69/7/14 | 14.3% |
| Hunting technology | – | – | – | – | – | – | – | – | 1 | 0.1% | 0/3/0 | 0.03% |
| Tools and other technology | 3 | 11.1% | 0/3/9 | 2.8% | 12 | 18.5% | 1/11/2 | 1.3% | 46 | 6.0% | 26/52/17 | 5.9% |
| Household items | 4 | 14.8% | 1/1/1 | 15.8% | 15 | 23.1% | 2/3/0 | 1.8% | 182 | 23.9% | 24/62/25 | 5.6% |
| Clothing, total | 8 | 29.6% | 3/11/0 | 53.1% | 10 | 15.4% | 2/7/0 | 2.5% | 222 | 29.1% | 70/91/12 | 15.4% |
| Clothing, unspecified | 5 | 18.5% | 2/10/0 | 37.4% | 3 | 4.6% | 0/18/6 | 0.8% | 122 | 16.0% | 34/81/12 | 7.8% |
| Clothing, men's | 3 | 11.1% | 1/1/0 | 15.7% | 6 | 9.2% | 1/17/0 | 1.6% | 92 | 12.1% | 30/64/6 | 6.8% |
| Clothing, women's | – | – | – | – | – | – | – | – | 5 | 0.7% | 2/26/0 | 0.7% |
| Clothing, child's | – | – | – | – | 1 | 1.5% | 0/3/0 | 0.1% | 3 | 0.4% | 0/11/0 | 0.1% |
| Sewing materials | – | – | – | – | 5 | 7.7% | 0/9/6 | 0.4% | 74 | 9.7% | 18/51/18 | 5.2% |
| Food, total | 6 | 22.2% | 0/14/6 | 10.8% | 4 | 6.2% | 0/11/6 | 0.5% | 21 | 2.8% | 13/45/29 | 3.2% |
| Food, imported | 6 | 22.2% | 0/14/6 | 10.8% | 4 | 6.2% | 0/11/6 | 0.5% | 17 | 2.2% | 10/53/29 | 2.6% |
| Food, country produce | – | – | – | – | – | – | – | – | 4 | 0.5% | 2/12/0 | 0.5% |
| Alcohol | – | – | – | – | 4 | 6.2% | 108/2/0 | 91.9% | 133 | 17.5% | 220/39/21 | 45.7% |
| Tobacco | 3 | 11.1% | 1/1/6 | 16.1% | 5 | 7.7% | 0/13/10 | 0.6% | 25 | 3.3% | 11/66/36 | 3.0% |
| Personal hygiene | – | – | – | – | 6 | 9.2% | 0/12/0 | 0.5% | 20 | 2.6% | 0/39/6 | 0.4% |
| Miscellaneous | 3 | 11.1% | 0/2/0 | 1.5% | 3 | 4.6% | 0/7/6 | 0.3% | 24 | 3.1% | 4/44/12 | 1.3% |
| **Total** | **27** | | **6/13/10** | | **65** | | **117/11/6** | | **762** | | **483/71/66** | |

At times, these small numbers skew the trends that appear in the data; thus, care has been taken in this analysis to note when data in these years influence any trends disproportionately.

There is a general decline in the number of purchases at the store by Maori over time. This decline is not unexpected given the diminishing whaling operations. Three years stand out as having particularly low numbers of transactions between Maori and Harwood – 1842, 1844 and 1847 – and no transactions with Maori were recorded by Harwood in 1846. In 1842, Joseph Crocome (a physician formally employed as the Otakou whaling station's doctor) opened a store in nearby Waikouaiti and Harwood became his main supplier. It is possible that Maori were trading more frequently in Waikouaiti this year as whaling operations were stronger there than at Otakou at this time.[24] Unfortunately, no accounting records remain from Waikouaiti that I could find, so this hypothesis cannot be verified. Nonetheless, Maori appeared to have resumed regular trade with Harwood at Otakou by the following year. It is not clear why there were so few transactions in 1844 and 1847 and no transactions in 1846, although incomplete accounting records remaining from Harwood's store is one possible explanation.

In all years except 1842, household items or clothing were the most frequently purchased items.[25] In 1842, alcohol was the most frequently purchased item. Thus, it would seem that by the 1840s, Maori had become accustomed to at least some European fashions and household comforts. The consumption of alcohol was noted by many contemporaries as a particular characteristic of whaling culture, and thus it would seem from the accounting records that, in some cases at least, the Maori most closely connected to whaling also consumed alcohol.

As with the number of transactions, there is a decline in the cost of transactions over time. Interestingly, despite there being fewer transactions in 1842 than in 1841 and 1843, the cost of the purchases in 1842 is less than 1841 but more than 1843. Thus, even though fewer overall transactions were made in 1842, the decline in trade is steadier when looking at the cost rather than the simple numbers. As before, in 1844 and 1847 little trading was recorded between Maori and Harwood's store and in 1846 there were no recorded transactions with Maori, for unknown reasons.

Comparing the cost of purchases to the number of purchases each year reveals some interesting differences. Although Maori most frequently purchased items of clothing in 1841, they spent the most on alcohol in that year. Similarly, in 1842 they most frequently purchased alcohol but spent the most on whaling technology.[26] In 1843, Maori most frequently purchased household items but again spent the most on alcohol. In fact, the highest number of purchases and the highest cost of purchases are for different categories of items in all years except 1844. While household and personal items were the most frequently purchased items in all years except 1842, Maori spent the most money on these items only in the last four years accounted for in the ledgers and notebooks

(1844–1848). Prior to that, the most money was spent on alcohol in 1841 and 1843 and whaling technology in 1842. It would seem that as the whaling industry declined in the Otakou region, the Maori were most interested in continuing to purchase household and personal items, suggesting that these items had been well incorporated into their lifestyles by the mid-nineteenth century.

Certain individual items demonstrate basic trends over this time period as well. For example, the number of items of food purchased by Maori at the Otakou station increased steadily over the years, with the exception of 1844 when there were no purchases of food items. However, only 15 transactions by Maori in total were recorded that year, and thus this anomaly might reflect missing data from the accounting records. The cost of the food items purchased by Maori also shows a general increase over time, with the exception of 1843. In this year, Maori spent £8/12/7 on food items, while they spent only £2 on food items in 1842 and £3/4/6 in 1845. Most of the money was spent on a one-time purchase of coffee, estimated at a value of £5, and on a one-time purchase of flour, estimated at a value of £3/8/1. Nonetheless, it may be that the Maori became more accustomed to, and more willing to purchase, European-style food over time in the Otakou region.

Similarly, both the number and the cost of personal hygiene items purchased by Maori at the Otakou whaling station increased over time. Personal hygiene items included such things as soap, mirrors, combs and handkerchiefs. Again, these data suggest that the Maori were increasingly interested in certain European manufactured goods in the Otakou region. At the same time, more sporadic purchases of various forms of European technology suggest that the Maori were selective in what they chose to incorporate into their lifestyle.

In addition to recording the detailed items purchased by Maori at his store, Harwood also recorded the items that Maori brought in to trade and/or sell at his store. Table 5.4 presents the total number and value (i.e. the amount paid to Maori) of items traded by Maori at the Otakou whaling station from 1841 to 1848. Again, while Harwood recorded the detailed and specific items traded by Maori, I have grouped these items into five basic categories – whale bone, country produce, country manufactured goods, cash and miscellaneous.[27] There are fewer records indicating what the Maori brought in for trade than indicating what they purchased. In particular, Harwood recorded very few items traded by Maori in the years 1847 and 1848 and no transactions in the years 1844 and 1846. It may be that Harwood made more careful record of the items brought in for trade from the Maori in ledgers or notebooks that have not been retained in any archives or libraries, at least that I could find, or detailed the trade items on shipping lists when goods were sent to Sydney.

As with the purchases made by Maori, there was a general decline in the number of items traded by Maori, although this decline is more sporadic and may reflect missing records from the accounting data. In most years, country produce accounted for the most frequent item traded by Maori. However, in 1841 and 1848, cash was used most frequently to pay for items purchased, and in 1847 'rent' (categorised as 'miscellaneous') was used most frequently to pay for items purchased. Unfortunately, Harwood did not specify in the accounting records to what the term 'rent' specifically referred. Perhaps the Maori had negotiated use of lands or goods to Harwood in exchange for repayment or forgiveness of debt, but it is not detailed or clear in the records. Unlike in the fur trade where cash was used infrequently, whalers and shore whaling station employees in New Zealand were usually paid according to the 'lay system'. In other words, employees were paid in both goods and cash based on each individual's rank and thus his share in the profits of the whaling season (his 'lay').[28] While it is not specified where these Maori received their cash initially, it is possible that this cash was from lays or other wages paid to the individual or a family member.

Interestingly, the value of items traded is significantly different than the number of items traded. In fact, the value of items traded increased between 1841 and 1843 before dropping considerably in 1845. This difference is likely a result of counting transactions instead of individual items. In other words, no matter how much of any item was traded by a Maori, it was still recorded as only one transaction. The value, however, would vary considerably depending on the amount of any particular item traded.

In four of the seven years, country produce was the most highly valued item traded. The most commonly traded country produce was potatoes. Only in 1842 and 1843 did other items of country produce exceed potatoes in the number of transactions. These two years also represent the highest value of items being traded in the time period covered. In both of these years, Maori were most often bringing in flax for trade, although they also brought in mutton birds (also called titi birds), pork and potatoes at a lesser frequency in these years. While the amounts that Harwood paid for most items remained relatively stable throughout this time period, flax was generally traded at a higher volume than the other common products (potatoes, pork and mutton birds), which might explain the significantly higher value of items traded in these two years as compared to the other years.

The highest value items traded by Maori in the final two years of the time period covered by Harwood's accounting records were no longer items of country produce. In 1847, 'rent' was the highest number and highest value of transactions, and in 1848, cash was used most frequently to pay for items purchased at the store, although the highest price was attributed to a miscellaneous entry that Harwood recorded as 'credit by subscription'. No further explanation was given for this entry. This trend may reflect a shift in Harwood's operations as the whaling industry declined in the Otakou region and was steadily replaced by agricultural pursuits. Harwood may have had less need for country produce that he could resell to local residents or ship to Australia as agriculture became entrenched in the region. Harwood may also have started purchasing agricultural products from local *pakeha* residents to trade to deep-sea whalers

*Table 5.4* Number and value of items traded by Maori, Otakou Whaling Station, 1841–1848.

| *Category of item* | *1841* | | | | *1842* | | | | *1843* | | | |
|---|---|---|---|---|---|---|---|---|---|---|---|---|
| | *Number of items purchased* | *Percent of total* | *Value of items traded purchased (£/s/d)* | *Percent of total* | *Number of items purchased* | *Percent of total* | *Value of items traded purchased (£/s/d)* | *Percent of total* | *Number of items purchased* | *Percent of total* | *Value of items traded purchased (£/s/d)* | *Percent of total* |
| Whale bone | – | – | – | – | 1 | 4.5% | 34/9/6 | 21.6% | – | – | – | – |
| Country produce | 43 | 29.7% | 12/12/0 | 19.3% | 16 | 72.7% | 122/7/0 | 76.7% | 24 | 100.0% | 310/13/8 | 100.0% |
| Country manufactured goods | 1 | 0.7% | – | – | 1 | 4.5% | 1/10/0 | 0.9% | – | – | – | – |
| Cash | 101 | 69.7% | 52/16/11.5 | 80.7% | 3 | 13.6% | 1/1/0 | 0.7% | – | – | – | – |
| Miscellaneous | – | – | – | – | 1 | 4.5% | 0/1/0 | 0.03% | – | – | – | – |
| **Total** | **145** | | **65/8/11.5** | | **22** | | **159/8/6** | | **24** | | **310/13/8** | |

and other shore whalers who came into Otago Harbour as time went on, lessening his dependence on Maori to bring in country produce that he could resell in other markets.

Figure 5.5 presents the proportion of items purchased by Maori at the Otakou whaling station during the entire time period from 1841 to 1848 combined. During this time, clothing was the most frequently purchased item (just over 29 per cent), followed closely by household items (nearly 24 per cent). Maori also purchased sewing materials almost 10 per cent of the time, suggesting that by the mid-nineteenth century, Maori had incorporated European-style clothing and household items into their lifestyles. European-style food (with the exception of alcohol) and technology, however, accounted for just over 10 per cent of their purchases combined, and thus would seem to be less important to the Maori lifestyle at this time.

Similarly, Figure 5.6 presents the proportion of the cost of items purchased by Maori during the entire time period combined.[29] Although alcohol only accounted for roughly 17.5 per cent of the number of items purchased, it accounted for just over 45 per cent of the cost of items purchased by Maori. Likewise, clothing accounted for nearly 30 per cent of the number of items purchased, but only roughly 15 per cent of the cost of items purchased. Thus while whaling technology was only purchased around 1 per cent of the time, it accounted for roughly 15 per cent of the cost of items purchased. Whaling technology was purchased quite rarely, possibly because it was so expensive; however, it does suggest that the Maori were actively engaged in the whaling industry and were making use of this technology on their own, although they were not necessarily using the technology exclusively for whaling, especially the boats.

| *1845* | | | | *1847* | | | | *1848* | | | |
|---|---|---|---|---|---|---|---|---|---|---|---|
| *Number of items purchased* | *Percent of total* | *Value of items traded purchased (£/s/d)* | *Percent of total* | *Number of items purchased* | *Percent of total* | *Value of items traded purchased (£/s/d)* | *Percent of total* | *Number of items purchased* | *Percent of total* | *Value of items traded purchased (£/s/d)* | *Percent of total* |
| – | – | – | – | – | – | – | – | – | – | – | – |
| 46 | 100.0% | 39/0/0 | 100.0% | 1 | 25.0% | 0/6/0 | 13.0% | 2 | 28.6% | 0/18/6 | 7.4% |
| – | – | – | – | – | – | – | – | – | – | – | – |
| – | – | – | – | – | – | – | – | 4 | 57.1% | 5/9/0 | 43.5% |
| – | – | – | – | 3 | 75.0% | 2/0/0 | 87.0% | 1 | 14.3% | 6/2/10 | 49.1% |
| **46** | | **39/0/0** | | **4** | | **2/6/0** | | **7** | | **12/10/4** | |

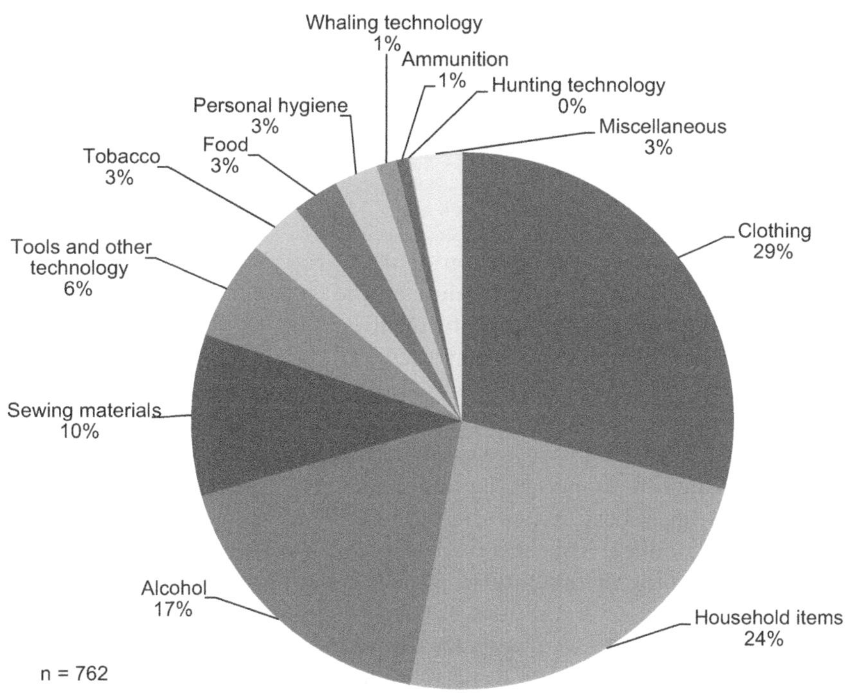


*Figure 5.5* Proportion of the number of items purchased by Maori, Otakou Whaling Station, 1841–1848.

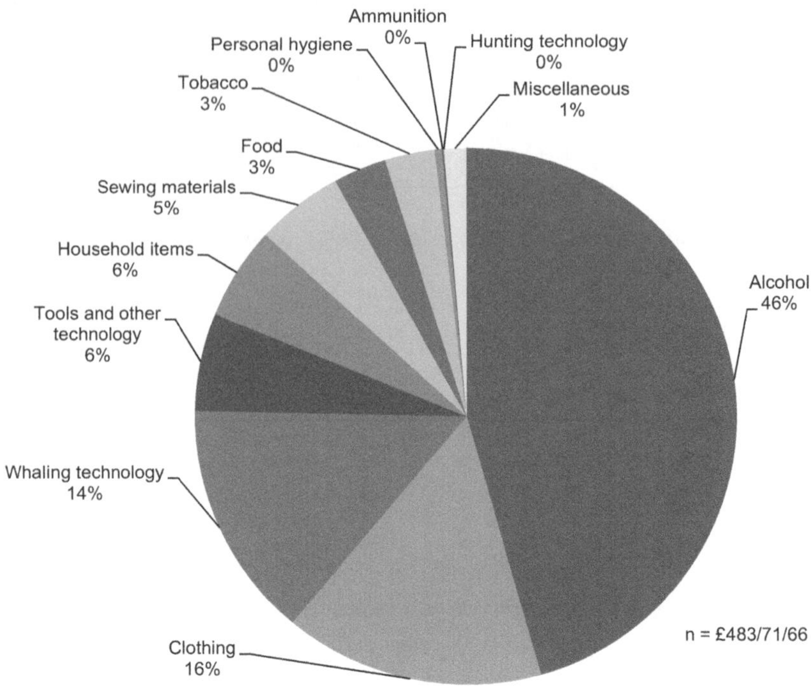


*Figure 5.6* Proportion of the value of items purchased by Maori, Otakou Whaling Station, 1841–1848.

Figure 5.7 presents the proportion of all items traded by Maori at the Otakou whaling station over the entire time period of 1841–1848. Over half of the items traded by Maori were some form of country produce, mostly potatoes but also flax, pork, mutton birds and a few other items. Cash was also used to purchase items at Harwood's store, accounting for just over 40 per cent of the transactions over the entire time period. Figure 5.8 presents the value of items traded by Maori at the Otakou whaling station over the entire time period of 1841–1848. The importance of the trade in country produce is even more evident in these data as over 80 per cent of the value of items traded by Maori was from country produce, while less than 10 per cent of the value was in the form of cash. While some of the country produce was probably used at the whaling station, mutton birds and pork in particular, correspondence from George Weller to his brother Edward suggests that at least some of the products, potatoes and flax specifically, were shipped for sale in Sydney, a practice common amongst many of the shore whaling stations in New Zealand.[30] Harwood's accounting records make it clear that while the main purpose of the Otakou station was the collection and shipment of whale products, the supplementary trade in flax, potatoes and other country produce was substantial.

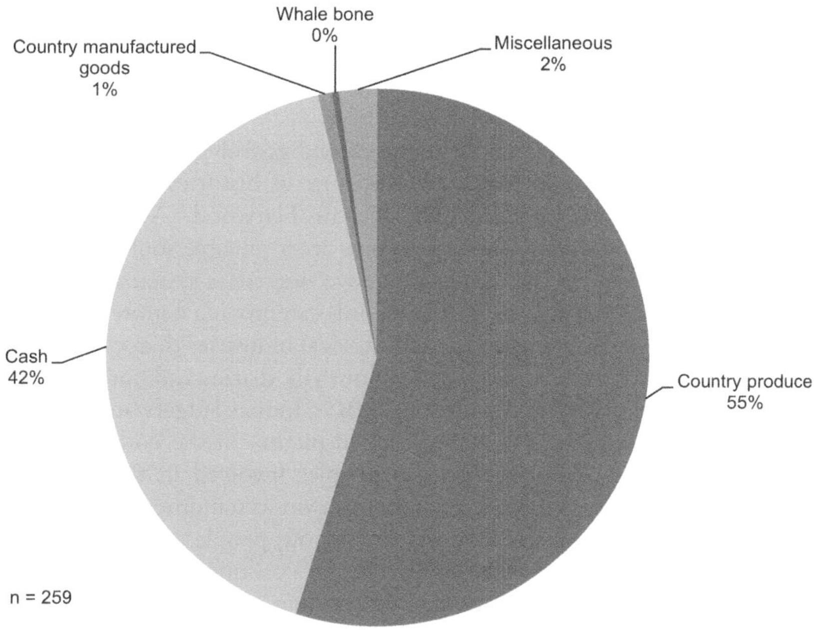


*Figure 5.7* Proportion of the number of items traded by Maori, Otakou Whaling Station, 1841–1848.

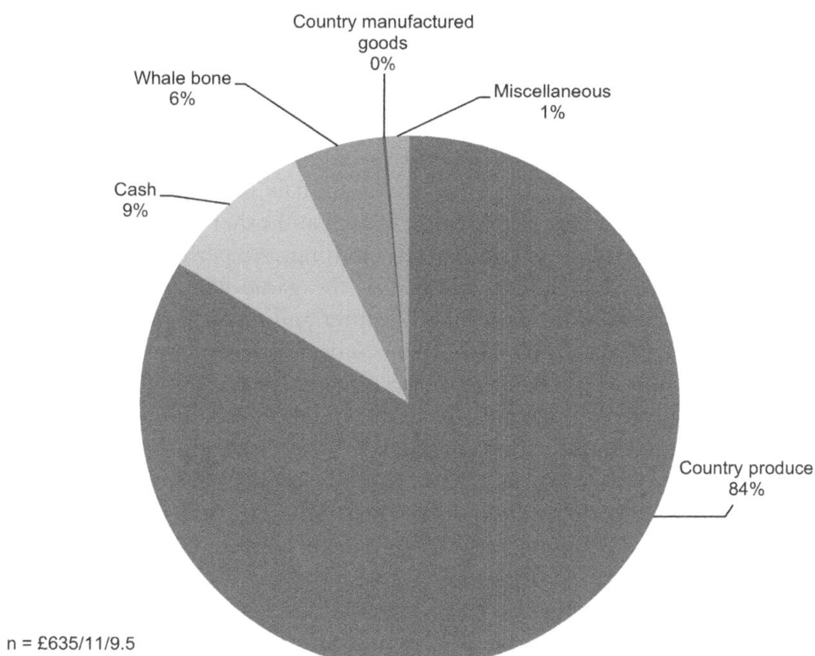


*Figure 5.8* Proportion of the value of items traded by Maori, Otakou Whaling Station, 1841–1848.

## Comparative analysis of the accounting data, Ile a la Crosse and Otakou

Few scholars studying the involvement of Indigenous peoples in historical commercial industries have made extensive use of historical accounting data, such as the records kept by HBC and Octavius Harwood.[31] While difficult to work with at times, these accounting records are a valuable source of information and rich in detail. As the discussion above suggests, a systematic analysis of even a small portion of the accounting records can provide a more comprehensive understanding of certain aspects of historical industries than can an analysis of more commonly used records such as journals, diaries and correspondence. In this case, a systematic analysis of the HBC's Indian ledgers and Harwood's ledgers and notebooks has created a detailed picture of the consumption and production patterns of the Indigenous peoples involved in these industries, which in turn provides a more comprehensive understanding of the impact of participation in these industries on the Indigenous peoples.

Interestingly, there are several similarities in consumption and production patterns between the Indigenous peoples trading at Ile a la Crosse and the Maori trading at Otakou. For example, in both places, the Indigenous peoples increasingly purchased European-style clothing over time, suggesting a change to pre-contact Indigenous lifestyles in both locales. At Ile a la Crosse, the purchase of clothing, and even more noticeably sewing materials, increased in the 1860s and 1870s compared to the 1830s. It would seem that by at least the mid-nineteenth century, European-style clothing and fabric had been incorporated into the lifestyles of Indigenous peoples in this region.[32] A number of factors might have contributed to this shift. As the Indigenous peoples became more entrenched in the fur trade, more effort would have been focussed on trapping fur-bearing animals rather than the game animals used in clothing production previously.[33] As well, cotton, wool, flannel and other materials would have been less labour-intensive to fashion into clothing, and perhaps also less labour-intensive to obtain, than hides. Further, as the game and fur-bearing animal populations declined in the region, less leather and fur would have been available to the Indigenous peoples. In other words, European clothing represented a lower opportunity cost as it was more efficient to trade hides for European clothing than to make clothing from the hides, especially as the game and fur-bearing animal populations declined. Finally, changing fashion-sense as a result of contact with Europeans, and possibly a growing Métis presence in the region, might have encouraged a shift to purchasing or making European-style clothing over time.[34] A change in clothing material would have facilitated participation in the fur trade; at the same time, however, it also would have made continued participation in the trade necessary as resources declined over the years forcing the Indigenous peoples to maintain this change in lifestyle.

Similar to the trends evident in the Indian ledgers, a significant and relatively consistent trade in clothing and, to a lesser extent, sewing materials suggests that European-style clothing had become a regular element in the Maori lifestyle by at least the mid-nineteenth century.[35] This trend is even more suggestive for the Maori as their traditional materials for clothing and other household items had not become important commodities for trade; they seem to have simply incorporated European clothing into their lifestyles.

There are also similar trends in the purchase of foodstuffs in both cases. The purchase of food by Indians at Ile a la Crosse increased somewhat in the 1860s, especially the sale in imported foods, but this increase also coincides with more frequent reports of declining game and populations of fur-bearing animals.[36] But even then, the types of imported food most frequently purchased – tea, sugar and flour – do not suggest that imported food was a main source of sustenance, even in the 1860s and 1870s. Even the less frequently purchased imported food items were more luxury items (raisins, peppermint, chocolate, caraway, salt, pepper and, very infrequently, rice and cured pork) than what one might expect if purchased food had become a main source of sustenance for the Indigenous peoples in the region. Thus, the Indian ledgers do not suggest significant changes to the Indigenous peoples' sustenance patterns and choice of food, although some new types of luxury foods (particularly tea, sugar and flour) had been incorporated by at least the mid-nineteenth century. At the same time, there is no strong evidence of declining participation in the trade; thus, the fur trade had become an important element of the Indigenous peoples' economy and even declining resources did not prompt a shift away from involvement in the trade.

Maori in the Otago region also increasingly purchased food from Harwood's store over the time period analysed. However, much like at Ile a la Crosse, the type and amount of food purchased do not suggest that the Maori had abandoned their pre-contact food sources entirely. The most commonly purchased food items at Otakou were flour and sugar, although to a lesser degree Maori also purchased rice, coffee and molasses. Interestingly, in 1845, Maori purchased pork and potatoes from Harwood's store – items that they would have normally grown or harvested themselves, some of which would have been traded to Harwood. Unfortunately, there are no journals from this year to suggest if there was famine or disease affecting the Maori in this region in that year. Nonetheless, these data suggest that Maori had begun to incorporate European-style food, either as a matter of choice or necessity as a result of increased pressure on local food resources from both shore-based whalers and deep-sea whalers, but not to the point of completely abandoning their pre-contact food sources.[37]

The importance of the introduction of metal ware to Indigenous populations through contact with Europeans, especially pots, pans, knives, axes and other such goods, has been discussed by many historians. In the fur trade, some historians have suggested that, in general, metal pots, pans and other such items were superior to pre-contact Indigenous technology and were thus readily absorbed into the Indigenous peoples' lifestyles.[38] While this pattern may have been true in some regions, the Indian ledgers of the Ile a la Crosse post do not show a substantial trade in metal goods, although the variety of metal goods purchased might have increased over time.[39] In the 1830s, Indians purchased traps, files, axes, knives, pots, pans and kettles but not to any great extent. Those items accounted for less than 10 per cent of the items purchased in most outfit years during this decade. The volume of trade increased slightly in the 1860s, sometimes accounting for slightly more than 10 per cent of the items purchased, but the type of items purchased remained very similar.

The amount of metal ware purchased by Maori in the 1840s was also not that substantial. Pots were a common item purchased by Maori in this decade, as well as knives. Occasionally, files, saws and nails were also purchased, but there does not appear to have been an extensive trade in metal ware at Otakou. Schaniel has argued that it actually took quite some time for the Maori to begin to see iron as a valuable trade good. Captain Cook found that initially the Maori, unlike other Polynesians, were not interested in metal ware; however, by the beginning of the nineteenth century, Maori were trading for a 'wide range of iron goods, including hatchets, axes, knives, and iron hoops'.[40] Interestingly, Schaniel further argued that despite the importance of the introduction of the white potato to Maori agriculture in the late eighteenth century, European agricultural tools (such as the hoe and the spade) were not widely adopted by the Maori until 1818.[41] Harwood's accounting records support the idea that metal ware was not a main focus of Maori trading efforts, at least in the 1840s at Otakou.

There were two very noticeable differences in consumption patterns at Ile a la Crosse and Otakou regarding the purchase of alcohol and the purchase of firearms and ammunition by Indigenous peoples at these sites. While some of the fur trade literature discusses the use of alcohol as an inducement to trade during the period of intense competition between the HBC and the NWC, it is generally accepted that after the 1821 merger, the trade in alcohol declined substantially.[42] The Indian ledgers and the post journals at Ile a la Crosse also support this notion. The early Ile a la Crosse post journals make frequent reference to Indians drinking at the nearby NWC post; however, references to Indians drinking disappear in the post journals after the 1821 merger. The earlier post journals did not make any reference to the HBC providing alcohol to Indians though, and so one might suggest that the journals simply did not record HBC activity of this nature. While Indian ledgers could not be found prior to the 1830s in the Ile a la Crosse post accounting records, no purchase of alcohol by Indians is found in the ledgers that were analysed. Alcohol was provided to tripmen (some of whom would have been Indigenous men from the region) and was included on lists of goods to be sent to other posts;[43] however, alcohol clearly did not represent an important trade item at Ile a la Crosse in the nineteenth century. This pattern was very different in the whaling industry.

Many of the early missionaries, officials and visitors to New Zealand commented extensively on the excessive consumption of alcohol by the whalers and the influence the whalers had on the Maori to do the same.[44] However, many of these early commentators seemed to believe that the number of Maori who drank excessively was actually quite small. For example, Edward Jerningham

Wakefield, the son of one of the main advocates for colonising New Zealand, noted in his memoirs that

> The bad points of the whaler's character have also passed, with the very worst effect, into the disposition of some of the natives. They have acquired, *in some few cases*, the habits of drinking; in many, boastful and insolent behaviour, and callousness to feeling.[45]

Similarly, Edward Shortland, Protector of the Aborigines for the Colonial Government of New Zealand, wrote: 'I was glad to find that spirits were not generally drunk by the natives. Those who had acquired the habit, however, although *few in number*, appeared to be as much slaves to it as their European neighbours.'[46]

Harwood's accounting records demonstrate that at least for those Maori most closely connected to the whaling station, alcohol was an important trade item, even as whaling declined in the region. Alcohol was the most frequently purchased item in 1842 but was also frequently purchased in 1843. In fact, Maori purchased alcohol in all years except 1844 and 1848, years in which there are few transaction records for Maori in total. Moreover, the highest cost of purchases by Maori was for alcohol in 1841, 1843 and in the unknown years. Thus, while the records cannot provide any real sense of the rate of consumption of alcohol by Maori, the shore whalers had clearly introduced Maori to alcohol and the consumption of alcohol continued even after whaling had started to decline at Otakou.

The purchase of firearms and ammunition also differed significantly at Ile a la Crosse and Otakou. At Ile a la Crosse, firearms were not commonly purchased in the nineteenth century, although this pattern is not unexpected. Some historians have discussed the importance of the introduction of firearms to Indigenous peoples in Canada. Firearms changed both the hunting patterns of some Indigenous peoples as well as the patterns of conflict between some Indigenous peoples (at least early on in the trade).[47] By the nineteenth century, however, only a small number of firearms were purchased by Indians at the Ile a la Crosse post, and in some years none at all (see Table 5.1). Not surprisingly, after several decades of trade, it would seem that firearms had been well integrated into the Indigenous communities of the region and/or firearms were of a higher quality and taken care of in such a way as they did not deteriorate quickly. Thus, numerous guns and rifles did not have to be purchased each year. This idea is substantiated by the considerable trade in ammunition throughout the time period analysed. Ammunition, which had to be replenished consistently, would not have been purchased if the Indigenous peoples were not using firearms regularly.

Similarly, much of the historical literature in New Zealand discusses the importance of the trade in firearms between Maori and whalers or other Europeans; some historians even suggest that securing access to guns and ammunition was the main motivation of Maori to engage in trade with Europeans, particularly in the 1820s but even as late as 1840.[48] Harwood's account books, however, suggest that while this desire to purchase firearms may have been important early on, particularly at times when inter-tribal warfare was extensive, it was not a primary motivation for trade in the 1840s in the Otago region. In fact, Harwood recorded Maori purchasing ammunition five times throughout the entire period covered in the account books, once in 1841 and four times in 1842. No purchases of guns or rifles by Maori were recorded in the account books in this period. Thus, the extensive trade in firearms was perhaps limited in time and place in New Zealand. It is also possible that Maori in the Otago region found alternate sources for a supply of firearms and ammunition other than Harwood, such as other whaling vessels coming into harbour.[49] Schaniel, however, argued that the Maori were insistent that they would only trade potatoes and pork for firearms and ammunition and were prepared not to trade at all if the Europeans refused to provide the desired goods. Thus, even missionaries and traders who objected morally to the trade in firearms were forced to engage in this trade if they needed potatoes and pork from the Maori.[50] Considering the large quantities of potatoes Harwood received in exchange for other goods, it is curious that no trade in firearms is evident in his accounting records. It was either not a significant issue for Harwood's business or it remained 'off the books'.

The trade in firearms also demonstrates a difference between Indigenous peoples' participation in the whaling industry and the fur trade. While hunting with guns and rifles was an important element in the fur trade, as well as in the Indigenous economy in the English River District, hunting was not important to Maori participation in the whaling industry. Whaling itself was conducted in a much different fashion and even the provisions trade to the Otakou whaling station, in which the Maori were actively involved, did not require hunting in the same sense as the provision trade in the English River District.[51] So while firearms may have been important during periods of Maori warfare, they were not used extensively in other aspects of Maori life. As such, when warfare declined in the 1830s, the importance of obtaining firearms might have declined as well, despite the continued discussion in the literature of the firearm trade continuing into the 1840s. Thus, in some ways, it is not surprising that items of trade that are found commonly in the Indian ledgers (ammunition and, to a lesser extent, firearms) are practically non-existent in Harwood's ledgers.

As this discussion suggests, the patterns of consumption and production evident in the accounting records at Ile a la Crosse and Otakou provide general insight into some of the impacts of participation in commercial industries on Indigenous peoples. At Ile a la Crosse, the trade in ammunition, food, clothing and sewing materials suggests some stability and some changes to the Indigenous peoples' lifestyles in the English River District by the nineteenth century. For example, the consistent sale of ammunition throughout the time period analysed suggests that hunting remained an important element of the Indigenous economy. While some of this hunting was certainly carried out as part of their participation in the fur and provisions trade, the limited amount of food purchased at the post, particularly in the 1830s, suggests that some of this hunting was also carried out for sustenance of the household. Similarly, while the Maori consistently purchased European-style food from Harwood's store, the amount and type of food purchased – mainly sugar, flour and coffee – suggests that Maori continued to consume country foods for their main sustenance.

As the above analysis of the HBC Indian ledgers and Harwood's store ledgers demonstrates, the patterns of consumption and production of Indigenous peoples involved in the fur trade and the whaling industry differ to some extent in their details, but both demonstrate some of the potential impacts of participation in these industries on the Indigenous peoples' economies and lifestyles. The patterns demonstrate both stability and change in the Indigenous peoples' economies and lifestyles but also suggest that participation in the industries had been integrated into the Indigenous economies by at least the early to mid-nineteenth century. The patterns suggest that enough changes had been made to the Indigenous peoples' lifestyles that not only was participation in these industries active and stable, rather than sporadic or occasional, but that this participation over time caused a need to continue active participation in the industries as these lifestyle changes became more entrenched and as local resources declined.

## Conclusion

Although historical accounting records, such as those kept by HBC and by Octavius Harwood, can be complex, difficult and time-consuming to analyse, detailed analysis of such records provides a more complex understanding of the consumption and production patterns of Indigenous peoples than can an examination of journals, memoirs and correspondence alone. The consumption and production patterns of the Indigenous peoples actively engaged in the fur and whaling industries demonstrate that the Indigenous economies were modified to incorporate new opportunities and changing circumstances introduced by these commercial industries. These modifications were not temporary or minimal as demonstrated by continual adaptations by the Indigenous people to adjust to changes in the broader colonial economies to maintain access to the goods to which they had become accustomed and, in some cases, upon which they may have come to rely as natural resources in their territories dwindled and changed over time. In particular, the consumption of specialty or luxury items was the means through which Indigenous peoples were drawn into the British colonial economy and through which a dependency to continue engaging in the colonial capitalist economy was created.

## Archival sources

### *Hudson's Bay Company Archives*

The Hudson's Bay Company Archives (HBCA) are an extensive collection of HBC and Northwest Company historical documents housed in Winnipeg,

Manitoba. The collection includes correspondence, post journals, accounts and ledgers and reports from many of the HBC posts that spread across Rupertsland. This extensive archival collection contains a variety of archival materials, although many historians have focussed predominantly on the post journals, correspondence and district reports for their analyses.

For this chapter, I have focussed most of my analyses on the account records for the Ile a la Crosse post, specifically the 'Indian ledgers', with some additional details gathered from post journals and district reports to aid in the interpretation of the accounting data. More specific discussion of the materials used for this chapter is contained in the relevant endnotes.

B.89/a/2 Ile a la Crosse Post Journal 1810–1811.
B.89/a/3 Ile a la Crosse Post Journal 1815–1816.
B.89/a/7 Ile a la Crosse Post Journal 1823–1824.
B.89/a/8 Ile a la Crosse Post Journal 1824–1825.
B.89/a/13 Ile a la Crosse Post Journal 1831–1832.
B.89/a/14 Ile a la Crosse Post Journal 1831–1832.
B.89/a/23 Ile a la Crosse Post Journal 1843–1845.
B.89/a/29 Ile a la Crosse Post Journal 1855–1856.
B.89/a/31 Ile a la Crosse Post Journal 1860–1861.
B.89/a/32 Ile a la Crosse Post Journal 1862.
B.89/a/33 Ile a la Crosse Post Journal 1862–1863.
B.89/a/34 Ile a la Crosse Post Journal 1863.
B.89/a/35 Ile a la Crosse Post Journal 1864–1865.
B.89/a/36 Ile a la Crosse Post Journal 1889–1891.
B.89/c/4 Ile a la Crosse Correspondence Book 1872–1875.
B.89/c/5 Ile a la Crosse Correspondence Book 1875–1877.
B.89/c/6 Ile a la Crosse Correspondence Book 1877–1881.
B.89/d/34 Ile a la Crosse Account Book 1832–1833.
B.89/d/36 Ile a la Crosse Account Book 1833–1834.
B.80/d/38 Ile a la Crosse Account Book 1834–1835.
B.89/d/40 Ile a la Crosse Account Book 1835–1836.
B.89/d/43a Ile a la Crosse Account Book 1832–1837.
B.89/d/43b Ile a la Crosse Account Book 1836–1837.
B.89/d/49 Ile a la Crosse Account Book 1839–1840.
B.89/d/51a Ile a la Crosse Account Book 1839–1841.
B.89/d/51b Ile a la Crosse Account Book 1840–1841.
B.89/d/53 Ile a la Crosse Account Book 1841–1842.
B.89/d/55a Ile a la Crosse Account Book 1841–1843.
B.89/d/55b Ile a la Crosse Account Book 1842–1843.
B.89/d/60 Ile a la Crosse Account Book 1843–1844.
B.89/d/85 Ile a la Crosse Account Book, 1854–1855.
B.89/d/86 Ile a la Crosse Account Book 1854–1855.
B.89/d/92 Ile a la Crosse Account Book 1860–1861.
B.89/d/93 Ile a la Crosse Account Book 1860–1861.

B.89/d/95 Ile a la Crosse Account Book 1862.
B.89/d/96 Ile a la Crosse Account Book 1862–1863.
B.89/d/98 Ile a la Crosse Account Book 1863–1864.
B.89/d/108a Ile a la Crosse Account Book 1863–1866.
B.89/d/113 Ile a la Crosse Account Book 1866.
B.89/d/118 Ile a la Crosse Account Book 1865–1867.
B.89/d/182 Ile a la Crosse Account Book 1875.
B.89/d/188 Ile a la Crosse Account Book 1875–1876.
B.89/d/192 Ile a la Crosse Account Book (Packing Account – Returns) 1876.
B.89/d/205 Ile a la Crosse Account Book 1877.
B.89/d/213 Ile a la Crosse Account Book 1878.
B.89/d/215 Ile a la Crosse Account Book (Fur Returns) 1873–1877.
B.89/d/216a Ile a la Crosse Account Book 1876–1879.
B.89/d/221 Ile a la Crosse Account Book 1879.
B.89/e/1 English River District Report 1822–1823.
B.89/e/2 English River District Report 1823.
B.89/e/5 Post Reports – Ile a la Crosse 1886.
B.239/z/10 Indian Population of Sundry Districts.

### *Hocken library references*

The Hocken Library in Dunedin, New Zealand, houses the collection of the remaining archival materials from Harwood's store at the Otakou Whaling Station. The collection includes journals, notebooks, ledgers and correspondence related to Harwood's store. The Hocken Library also houses collections of other archival materials related to the whaling industry in New Zealand.

For this chapter, I have focussed most of my analyses on the ledgers and notebooks maintained by Harwood that detail the transactions at his store. I have also gathered additional details from his journal and correspondence to support my analyses. More specific discussion of the materials used for this chapter is contained in the relevant endnotes.

MS-0404/001 Harwood Family Papers, Correspondence including letters from Octavius's father, Robert Harwood.
MS-0438/001, G.C. Thomson Collection Journal Apr. 1838 – Jan. 1840.
MS-0438/002, G.C. Thomson Collection Journal Oct. 1840 – July 1842.
MS-0438/003, G.C. Thomson Collection Copy of Octavius Harwood Journals.
MS-0438/007 G.C. Thomson Collection Notebook number 4.
MS-0438/009 G.C. Thomson Collection Notebook number 6.
MS-0438/010 G.C. Thomson Collection Notebook number 7.
MS-0438/011 G.C. Thomson Collection Notebook number 8.
MS-0438/012 G.C. Thomson Collection Notebook number 9.
MS-0438/014 G.C. Thomson Collection Notebook number 11.

MS-0438/018 G.C.Thomson Collection Notebook number 15.
MS-0438/019 G.C.Thomson Collection Notebook number 16.
MS-0440/005 G.C.Thomson Collection George and Edward Weller, Transcript of Letters, 1832–1861.
MS-0604/003 Harwood Family Papers Accounts ledger of store customers and any debts incurred.

### *Library and Archives Canada references*

The Library and Archives Canada is the national archive of Canada and houses extensive collections of archival materials related to a wide range of topics relevant to Canadian history, including Canada's relationship to and interactions with Indigenous peoples.

For this chapter, I used some of the census data housed by Library and Archives Canada to develop an understanding of changing populations in the Ile a la Crosse region to support my analyses. More specific discussion of the census material used for this chapter is contained in relevant endnotes.

RG 15, Vol. 230, file 614, Hudson's Bay Census of Indians, Whites, and Half-breeds of the Northern Department, Aggregate, 1872.

## Notes

1 I use the term 'commercial industries' here to highlight two key differences between the extensive trade networks that Indigenous peoples were a part of prior to contact with Europeans and the trade Indigenous peoples engaged with Europeans in the fur trade and the shore-based whaling industry. Unlike the pre-contact exchange networks, the fur trade and whaling industry were commercial enterprises for the Europeans. In other words, the Europeans were engaged in industries that were trying to make a profit for the owners. Additionally, the Europeans, in both the fur trade and the whaling industry, were trying to procure raw materials that would be transformed into finished products (i.e. industries). In the fur trade, Europeans were trading with Indigenous peoples directly for the raw materials they were seeking. In the shore-based whaling industry, Europeans were trading for supplies that would allow them to continue harvesting the raw materials they sought without having to import their own food and materials. To a certain extent, this type of exchange also occurred in the fur trade. What is important is to note that these trading systems were unequal and the Europeans were trying to obtain raw materials and supplies for as cheaply as possible while exchanging goods that did not diminish their profit margins greatly. This motivation is important to understand when considering how Europeans approached the trade in both industries. Thus, using the term 'commercial industries' is meant to draw attention to the two elements of the fur trade and the whaling industry that influenced the actions of the Europeans – the for-profit nature of the trade and the collection of raw materials for use in the manufacturing process.

2 For a more complete list and discussion of HBC accounting records prior to 1763, see A. J. Ray, 'The Early Hudson's Bay Company Account Books as Sources for Historical Research: An Analysis and Assessment', *Archivaria*, 1:1 (1975–1976), pp. 3–38; and A. J. Ray and D. Freeman, *'Give Us Good Measure': An Economic Analysis of Relations Between the Indians and the Hudson's Bay Company Before 1763* (Toronto: University of Toronto

Press, 1978), especially chapter 9, 'The Early Hudson's Bay Company Account Books', pp. 81–119. Although the accounting records changed somewhat over time, these discussions provide a basic context for understanding the records.

3 The Indian ledgers do not appear to capture all of the transactions between Indigenous people and the HBC in the English River District. Thus, the data set should not be considered a comprehensive collection of all relevant transactions.

4 Unless otherwise noted, information and data in this section are from Hudson's Bay Company Archives (HBCA), B.89/d/43a, Ile a la Crosse Account Book, 1832–1837; B.89/d/51a, Ile a la Crosse Account Book, 1839–1841; B.89/d/55a, Ile a la Crosse Account Book, 1841–1843; B.89/d/86, Ile a la Crosse Account Book, 1854–1855; B.89/d/95, Ile a la Crosse Account Book, 1862; B.89/d/108a, Ile a la Crosse Account Book, 1863–1866; B.89/d/188, Ile a la Crosse Account Book, 1875–1876; and B.89/d/216a, Ile a la Crosse Account Book, 1876–1879.

5 R. Jarvenpa and H. Brumbach, 'Occupational Status, Ethnicity, and Ecology: Metis Cree Adaptations in a Canadian Trading Frontier', *Human Ecology*, 13:3 (1985), p. 314; R. Jarvenpa and H. Brumbach, 'The Microeconomics of Southern Chipewyan Fur Trade History', in S. Krech III (ed.), *The Subarctic Fur Trade: Native Social and Economic Adaptations* (Vancouver: University of British Columbia Press, 1984), p. 155.

6 H. A. Innis, *The Fur Trade in Canada: An Introduction to Canadian Economic History*, rev. ed. (Toronto: University of Toronto Press, 1970), pp. 341–79.

7 Innis, *The Fur Trade in Canada*, pp. 341–79; and, A. J. Ray, *The Canadian Fur Trade in the Industrial Age* (Toronto: University of Toronto Press, 1990), pp. 30–49.

8 I am using the term 'Indians' here in the same sense used by the HBC to identify Indigenous people not formally employed by the company. At Ile a la Crosse, Indians could be Cree, Dene or Métis. The term is not meant to denote the legal definition of Indian provided by the Indian Act in Canada.

9 Household items include blankets, comforters, buffalo robes, pots, pans, kettles, teapots, cups, mugs, plates, knives and forks, lamps, etc.

10 Discussion of a decline in the fur-bearer and game animal populations in the region can be found in much of the post journals and correspondence from Ile a la Crosse. See for example, HBCA, B.89/a/29 Ile a la Crosse Post Journal 1855–1856, 19 June 1855, 8, 12, 17, 21, 23 and 31 July 1855, and 1, 6, 9, 10, 11, 13, 14, 15, 16, 17, 18, and 21 August 1855; B.89/a/31 Ile a la Crosse Post Journal 1860–1861, 23 October 1860, 17 December 1860, 6 and 16 January 1861, 13 and 27 March 1861, and 1 and 17 May 1861; B.89/a/33 Ile a la Crosse Post Journal 1862–1863, 10 December 1862; B.89/c/4 Ile a la Crosse Correspondence Book, 1872–1875, letter dated Ile a la Crosse 20 January 1872 to Donald A. Smith, Chief Commissioner from Samuel McKenzie, fo. 2; letter dated Ile a la Crosse English River District, 1 June 1872, Report to the Chief Commissioner, fo. 11; letter dated Green Lake Store, 9 September 1873, to Donald A. Smith from W. McMurray, fo. 44–45; and, B.89/c/6 Ile a la Crosse Correspondence Book, 1877–1881, letter dated Ile a la Crosse 14 January 1878, to James A. Grahame from Ewen Macdonald, fo. 61–63. One letter in particular noted that, as a result of the scarcity of game and fur-bearing animals in the region, the post was required to provide more provisions and ammunition to induce the Indians to go further afield to hunt and trap. The provision of ammunition during times of hardship might also provide an explanation of why ammunition was no longer the most frequently purchased item at Ile a la Crosse in the later years. B.89/c/6 Ile a la Crosse Correspondence Book, 1877–1881, letter dated Isle a La Crosse English River District, 1 June 1880 to James A. Grahame from Ewen Macdonald, fo. 145–146.

11 Country produce included such items as pemmican, grease, barley, potatoes and Athabasca salt. Imported food included such items as tea, sugar, flour, chocolate, raisins, peppermint, cured pork and pepper.

12 See, for example, B.89/c/6 Ile a la Crosse Correspondence Book, 1877–1881, letter dated Isle a La Crosse 1 June 1880 to James A. Grahame from Ewen Macdonald, fo. 145–146.

13 HBCA B.89/a/31 Ile a la Crosse Post Journal 1860–1861, 17 November 1860; B.89/a/33 Ile a la Crosse Post Journal 1862–1863, 10 December 1862.

14 Much like with the purchase of various commodities, the number of items traded records the number of times Indians brought goods in for trade, regardless of the number of items that were brought in. It was necessary to record transactions in this way because the early records did not often provide a detailed list of all the items brought in for trade.

15 Country produce includes such items as castorum, meat, fish, provisions and dogs. Country manufactured goods include such items as leather, babiche, sinew and pack cord. The miscellaneous category includes such items as sundries, adjustments in the accounts, unspecified payments at other posts or outposts and, rarely, returned merchandise.

16 In many cases, the clerks did not record the exact number of furs or skins being brought in for trade. Thus, the number of transactions (i.e. groups of items brought in for trade) has been counted, rather than the number of items. Thus, when an Indian brought in 'furs' to trade, one transaction was recorded, regardless of the number of pelts that were brought in.

17 The district accounts were the accounting records for an HBC district. These records would include details about the number of furs collected, goods traded to Indians, goods provided to employees and a general description of the fur trade in the district for the period covered in the accounts.

18 See for example, HBCA B.89/d/34 Ile a la Crosse Account Book 1832–1833; B.80/d/38 Ile a la Crosse Account Book, 1834–1835; B.89/d/93 Ile a la Crosse Account Book, 1860–1861; B.89/d/98 Ile a la Crosse Account Book, 1863–1864; B.89/d/118 Ile a la Crosse Account Book, 1865–1867; B.89/d/192 Ile a la Crosse Account Book (Packing Account – Returns), 1876; B.89/d/215 Ile a la Crosse Account Book (Fur Returns) 1873–1877.

19 The pound sterling values in Figures 5.2 and 5.4 have been converted to decimal pounds for ease of calculation with percentages and for presentation purposes.

20 Looking at the purchases of four individual Dene trappers trading at Ile a la Crosse in the decades following the time period analysed in this chapter, Jarvenpa and Brumbach noted a somewhat similar proportion of expenditures for some individuals. For example, in 1889–1890, Bernard Chayauyazie purchased mostly imported food, followed by clothing and textiles. In 1894–1895, Willibert Grandfarrand purchased mostly clothing and textiles, followed by imported foods. In 1900–1901, Ehtengoo Campbell purchased mostly imported food, followed by clothing and textiles. Finally, in 1908–1909, Deaf Isaac purchased mostly clothing and textiles, followed by imported food. Jarvenpa and Brumbach, 'The Microeconomics of Southern Chipewyan Fur Trade History', p. 165, p. 171, p. 173, p. 175. Thus, even in the following decades, clothing and sewing materials remained important trade items, although the importance of imported food might have increased, at least for some individuals. These authors had similar findings for Métis Cree in this region as for the Chipewyan. Jarvenpa and Brumbach, 'Occupational Status, Ethnicity, and Ecology', pp. 315–23.

21 Unless otherwise noted, information and data in this section are from Hocken Library, MS-0604/003 Harwood Family Papers Accounts ledger of store customers and any debts incurred, MS-0438/007 G.C. Thomson Collection Notebook number 4, MS-0438/009 G.C. Thomson Collection Notebook number 6, MS-0438/010 G.C. Thomson Collection Notebook number 7, MS-0438/011 G.C. Thomson Collection Notebook number 8, MS-0438/012 G.C. Thomson Collection Notebook number 9, MS-0438/014 G.C. Thomson Collection Notebook number 11, MS-0438/018 G.C. Thomson Collection Notebook number 15, and MS-0438/019 G.C. Thomson Collection Notebook number 16.

22 E. Shortland, *The Southern Districts of New Zealand; a Journal, with Passing Notices of the Customs of the Aborigines* (London: Longman, Brown, Green and Longmans, 1974, originally published 1851), pp. 11, pp. 300–1; and F. Tod, *Whaling in Southern Waters* (Dunedin: New Zealand Tablet Co., 1982), pp. 21–36, pp. 66–68 and pp. 87–99.

23 As much as possible, I have kept the categories of analysis as similar as possible for the whaling records and the HBC records; however, there are differences in the categories that reflect differences in the nature of the two industries.

24 Tod, *Whaling in Southern Waters*, p. 93.

25 Household items include blankets, comforters, tablecloths, dishes, cups, knives, pots, kettles, jars, boxes, pipes, books, etc.

26 Interestingly in this year, much of the whaling technology was purchased by 'Toawaik' (probably Tuhawaiki), a Ngai Tahu leader who owned and operated a shore whaling station. H. Morton, *The Whale's Wake* (Honolulu: University of Hawaii Press, 1982), p. 172; E. Olssen and M. P. J. Reilly, 'Te tutakitanga o nga ao e rua: Early Contacts Between Two Worlds', in T. M. Ka'ai, J. C. Moorfield, M. P. J. Reilly, and S. Mosley (eds.), *Ki Te Whaiao: An Introduction to Maori Culture and Society* (Auckland: Pearson Education New Zealand, 2004), p. 142.

27 Country produce includes such items as fish, birds, flax, potatoes, pork and greenstone. Country manufactured goods include such items as mats and baskets. The miscellaneous category includes such items as rent, credit and 'trade'. Again, I have tried to keep these categories as consistent with the categories used in the fur trade analysis as possible, bearing in mind the different natures of the industries.

28 Morton, *The Whale's Wake*, pp. 75–78. Morton further argued that by the mid-1830s, at least in the Bay of Islands, Maori were quickly adapting to using cash instead of other goods for trade. Morton, *The Whale's Wake*, p. 216.

29 Although Harwood's ledgers and notebooks recorded values in pound sterling, these values have been converted to decimal pounds for Figures 5.6 and 5.8 for ease of calculating percentages.

30 Hocken Library, MS-0440/005 G.C. Thomson Collection, George and Edward Weller, Transcript of Letters, 1832–1861, Letter from George Weller to Edward Weller, dated 16 March 1835 and Letter from George Weller to Edward Weller, dated 23 July 1835. See also, A. H. Clark, *The Invasion of New Zealand by People, Plants and Animals, the South Island* (Westport, CT: Greenwood Press, 1949), p. 68; R. McNab, *The Old Whaling Days: A History of Southern New Zealand from 1830 to 1840* (Christchurch: Whitcombe and Tombs, 1913), pp. 98–288; Morton, *The Whale's Wake*, pp. 188, pp. 279–80; and Tod, *Whaling in Southern Waters*, p. 23.

31 Some notable exceptions include: A. M. Carlos and F. D. Lewis, 'Trade, Consumption, and the Native Economy: Lessons from York Factory, Hudson Bay', *Journal of Economic History*, 61:4 (2001), pp. 1037–64; Jarvenpa and Brumbach, 'Occupational Status, Ethnicity, and Ecology'; Jarvenpa and Brumbach, 'The Microeconomics of Southern Chipewyan Fur Trade History'; A. J. Ray, *Indians in the Fur Trade: Their Role as Hunters, Trappers and Middlemen in the Lands Southwest of Hudson Bay 1660–1870* (Toronto: University of Toronto Press, 1974); Ray, 'Early Hudson's Bay Company Account Books'; Ray and Freeman, 'Give Us Good Measure'; and F. Tough, 'Indian Economic Behaviour, Exchange and Profits in Northern Manitoba During the Decline of Monopoly, 1870–1930', *Journal of Historical Geography*, 16:4 (1990), pp. 385–401.

32 Helm, Rogers and Smith suggest that the increasing purchase of European-style clothing and sewing materials was quite common for all Indigenous peoples involved in the Rupertsland fur trade. J. Helm, E. S. Rogers and J. G. E. Smith, 'Intercultural Relations and Cultural Change in the Shield and Mackenzie Borderlands', in J. Helm (ed.), *Handbook of North American Indians*, vol. 6 (Washington: Smithsonian Institute, 1981), pp. 153–54.

33 Jarvenpa and Brumbach reach a similar conclusion in their study of Chipewyan trappers trading at the Ile a la Crosse Post in the late nineteenth and early twentieth centuries, although they also suggested that the Chipewyan probably only wore such clothing during religious holidays and other special occasions in Ile a la Crosse. Jarvenpa and Brumbach, 'The Microeconomics of Southern Chipewyan Fur Trade History', p. 170, p. 176. See also, Helm, Rogers, and Smith, 'Intercultural Relations and Cultural Change

in the Shield and Mackenzie Borderlands', pp. 150–51, for a more generalised discussion of changes in hunting patterns of Indigenous groups in the Canadian Shield and Mackenzie borderlands.

34 While the HBC did keep a census of the population of each district, the early data refer simply to 'Indians frequenting the post' and thus do not attempt to identify more specific Indigenous peoples. However, the census taken of the English River District in 1872 identified 131 'French Halfbreeds' in the district, representing 8 per cent of the total population in the district (1,625, including 'Whites' and 'Chepewyans'). Library and Archives Canada (hereafter LAC), RG 15, vol. 230, file 614, Hudson's Bay Census of Indians, Whites, and Half-breeds of the Northern Department, Aggregate, 1872. For a discussion of Métis use of European fashions, see J. Teillet, 'The People and Territory of the Métis Nation' (paper presented at conference 'The Powley Legacy: Mapping the History of Métis Nation Rights', Saskatoon, SK, 16–17 July 2010). Macdougall also mentions Métis women wearing tartan shawls as being a common depiction of Métis in the nineteenth century. B. Macdougall, *One of the Family: Metis Culture in Nineteenth-Century Northwestern Saskatchewan* (Vancouver: University of British Columbia Press, 2010), p. 94.

35 Shaniel also finds that clothing was a common trade item between Maori and whalers in his study, although he places more emphasis on the trade in muskets and powder prior to 1840. W. Schaniel, 'The Maori and the Economic Frontier: An Economic History of the Maori of New Zealand, 1769–1840' (PhD dissertation, University of Tennessee, 1985), p. 303.

36 HBCA, B.89/a/29 Ile a la Crosse Post Journal 1855–1856, 19 June 1855, 8, 12, 17, 21, 23 and 31 July 1855, and 1, 6, 9, 10, 11, 13, 14, 15, 16, 17, 18, and 21 August 1855; B.89/a/31 Ile a la Crosse Post Journal 1860–1861, 23 October 1860, 17 December 1860, 6 and 16 January 1861, 13 and 27 March 1861, and 1 and 17 May 1861; B.89/a/33 Ile a la Crosse Post Journal 1862–1863, 10 December 1862; B.89/c/4 Ile a la Crosse Correspondence Book, 1872–1875, letter dated Ile a la Crosse 20 January 1872 to Donald A. Smith, Chief Commissioner from Samuel McKenzie, fo. 2; letter dated Ile a la Crosse English River District, 1 June 1872, Report to the Chief Commissioner, fo. 11; letter dated Green Lake Store, 9 September 1873, to Donald A. Smith from W. McMurray, fo. 44–45; and, B.89/c/6 Ile a la Crosse Correspondence Book, 1877–1881, letter dated Ile a la Crosse 14 January 1878, to James A. Grahame from Ewen Macdonald, fo. 61–63; and, B.89/c/6 Ile a la Crosse Correspondence Book, 1877–1881, letter dated Isle a La Crosse English River District, 1 June 1880 to James A. Grahame from Ewen Macdonald, fo. 145–146.

37 It would be interesting and useful to compare the caloric values of the food purchased by Indigenous peoples at Ile a la Crosse and Otakou with what would have been their daily needs, but with limited population data this avenue of analysis is beyond the scope of this chapter. Jarvenpa and Brumbach have done these calculations for four individual trappers at Ile a la Crosse covering four different outfit years (1889–1890, 1894–1895, 1900–1901, and 1908–1909). Although imported foods were accounting for a greater share of purchases in these years for these individuals (and increasing over time), when comparing the caloric values obtained through the purchase of imported foods to the caloric needs of a family of five, these scholars found that imported foods only accounted for between 3 and 15 per cent of the family's caloric needs, and still only between 7 and 38 per cent of the caloric needs of a family of two. Jarvenpa and Brumbach, 'The Microeconomics of Southern Chipewyan Fur Trade History', p. 169, p. 172, p. 174, p. 177.

38 Helm, Rogers, and Smith, 'Intercultural Relations and Cultural Change in the Shield and Mackenzie Borderlands', p. 151; Innis, *The Fur Trade in Canada*, pp. 16–22, p. 388; and, Ray, *Indians in the Fur Trade*, pp. 81–85. Calvin Martin has gone so far as to suggest that some items, such as the copper kettle for the Mi'qmaq, allowed Indigenous groups to change substantially their pre-contact livelihoods and settlement patterns. C. Martin, 'The Four Lives of a Micmac Copper Pot', *Ethnohistory*, 22:2 (1975), pp. 111–33. For an alternative view that metal goods were not used extensively by the Cree and did not

always replace pre-contact tools, at least early in the fur trade, see P. C. Thistle, *Indian-European Trade Relations in the Lower Saskatchewan River Region to 1840* (Winnipeg: University of Manitoba Press, 1986), pp. 34–39.

39 The inventory lists at the Ile a la Crosse post change very little in the variety of metal goods listed over the decades in consideration here. See, for example: HBCA B.89/d/34 Ile a la Crosse Account Book, 1832–1833; B.89/d/36 Ile a la Crosse Account Book, 1833–1834; B.89/d/38 Ile a la Crosse Account Book, 1834–1835; B.89/d/40 Ile a la Crosse Account Book, 1835–1836; B.89/d/43b Ile a la Crosse Account Book, 1836–1837; B.89/d/49 Ile a la Crosse Account Book, 1839–1840; B.89/d/51b Ile a la Crosse Account Book, 1840–1841; B.89/d/53 Ile a la Crosse Account Book, 1841–1842; B.89/d/55b Ile a la Crosse Account Book, 1842–1843; B.89/d/60 Ile a la Crosse Account Book, 1843–1844; B.89/d/85 Ile a la Crosse Account Book, 1854–1855; B.89/d/92 Ile a la Crosse Account Book, 1860–1861; B.89/d/96 Ile a la Crosse Account Book, 1862–1863; B.89/d/98 Ile a la Crosse Account Book, 1863–1864; B.89/d/113 Ile a la Crosse Account Book, 1866; B.89/d/118 Ile a la Crosse Account Book, 1865–1867; B.89/d/182 Ile a la Crosse Account Book, 1875; B.89/d/205 Ile a la Crosse Account Book, 1877; B.89/d/213 Ile a la Crosse Account Book, 1878; and, B.89/d/221 Ile a la Crosse Account Book, 1879.

40 Schaniel, 'The Maori and the Economic Frontier', p. 41.

41 Schaniel, 'The Maori and the Economic Frontier', p. 209.

42 Innis, *The Fur Trade in Canada*, pp. 82–87, pp. 306–7; and Ray, *Indians in the Fur Trade*, p. 85, pp. 142–44, pp. 197–98. Looking at expenditures at York Factory from 1716 to 1770, Carlos and Lewis note that early in this period no alcohol was traded for by Natives, but gradually alcohol did become a trade item. Then, after 1738, the proportion of expenditures by Natives on alcohol started to grow, equalling or surpassing the purchase of tobacco, until the end of the study period. They argue, however, that the increase in purchase of alcohol by Natives was related to a decline in the HBC providing brandy as a gift in the trading ceremonies. Carlos and Lewis, 'Trade, Consumption, and the Native Economy', pp. 1050–51.

43 Tripmen were the men hired by the HBC to transport the furs and skins from the post where they were collected to a port where they could be sent to Europe and bring trade goods back to the post. See, for example, HBCA B.89/d/85 Ile a la Crosse Account Book, 1854–1855; B.89/d/92 Ile a la Crosse Account Book, 1860–1861; B.89/d/96 Ile a la Crosse Account Book, 1862–1863; B.89/d/98 Ile a la Crosse Account Book, 1863–1864; and B.89/d/118 Ile a la Crosse Account Book, 1865–1867.

44 See, for example, F. T. Bullen, *The Cruise of the 'Cachalot': Round the World After Sperm Whales* (London: Smith, Elder and Co., 1898), p. 314; D. A. Chappell, *Double Ghosts: Oceanian Voyagers on Euroamerican Ships* (Armonk, NY: M. E. Sharpe, 1997), p. 47; and Morton, *The Whale's Wake*, p. 201, p. 247.

45 Emphasis added. E. J. Wakefield, *Adventure in New Zealand* (Auckland, NZ: Viking Penguin Books, 1987 [1845]), p. 143.

46 Emphasis added. Shortland, *The Southern Districts of New Zealand*, p. 116.

47 Innis, *The Fur Trade in Canada*, pp. 17–22, pp. 53–57, p. 388; and Ray, *Indians in the Fur Trade*, pp. 19–25, pp. 73–78. Carlos and Lewis found that from 1716 to 1770, 70 to 80 per cent of the purchases made by Natives trading at York Factory were for firearms and related goods, although they also note that over this time period, the proportion of expenditure on producer and household goods declined, while the proportion of expenditure on luxury goods (alcohol, tobacco, beads, cloth, etc.) increased. Carlos and Lewis, 'Trade, Consumption, and the Native Economy', p. 1049. For an alternative perspective that firearms were not readily adopted by Indigenous people in the early fur trade see E. M. Blaine, 'Dependency: Charles Bishop and the Northern Ojibwa', in K. Abel and J. Friesen (eds.), *Aboriginal Resource Use in Canada: Historical and Legal Aspects* (Winnipeg: University of Manitoba Press, 1991), pp. 97–100; and, Thistle, *Indian-European Trade Relations*, pp. 38–39.

48 J. R. Elder, *The Pioneer Explorers of New Zealand* (London: Blackie and Son Limited, 1929), p. 4. See also, Morton, *The Whale's Wake*, p. 127, p. 184, pp. 201–4; Schaniel, 'Maori and the Economic Frontier', p. 148, p. 178, p. 180, pp. 185–86, p. 303; W. C. Schaniel, 'European Technology and the New Zealand Maori Economy: 1769–1840', *Social Science Journal*, 38 (2001), pp. 142–43.

49 Morton even argues, 'Whaleship captains were a major, perhaps the major source of arms for the Maoris, and sold guns to them long after British annexation.' Morton, *The Whale's Wake*, p. 204.

50 Schaniel, 'The Maori and the Economic Frontier', pp. 158–60. Morton similarly noted that ships' captains who refused to trade in firearms were not successful in obtaining potatoes or pork from the Maori, even into the late 1840s. Morton, *The Whale's Wake*, p. 204.

51 Even pre-contact Maori subsistence was not hunting-based in the same manner as pre-contact Cree and Dene subsistence. Maori subsistence focussed on fish, birds, fern root and to a lesser extent kumara (sweet potato). Clark, *The Invasion of New Zealand*, pp. 42–43.

# 6 Economic intelligence and fur trade management by the Hudson's Bay Company

## An examination of district reports in the nineteenth and early twentieth centuries

*Arthur J. Ray*

### Laying the groundwork for long-distance management

When the Hudson's Bay Company (HBC) began establishing permanent posts in present-day Canada towards the late seventeenth century, its London directors, known as the Governor and Committee (GC), faced numerous business challenges related to building construction and maintenance, labour management, and inventory control. They also had to deal with fluctuating local environmental circumstances and ever-changing fur and 'country produce' markets. When the company moved inland from its bases on the shores of Hudson and James Bays beginning in 1774, it faced the enormous additional task of maintaining an ever-expanding canoe and Yorkboat transportation system that was anchored on Hudson and James Bays. To meet these management challenges, the GC established a comprehensive reporting and record-keeping system. The latter survives today as the HBC Archives, which spans more than three centuries.[1] The UN has designated it as a world heritage resource.

### Business reporting in the seventeenth and early eighteenth centuries

From the earliest days of the company's operations, the GC expected its post managers to keep two primary sets of records, a post journal and a general account book. Apparently the requirement to keep post journals began in 1683. In that year the London committee wrote to Governor Henry Sergeant at Fort Albany and informed him: 'We doe expect and accordingly doe hereby expressly require you to sende us home every year exact Jounralls of what hath been Done both at the place where you shall reside your selfe and at all our other Factories [. . .]'[2] In their daily journal entries post managers were expected to include the following array of information: (1) date; (2) the employment of the men; (3) every event of importance, such as arrival and departures of aboriginal clients; (4) the state of the weather; (5) the arrival and departure of geese, ducks, salmon, etc.; and (6) major climate events such as the break-up of lakes and rivers, freeze-up in the autumn, the first snow, etc. This practice continued into the twentieth century. As late as 1929, for example, the instructions printed on the inside covers of the blank journals, which the Winnipeg Fur Trade Commissioner's office sent to its post managers, stated that, in addition to recording the above range of information, it was

> important that [the] year, month, and day of [the] month be shown on each page in [the] column provided for that purpose. At the close of the outfit [business year] [a] duplicate copy should be detached and filed in your office and the original left in [the] book, and the book promptly mailed to the District Manager.[3]

The fact that duplicates were kept of this and other records helps explain why so many HBC files have survived.

To make sure that its managers took their recording obligations seriously, the fur trade commissioner's instructions warned: 'Your ability to keep this book in a neat and intelligent manner will be an indication of your character and ability as a Post Manager.'[4] Of great importance for economic historians and historical economic geographers, the post journals provide invaluable information about local seasonal cycles of economic activities, thereby providing critical clues about the changing temporal and spatial dynamics of local aboriginal economies. Journal entries frequently also provide important information about various aspects of the collective and individual economic behaviour of local aboriginal people.

It is unclear when post managers began keeping detailed post account books. The oldest surviving records are those for Fort Albany (from 1692) and York Factory (from 1688), albeit the latter are not continuous until 1714.[5] There are indications that post accounts were being kept earlier than these dates, however. By the early 1680s, for example, the GC's annual letters of instructions to its post commanders included extended commentaries on accounts they had received in London. This correspondence also suggests that the format of the post accounts was evolving in response to criticisms from the London committee. This is made clear by the letter the GC sent to Governor Sergeant on 16 May 1684. In this letter the London committee informed Sergeant that his invoice for 1,150 guns of all sizes seemed excessive considering that 'by your Accte. there are 962 remaining in the country (though our bookes mentions 991)'.[6] The GC noted that Sergeant's past sales figures indicated that the stock on hand was sufficient for two and a half years. The committee went on to note that it wanted Sergeant to provide more detailed accounting of trading goods sales:

> In the account of sales you sent us we are satisfied as it is an account Currant or a Collection of the whole which we wold have you constantly follow yet we must tell you we are not sattisfyed in that only because it is not particular enough for take that account of Albany River you mention 243 guns sold at 8 beavor 51 at 9 beavor & 30 at 10 beavor not expressing what kinde of guns they are whither 3 ½ foote guns, 4, 4 1'2 or 5 foote.[7]

The GC noted similar problems with the sales reports for other trade goods. Subsequent accounts provided the more detailed information the GC requested.[8]

The surviving account books reveal that by the early eighteenth century they were comprised of two basic parts. The first section dealt with trade goods accounts and the second concerned the 'stores accounts'.[9] The latter were detailed inventories of provisions and the craftsmen/tradesmen 'stores' such as 'armourer's (gunsmith) store, 'blacksmith's store, carpenter's store, etc.[10] Keeping control of inventories remained a key objective of the company's accounting system. Accordingly, section one of the annual account books concerning trading goods included four crucial inventories: (1) the closing inventory of trading goods from the previous year; (2) the invoice of trading goods shipped from London for the current year; (3) the 'general charge', which was a compilation of the previous two lists and represented all of the trading goods and supplies that were on hand for the current year; and (4) a closing inventory that was carried over to the following outfit.

The annual account books also listed two 'official' price lists. The first was the 'standard of trade', which priced the company's trade goods in 'Made Beaver' (MB). The latter was equivalent to the market value of one prime winter beaver. The second was the 'comparative standard', which priced in MB all of the commodities native people brought to trade. Research has shown that these two official standards did not change substantially over the short term, but that the actual rates of exchange varied in relation to the intensity of local competition offered by the HBC's opponents.[11] The GC insisted that its men not exchange company goods at rates that were lower than those specified.[12] In fact, usually they exceeded those rates and reported the gain as 'overplus'.[13]

Post bookkeepers kept track of all of the goods the company men bought during the year and posted them to the 'men's debts' section of the accounts. Likewise, expenditures of trading goods for various purposes other than trade were listed in the 'expenses' segment. The company men did not keep daily records of the goods sold to native people. The GC had asked their post managers to keep such records in 1738,[14] but Richard Norton, who was in charge of Fort Churchill at the time, explained why this was not possible given the nature of the long-distance trade with their native clientele:

> We should have gladly complied to [your instructions], but your honours must know that the whole trade is brought by two or three bodies of Indians, and those people are obliged to get their trade and be gone as soon as possible they can in order to provide food for themselves, they never bringing with them more provisions than is sufficient to serve them a day or two.

Continuing, Norton explained that for this reason:

> I am never longer than sometimes two and sometimes three days in trading the whole cargo, and at same the same time for want of room the warehouse-keeper is obliged to pack the furs as they are traded, and each cask or bale is immediately marked and an exact account taken of the

> contents thereof, and so entered into the book of accounts. By this your honours may readily see that it is impracticable for the warehouse-keeper to take an account of the goods that is traded for each sort of furs etc. in the manner your honours has directed.[15]

In other words, the nature of the company's trade in western Canada before 1774, which involved native groups making long-distance trading voyages from inland areas to the shores of Hudson Bay and James Bay, required that transaction times (costs) be kept to a minimum. This precluded keeping point-of-sales information.

Rather, the bookkeepers determined the volume of each category of goods that had been traded in an outfit year in the following manner. Bookkeepers subtracted the closing inventory from the general charge (opening inventory) to determine the total quantities of each item that had been expended during the outfit. From this total the bookkeepers then subtracted the inventories of goods sold to the men and used in support of trade. The amounts of goods that had gone out of the warehouse and were still not accounted for had not been accounted for in sales to men and post expenses 'it appears hath been traded'.[16] After determining the quantities of goods that had been traded using this method of accounting, the bookkeepers tallied the 'furs and other commodities' that the company had received in exchange for those goods. As the company's operations expanded over time and the range of business activities increased at its growing number of posts, some of the above sections of the general account books became so extensive that they were kept as separate records.[17] This happened most commonly at department and district headquarters posts. Notable examples of such accounting records from the nineteenth century are company servants' debt books and Indian debt books. Also, once the company expanded inland after 1774, native people had access to posts locally and bookkeepers no longer faced the kinds of restraints that Norton described.

As noted, from the outset the GC paid close attention to the journals and account books. Prior to the 1770s, when the company's posts were few in number and were located on the shores of Hudson and James Bays, the London directors continued to send an annual letter to each manager commenting on their record keeping the previous year, paying particular attention to the accounts. The GC expected their managers to write their replies before the annual supply ship set sail back to London. This practice was refined beginning in 1737, when the GC adopted the practice of numbering the paragraphs in their outward letters (London Outward Correspondence) and they expected their post managers to make reference to these numbered paragraphs in their replies (the London Inward Correspondence).[18]

In 1774, the company's trading rivals from Montreal, who eventually formed the North West Company (NWC) in 1783, forced the HBC to abandon its practice of operating solely from bases located on the shores of Hudson and James Bays[19] and the company moved inland to meet its competitors head-on. This change of strategy sparked off a period of rapid expansion and cut-throat competition that was ruinous to both concerns. By 1810 the situation had deteriorated to the point that the HBC's directors were pondering two competing proposals about the course of action the company should take. One recommended withdrawing from active participation in the fur trade; the other advocated expanding operations to take on the NWC in new territories, most notably the fur-rich Athabasca District.[20]

While the GC was debating these opposing options, an influential new shareholder, Andrew Wedderburn (later Colvile), joined the committee.[21] He opposed both plans. According to E. E. Rich, who wrote the definitive history of the company's first 200 years, Wedderburn's prior experience as a West Indian sugar-broker led him to conclude that the key to the HBC's future success depended on good management, sound accountancy and making the existing operations more efficient. In Wedderburn's view the company should not challenge the NWC in new territories until these objectives had been achieved.[22] Wedderburn carried the day and the GC adopted his 'retrenching system'. According to Rich, it was based on 'a meticulous scrutiny of accounts' for the purpose of trimming unnecessary costs and determining which posts were profitable. Instead of analysing the trade as a whole, each post was now scrutinised and the results tabulated. To the company's surprise, this analysis seemed to reveal that its most efficient and profitable posts tended to be located in areas where its men battled the NWC, rather than in the more sheltered backwater regions such as along the shores of Hudson Bay and James Bay. This conclusion was erroneous in that the accounting system's emphasis on individual posts did not take into account the costs the Bayside posts incurred in their capacities as depots for the inland trading networks they serviced.[23] In any event, the account analyses undertaken at the time emboldened the company to be more aggressive vis-à-vis the NWC and it pushed into Athabasca where the latter company had held sway with impunity.

While these accounting and other reforms were underway, the GC made two other important changes. One involved reorganising the company's operations into the Northern and Southern departments in 1810.[24] In turn, they divided each department into fur trading districts. The committee also brought in a profit-sharing scheme for its commissioned officers that was designed to give them an incentive to pursue the trade more vigorously than they had in the past. This innovation reinforced the need to be able to determine which trading posts and districts turned profits.

## Reporting innovations in the early nineteenth century

It was during this period of major reforms that the GC introduced a new management tool – the district report. Beginning with the outfit year 1814–15, the GC requested district managers to file a narrative statement that addressed eight major topics: (1) a description of the district boundaries, (2) a description of the 'nature of the country, soil, and vegetable production', (3) an account of food obtained locally (termed 'country produce') and fur production, (4) a description of the native people, (5) a description of the post(s), (6) an analysis of the state of the trade, (7) evaluations of the officers and men, and (8) a discussion of the advantages and disadvantages of the district.[25] These topics were carried forward in the company's reports into the twentieth century. Understandably, the district managers drew upon the daily journals and account books of their local posts when they drafted their reports. For these reasons the reports often provide useful synopses of these two other crucial records. This makes the district reports a good place to start research on the various dimensions of the local fur trade economies.

Although the district managers were expected to cover this array of broad topics, in the early nineteenth century they were not given blank books or forms with these or similar headings as guidelines for drafting their reports. Consequently, district reports from this era are not entirely formulaic narratives. There are considerable variations in the range of subjects that different managers, or even the same manager, emphasised from one year to the next. Typically district managers dwelt extensively with issues that they currently confronted. An added reason for the variability of their reports over time is that the company sometimes asked its district managers to address a particular issue that was a general management concern. For example, in the closing years of the HBC-NWC rivalry, the GC wanted to know how many of the local aboriginal people were 'attached' to the company as opposed to its NWC rival.

Although district reports were variable in content, their coverage of the topics listed above usually is sufficiently detailed to provide a picture of the micro economic geographies of the various districts. Sometimes reports were illustrated with maps and statistics (see Figure 6.1). Frequently the commentary on the state of the trade included a comparative look at the returns from the current outfit with those of one or more previous years to highlight short-term trends.

As noted, district managers emphasised particular topics of concern in the course of their general survey. Their discussions often give us penetrating insights into the distinguishing aspects of the local economies at key points in time. I will now offer examples from two posts, Fort Edmonton and Fort Kilmaurs (Old Fort Babine), that cover the period 1815–22. I have selected these two posts because they were located in distinctly different cultural and environmental areas of western Canada.

## Fort Edmonton

Fort Edmonton, which was situated on the North Saskatchewan River, was one of the company's preeminent establishments in the parkland region of western Canada. This ecological zone separated the boreal forest environment/Subarctic Cultural area to the north from the grassland environment/Plains Culture area to the south. Native groups from both areas traded at the post. Five district reports survive for the period 1815–1825.[26]

In August 1815 district manager James Bird wrote the first Edmonton district report. Bird, who was from Middlesex, England, had joined the company service in 1788. From 1794 he had served at various locations in the parkland/grassland area. He had been stationed at Fort Edmonton since 1799, had been in charge of its inland posts since 1803 and served as Chief of District from 1813 to 1817.[27] In other words, Bird was very experienced with the company's business in this district when he wrote his report. In his narrative, Bird provided a lengthy description of the varied environment of the Saskatchewan District, which had its headquarters at Fort Edmonton. In his description Bird recounted the local resources; he described the territories of the various native groups who visited the post, and he made commentaries on their varied social and political organisations. Before concluding his discussion of the native people, Bird explained why he could not meet the company's request that he provide a list of the individual native people who frequented the post from the grasslands and those who regularly dealt with the NWC:

> It would be difficult to ascertain the names of all the Indians that occasionally trade at this District, and still more to distinguish those who trade with the company from those who trade with the Canadians [NWC], as many of them do not visit any House once in three years, and others will change houses twice or even thrice in the same season. They are [. . .] independent and alive to their own interest. Therefore they go in the greatest numbers to that house where the greatest value is set on the commodity they may have with them. Thus when they have wolves and kitts [fox] the greatest number of Indians will visit us, because we can pay for these furs a little more than the Canadians can afford to do; when they have only buffalo robes the greatest number will go to the Canadians who pay much better for the robes than we do. In short these Indians form very little attachment to particular Houses or to particular traders, but in general carry their goods to what they consider the best market.[28]

Subsequently Francis Heron[29] replaced Bird as District Master. In his report for 1818–1819, Heron confirmed his predecessor's observations:

> To make out a list of all the Indians who trade with us at this District would be a thing merely impossible, particularly of the [. . .] tribes who inhabit the plains, many of whom are at yet entirely unknown to us and even those with whom we have any acquaintance, are not regular traders, as they trade indiscriminately with us and the NWC, according as they are better or worse paid at our place than the other, but on the whole we obtain three fifths of all the beaver killed by these numerous tribes.[30]

Heron's statement implies that the trading behaviour of his Plains Indian clients were different from those from the northern woodlands. The former had no strong loyalties to either company, being more concerned about the prices they could obtain for their furs, buffalo hides and robes, and provisions (buffalo meat and pemmican). The latter were more dependable trading partners and supplied the company with most of its fur returns.

At the time these reports were written, the GC wanted their managers to discuss the advantages and disadvantages of the districts they administered. In his Edmonton district report for 1815, Bird made the following observations about the problems the company faced in the Saskatchewan District:

> The trade of this District is, perhaps, liable to greater fluctuations than that of any other in the northern department,[31] because it is seriously affected by circumstances which in other parts of the country have little influence on the fur trade. Here a very mild winter, which admits of the Buffalo wintering in the large plains of the south, an extraordinary depth of snow which renders it difficult or impossible for horses to travel, or the burning of the plains, as are occurancies [*sic*] which lessen in a very sensible degree that part of the trade which is procured from the Indians of the plains, viz., wolves, kitts, red foxes, musquash, and beaver as well as dry provisions. And, as the means employed and goods provided must always be adequate to the purchasing and conveying away a tolerably large trade, the expenses incurred in a poor year will appear disproportionate to the returns procured. I am unacquainted with any method by which the trade of this District can be improved unless wolves should increase [in price] and a channel opened for disposing of Buffalo Robes to advantage.[32]

In his report for 1818–1820, Heron cited two additional problems that the company faced in its attempt to expand the trade in the Saskatchewan District in the vicinity of Fort Edmonton.

First, the HBC and the NWC men had agreed not to poach on each other's business with woodland Cree and Stony First Nations. Thus, according to Heron, expansion of the trade in this quarter was not possible.[33] Second, and more problematic, NWC opponents obtained the bulk of their furs from Iroquois trappers they had brought into the region and from former NWC employees, or Canadian 'freemen' as they were known. According to Heron,

> The Canadians take out annually from this District about two thousand Beaver Skins, seven thousand Martins, and of all other furs nearly the same quantity as ourselves, but they obtain nearly two fifths of these furs from the Canadian Freemen and Iroquois trappers they retain in their service.

Heron added:

> These trappers are of great service to the North West Company, and give them a great advantage over us, for wherever there are Beaver to be found, there they immediately dispatch their trappers to hunt them, who have now nearly destroyed all the Beaver in this quarter.[34]

Heron tried to lure the Freemen and Iroquois away from the NWC, but he was unable to do so. Heron explained: 'They are kept in such a state of subjection by that concern that I have succeeded no farther as yet than getting a part of their hunts.'[35] The following year he described Canadians' relationship to the NWC as a kind of slavery that the latter sustained through threats and intimidation.[36]

## Fort Kilmaurs

Across the Rocky Mountains in present-day British Columba, HBC Chief Trader William Brown established Fort Kilmaurs on the north end of Babine Lake during Outfit 1822–1823. This was the first outfit after the merger of the HBC and the NWC in 1821. The district was located in the territory of the salmon fishing Babine people and it was adjacent to the territories of their Wet'suet'en relatives, who lived to the west in the Bulkley River valley, and the lands of the Gitxsan, whose villages were located in the Skeena River basin lying to the north and west of Babine Lake. The cultures of these three First Nations were very different from those of the fisher, hunter and gatherer peoples of the boreal forests, parklands and grasslands to the east of the Rocky Mountains. Brown, who was from the Scottish lowlands, had learned his skills as a trader amongst these latter First Nations. Consequently, the Babine and their neighbours posed major new challenges for this Scotsman. It became immediately apparent to Brown that he faced two paramount problems that were very different from the ones he previously had faced as manager of the Brandon and Athabasca districts to the east of the Rocky Mountains. First, his new clientele were members of extended lineages, who resided in communal longhouses. A hereditary chief managed the house's territory and tightly regulated the harvesting of resources from it. Second, Brown learned, to his considerable consternation, that Tshimshian people from the lower Skeena River, who were obtaining their trade goods from European ships on the Pacific Coast, were expanding their fur trading networks eastward up the river into the hinterland of his new post.[37]

Brown gave a remarkably full account of the local land tenure system and the socio-political-economic system that supported it. He undoubtedly did so because he quickly concluded that his success depended on understanding this complex system.[38] Thus, his post journals and his district reports for 1823 and 1826 dealt extensively with the hereditary chiefs and the house-territory system they managed.[39] Regarding the hereditary chiefs, who he characterised as being 'men of property', Brown described the various means by which these leaders obtained their furs and he commented on the roles that the chiefs played in regulating beaver harvests. His description of the chiefs of Babine Lake is an example:

> Ack koo shaw is the principal Chief of the Indians of the Lake and is possessed of the most influence which he in general uses to his own advantage. Still he is of great Service to his Country Men by preventing them from

> carrying their disputes (which are not unfrequent [*sic*]) to a length that might prove fatal to those concerned. He is now an old Man which renders him unfit for the more laborious parts of the chase: however he is generally possessed of more furs than any of his followers, these he either gains at play [gambling], [or] receives in presents [gift-exchange] or trades from others. Cabbah belongs to the same tribe as Caupin of which he is the principal chief, he is also an old Man, whose hunting days are nearly over, still he gives to the Fort from twenty to thirty skins yearly, part of which he kills himself and part he receives in presents from his young Men.[40] Hou chete tah kie is an inferior Chief connected with the tribe of Ack koo shaw having no independent band of his own. His lands are very extensive and are the best stocked with Beaver of any in the vicinity of the Lake, of which he is particularly careful neither killing too many himself nor allowing any others to do so, he generally gives into the Post from twenty to thirty skins in the course of a season.[41]

From this and other observations Brown made it clear that lineage heads both regulated the harvest of beaver in their territories and controlled trade with outsiders.

In his reports and journals[42] Brown indicated that his Tshimsian rivals on the lower Skeena River had two advantages vis-à-vis the HBC. First, they obtained goods on the coast more cheaply than the company could deliver them from the York Factory depot on Hudson Bay. This post was located half a continent away to the east on the western shores of Hudson Bay. Second, the Tshimsian already had well-established trading alliances with many of the hereditary chiefs in the area. Indeed, intertribal trade had been a prominent feature of all of the pre-contact societies on the Pacific coast. Under Brown's direction the HBC was attempting to break into this ancient network.

In his district report for 1826 Brown proposed a strategy for combating these rivals. This involved continuing to import moose hides from HBC trading districts that were located to the east of the Rocky Mountains. The reason was that the Babine and their neighbours prized moose hides as a very high status commodity. Families gave hides away at the critically important funeral potlatches.[43] An added reason for the high value of this commodity was that moose were scarce in Babine country and non-existent on the coast. Before the Europeans arrived on the scene local native people had obtained their hides mostly through trade with other aboriginal groups who lived farther to the east. When the NWC moved into the territory in the early nineteenth century it took over most of the importation of moose hides. The HBC continued the practice after the merger. In his district report for 1826, Brown noted that the company had imported 559.5 moose skins from 1822 to 1826. Of these, 491 had been traded to local native people and 68.5 had been sold to company servants. Twelve had been expended at his post. Brown complained that these supplies had been totally inadequate. He thought that the insufficiency was preventing him from expanding his trade:

> That the returns of this place [are] not increasing as might have been expected can be ascribed solely to the small quantity and inferior quality of the Leather that has been allowed for these last two years. The supply of prime skins, such as are calculated for the trade of this quarter, not being a tenth of the number required for the Indians of the Lake [Babine Lake] alone, consequently it was in vain to make derouines[44] to those of Simpsons River as the result could only have been to incur expences [*sic*] and receive nothing, and what is worse we would most probably have got ourselves involved into a quarrel with them, for they will not part with their Furs for any thing but leather, and when they saw us in their Country without the article they were in want of there is not a doubt they would be dissatisfied and give us as much trouble as possible.

Brown's comment makes it clear that the local native people were engaged in complex trading relations with the Coast Tshimshan and the HBC. By dividing their custom in this fashion they were able to obtain the full array of the trade goods and commodities that they desired. In this respect, their trading behaviour was similar to that of the plains tribes who visited Fort Edmonton.

In his 1826 report, Brown provided a list of the 107 native men who owed debts at Fort Kilmaurs at the close of the outfit. On this list he recorded the amounts that each individual owed and the place where they lived. Brown also wrote very brief 'character sketches'. The practice of including 'character sketches' on the lists of native debtors had become a fairly common practice for HBC traders by this time. They were, in effect, the traders' evaluations of the credit worthiness of their clients. Although the language is often harsh and Eurocentric, these sketches provide useful information about the trading behaviour of individuals, which cannot be obtained from the aggregate data concerning fur returns and goods traded. In particular, they indicate the extent to which an individual was a regular HBC trading partner or was associated with one of its rivals.

Taking into consideration the key words that Brown used in his sketches, I have grouped the individuals on his list into seven categories (see Table 6.1).

*Table 6.1* William Brown's categorisation of First Nations individuals who traded at Fort Kilmaurs, 1826.

| *Category* | *Percentage of total* |
|---|---|
| Trade with Hudson's Bay Company – of various ability | 28 |
| Trade mostly with Coastal Tshimshian | 17 |
| 'Useless-undependable' | 14 |
| 'Gamblers' | 12 |
| 'Poor hunters' | 12 |
| Fishermen or individuals who are not described | 11 |
| 'Lazy' | 6 |

The largest category, which comprised 28 per cent of the total, included those whom he depicted as being fair to good traders (without making any other qualifying remarks). These individuals probably traded mostly with him at Fort Kilmaurs and cleared their debts routinely. Not surprisingly, nearly all of those who are in this group were from Babine Lake. However, with only three exceptions, those who Brown specifically mentions as trading mostly with the Coast Tshimshian, who accounted for 17 per cent of the total listed in his debt book, were Gitxsan men from the 'Simpson's River' [the Skeena River]. Two of the three exceptions were from Hotset, which was the primary Wet'suet'en village situated on the Bulkley River to the west near present-day Morricetown, British Columbia. The other exception was an individual from Babine Lake. Brown described 14 per cent of his debtors as being either 'useless' and/or 'undependable'. He claimed another 6 per cent were 'lazy'. It is probable that the men in these two categories either were not engaged in the fur trade to a significant extent or rarely visited Fort Kilmaurs. Brown claimed that another 12 per cent of those who had outstanding debts were addicted to 'playing' (gambling) and regularly lost most of their furs by doing so.[45] It may well be that some of these men were addictive gamblers who lost heavily. It is more likely that their losses were not simply due to bad luck. The reason for this conclusion is that Brown also indicated that there were a few men who regularly gained some or all of their furs by playing.[46] This suggests that the games were not merely ones of chance and that 'gambling' may have been one of the ways that chiefs secured wealth from their followers. Of course, it is also possible that some of the local native men simply claimed they had lost their furs through play because they did not want to tell Brown bluntly that they did not want to trade with him.

## Reporting in the late nineteenth and early twentieth centuries

The practice of filing district reports continued throughout the nineteenth century, albeit most of the surviving reports are from 1815 to the early 1830s. In the closing decades of the century the fur trade underwent another period of rapid change. The driving forces for it were transportation improvements (most notably steamboats and railways) and the introduction of the telegraph, which linked fur-producing areas more closely to external markets. This facilitated cash fur buying and a renewal of intense competition from small and large operators.[47] During this time of transition the HBC altered district-reporting practices in several important respects. Most notably, instead of relying on district managers to compile reports, the company appointed inspectors who visited the posts for that purpose. Among the earliest surviving inspecting officers' reports are those of Richard Hardisty[48] for the Peace River district and E. K. Beeston[49] for the Rainy River District of present-day Northern Ontario.

*Table 6.2* Topics commonly discussed in Hudson's Bay Company district and post inspection reports, late 1880s and 1890s.

| *Main topic* | *Content* |
|---|---|
| Buildings | This section often has (1) sketch map of post, (2) photographs of buildings and provides information about their (3) age and (4) condition. |
| Stock | This section discusses (1) whether stock is properly taken and (2) assesses its suitability for the local trade. |
| Accounts | The accounts surveyed here were (1) cash account, (2) debts of settlers, (3) debts of 'Indians', (3) capital employed at post and (4) statement of profit/loss. Made comments on quality of bookkeeping. |
| Expenses | Totalled a variety of expenses: (1) mess, (2) gratuities, (3) taxes, (4) costs of sending men out to trade in Indian camps (termed 'tripping'), (5) fuel, (6) fur packing, (7) wages (full-time and seasonal) and (8) sundries. Usually a commentary is included about whether expenses are reasonable or need to be trimmed. |
| Personnel | Lists employees by name and provides (1) years of service, (2) rate of pay and (3) a performance evaluation. |
| General remarks | Provides an overall assessment of the trend of the business locally and at any outposts. |

Beeston's and Hardisty's reports are more outline-like in format rather than in the essay style of earlier years. They are organised in reference to a proscribed list of questions and topics. I have listed the major subject headings that these two men addressed in Table 6.2. It is readily apparent that most of the topics were the ones that had been covered in the eighteenth-century account books, correspondence to and from London, and, in the early nineteenth-century district reports. For instance, Beeston's discussion of the suitability of the local stocks of trade goods includes commentaries that are reminiscent of the letters from Hudson Bay to London during the early eighteenth century. He comments about brands and how saleable they were locally, and he talks about the prices stock items could fetch in the district. His 1890 report on Fort Francis, which was located in the old Rainy River District in present-day Northern Ontario, offers an example:

> Generally speaking, the stock appears well selected. The English Cottons supplied from W. Rumney & Co., ex. Bales 313/4, 90/K/2 were complained of: samples are attached. The Blue Druggets[50] supplied from England are said to be of much lighter weight than formerly. Turlington's

> Balsam[51] supplied is the Canadian make, costing about 6 ¼ [cents] per bottle, and selling for 25 cents. The English make costs about 36 cents, and sells readily for $1.00. There is a little more profit on the former, but the latter sells much more readily, and is preferred. Seidlitz Powders,[52] it is said, have been sent two years in succession from Winnipeg, instead of Butler's as asked for.[53]

The inspection reports included fur-buying standards, but they were expressed in Canadian dollars rather than MB[54] and included information about the highest prices paid (see Table 6.3). Beeston noted that prices reflected the fact that competition was 'active' in the vicinity because the post was located adjacent to the Canada-United States border. He also observed that few furs were actually bought with cash. Instead, most exchanges were barter transactions.

As noted above, in the 'General' section of their reports, Hardisty and Beeston included various kinds of information that was particularly relevant to the current outfit. In his 1890 report for Fort Francis, for instance, Beeston focussed on the profits and losses of the outposts. An example is his entry for the outpost of Little Forks:

> *Little Forks*, about 12 miles down the Rainy River, was all last winter in charge of an Indian. There was a loss by Indian debts of $145, and the Net Result was a loss of $138.89. The following is a statement for Outfit 1889:

| | | | |
|---|---|---|---|
| To goods | 627.48 | By valuation of furs | 410.52 |
| To wages | 127.75 | Cash, etc. | 118.14 |
| Goods returned | 89.68 | | |
| | | Loss | *136.89* |
| 755.23 | 755.23 | | |

*Table 6.3* Fur tariff, Fort Francis, 1890.

| *Fur/commodity* | *Tariff ($)* | *Highest prices paid* |
|---|---|---|
| Bears | 1.00–15.00 | 30.00 |
| Beaver | 1.00–5.00 | 9.00 |
| Fisher | 2.00–6.00 | 8.00 |
| Fox, Silver | 10.00–50.00 | 50.00 |
| Fox, Cross | 1.50–6.00 | 20.00 |
| Fox, Red | .50–1.25 | 1.75 |
| Lynx | 1.90–3.00 | 5.00 |
| Marten | .75–2.00 | 2.50 |
| Otter | 2.00–7.00 | 10.00 |
| Skunk | .25–.75 | .75 |
| Castorum | 1.00 | 1.00 |
| Isinglass | .50 | .50 |

After providing summary analyses of all of the outposts in this fashion, Beeston recommended that they should be closed, or, for 'such of the posts as are deemed advisable and necessary to keep up should be placed under the most responsible of these people [outpost managers], and the most definite and clear instructions should be given'.[55] He thought the greatest problems of the outposts were that they tended to compete with each other and the managers gave advances that were too large in relation to the returns that could reasonably be expected. In his closing remark to the final section of the Rainy Lake report he wrote that 'the poor result of this post is mainly attributable to the large advances made to Indians not repaid, and the expenses of keeping up the Out-Posts'.[56] It should be noted here that in the closing section of the late nineteenth-century reports, inspectors typically discussed the presence (if any) of competitors and their activities.

The most elaborate of the inspection reports filed, when measured in terms of modes of presentation and information provided, were those of inspector Louis Romanet for 1919 and 1920.[57] Romanet began his career in the fur trade with Revillon Frères at Fort Chimo in the arctic in 1903. In 1916 he joined the HBC and served as general inspector of the James Bay District for two years. In 1919 he began a two-year term as a general inspector of the Lake Superior District and Lake Huron districts. This was a critical transition period for the HBC. World War I had had a very negative impact on the company's trade for several reasons. Most notably, the anticipated collapse of the fur markets in Europe in the autumn of 1914 led the company to suspend its tradition of advancing credit to its native trading partners. This move alienated the company's native clients.[58] During the war, fur markets boomed in North America, which led American fur buyers to flock to the Canadian north and buy furs with cash at inflated prices. Thus, the HBC not only faced unbridled competition, but it also saw the traditional and highly lucrative barter trade decline relative to cash fur buying and merchandise sales. These problems were especially acute in the areas of Northern Ontario that are crisscrossed with railway lines, which provided easy access to the region for even small fur buyers and iterant merchandise sellers. Romanet's inspections reports on the company's posts in the region address all of these problems. In ways that recall the annual letters outward from Hudson Bay and James Bay in the eighteenth century, he talks about the suitability of the company's merchandise vis-à-vis that offered by local competitors. He analyses the company's competitiveness in terms of fur and trade goods prices. Recalling the district reports of Heron for Edmonton and Brown for Fort Kilmaurs, he discusses how the local native people were responding to new opportunities. Strikingly different from earlier reports, however, is that Romanet illustrated his reports with photographs of the posts, often including pictures of the HBC staff, drew graphs (he made his own graph paper using lined writing paper, see Figure 6.1) to show trends of key data, and made colour pencil sketch maps of the hinterland of each post to show the distribution of the local native population and the spatial trends of the trade (see Figure 6.2).

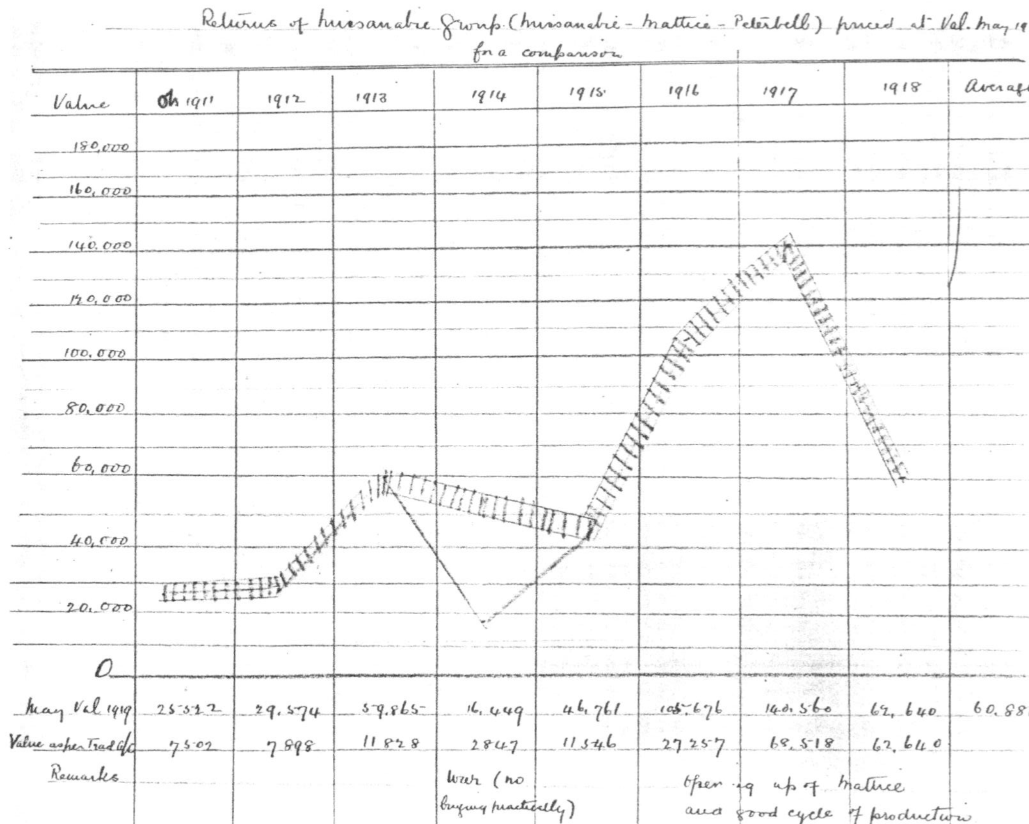


*Figure 6.1* Pencil graph of returns of the Missinaibi district group of posts, Northern Ontario, 1911–1918.

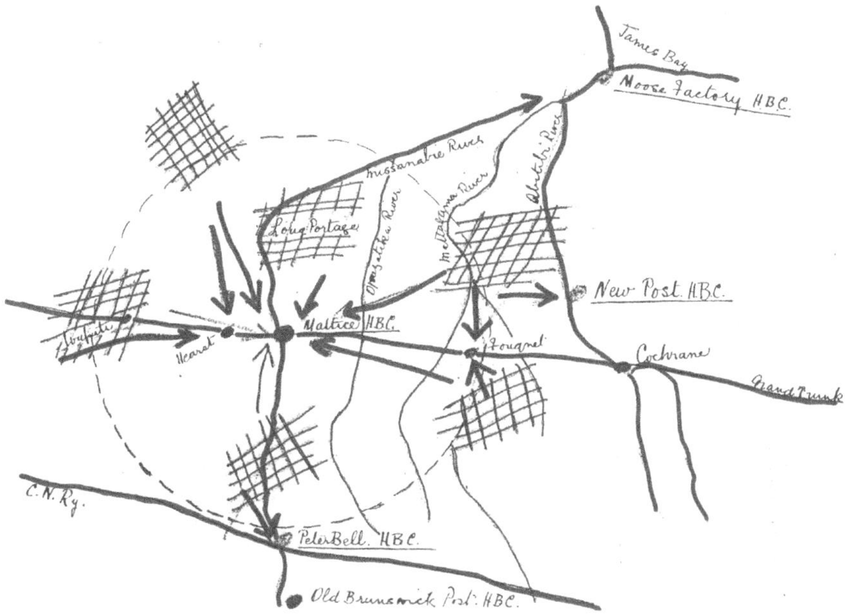


*Figure 6.2* Louis Romanet's map of Mattice post hinterland.

Romanet's report for the HBC post at Mattice, Ontario, is an example. This establishment was located southwest of James Bay on the Grand Trunk Railway (now part of the Canadian National [CN] network) where the latter crossed the Missinaibi River. The latter had long been a trading route to Moose Factory on James Bay. Romanet's sketch map shows the former railway as well as the Canadian Northern Railway (it also is now part of the district of CN), which is located farther south.[59] Additionally, he showed the major rivers and other railway settlements (Wapiti, Hearst, Fouquen, Cochrane and Peterbell). Romanet indicated the approximate hinterland of Mattice Post with a circle (dashed line) and the locations of primary hunting areas (crosshatched areas) of local native bands. He used arrows to show where these groups traded. As his map suggests, and his narrative makes clear, opponents were active all along the railways lines and in the settlements. According to his report, Mattice had been established in 1916 and was serving to draw local natives away from Hearst and Cochrane because it was situated on the Missanabie River. It also attracted native people from Moose Factory because they travelled up this river to trade at 'the line' where exchange rates were more favourable.[60]

Similar to the Hardisty's and Beeston's inspections of the late nineteenth century, Romanet's report opens with a discussion of the quality of accounting being done at the post. He then provided an extended analysis of the local business that was much more detailed than earlier reports. Most notably, he observed that the company was obtaining only about 50 per cent of the total fur harvest in the region, but he did not think it should try to obtain a greater share. Romanet explained:

> I maintain my old conviction – that is to say – the ability of the man in charge of a post is always the biggest asset of our success, and the prices second. It is easy enough to buy a big collection if we pay the price, but to secure it at a profitable rate is a much more difficult proposition.

He continued: 'We do not want furs at all costs, but to get a profit from the furs.'[61] Romanet's analysis led him to conclude that Mattice should be able obtain a 40 per cent gross profit margin overall given the current levels of competition provided that the company did not seek to increase its market share. He thought that the company could achieve this by pursuing three courses of action. First, native customers had to be 'treated in such a way that they will have no reason to go elsewhere'. Second, the company had to maintain a stock of basic provisions that native customers wanted at prices that were below those of any competitors within 50 miles. Third, the company had to maintain a stock of dry goods and hardware that was of superior quality to that offered by its opponents. According to Romanet, the company's native clientele were willing to pay 'stiff prices' for quality goods.[62] Therefore, he opposed reducing inventory costs by importing quality goods.

According to Romanet, the primary problems the company faced in the district were related to the intense level of competition. Competitors often sold alcohol illegally to the native people. He estimated that Mattice Post lost 20 per cent of the local cash trade for that reason.[63] Also, to obtain its fair share of native trappers returns the local post manager had to resort to the old practice of 'tripping', which involved sending men out to the trappers' camps. In 1918 this cost $600 or 25 per cent of the estimated total post expenses of $2,381.[64]

Romanet's report for Mattice is typical of the reports he filed in 1919 and 1920. Collectively they provide a remarkable snapshot of historical economic geography of fur trade in a broad swath of the Canadian north during the immediate aftermath of World War I when the economy of the region was undergoing a major transformation.

## Conclusion

The remarkable ability of the HBC to survive for almost three and a half centuries cannot be easily explained. During the age of long-distance management by correspondence, which lasted until well after the end of World War I, there is little question that the generation and monitoring of an array of accounts and narrative records were important keys to the company's success. For students of the economic history of the Canadian fur trade, the district accounts in their various formats are one of the management records that offers the researcher thumbnail sketches and analyses of local fur trading activities. Those of the late nineteenth and early twentieth centuries also provide assessments about the accuracy and utility of the various accounts that post and district managers kept. For these various reasons, when available, district reports offer economic historians excellent entry points into the massive HBC archives.

## Notes

1 For an online guide to these archives see: www.gov.mb.ca/chc/archives/hbca/resource/index.html.

2 E. E. Rich (ed.), *Copy-Book of Letters Outward &c: Begins 29th May, 1680 Ends 5 July 1687* (Toronto: Champlain Society for the Hudson's Bay Record Society, 1948), p. 79. None of the journals from the seventeenth century have survived. The oldest are those of Fort Albany, which begin in 1705.

3 Hudson's Bay Company, Fort George, Outfit 260, James Bay (1929); copy in author's possession.

4 Archives of Manitoba/Hudson's Bay Company Archives [AM/HBCA] B 77/a, Overleaf of Fort George Post Journal, James Bay, Outfit 260, 1929. The instruction was issued by the Fur Trade Commissioner's Office, Winnipeg, Manitoba, April 1929.

5 Continuous records do not begin at York Factory until 1714. Prior to that time the company battled with the French for control of the post. The French occupied it (renaming it Fort Bourbon) for 20 years ending in 1714. The Fort Albany accounts are continuous after 1692.

6 Rich, *Copy-Book of Letters Outward*, p. 127.

7 Rich, *Copy-Book of Letters Outward*, p. 127.

8 Fifty-four years later the GC returned to this topic in their general instructions for 1738. K. G. Davies (ed.), *Letters from Hudson Bay, 1703–40* (London: Hudson's Bay Record Society, 1965), p. 255.

9 I have discussed the nature of the post account books in A. J. Ray, 'The Early Hudson's Bay Company Account Books as Sources for Historical Research: An Analysis and Assessment', *Archivaria*, 1:1 (1976), pp. 3–38; A. J. Ray, 'The Hudson's Bay Company Account Books as Sources for Comparative Economic Analyses of the Fur Trade: An Examination of Exchange Rate Data', *Western Canadian Journal of Anthropology*, 6:1 (1976), pp. 30–45; and in A. J. Ray and D. B. Freeman, *Give Us Good Measure: An Economic Analysis of Relations Between the Indians and the Hudson's Bay Company Before 1763* (Toronto: University of Toronto Press, 1978), pp. 62–119.

10 It seems that during the first few years of the company's operations post managers did not keep inventories of these 'stores'. Accordingly, in the 1684 general letter to their governor in Hudson Bay, Henry Sergeant, the Governor and Committee in London wrote: 'We doe expect not only a just account of what they [other company traders] and you have traded for & Remaines of Merchantdizes but an account of all the stores & provisions which governour [John] Nixon did always decline to our Detriment.' Rich, *Copy-Book of Letters Outward*, p. 120.

11 Ray and Freeman, *Give Us Good Measure*, pp. 142–46.

12 For example, in their 1684 letter to Sergeant they complained: 'We are heartily troubled that Governour Nixon [Sergeant's predecessor] has altered the standard of Trade which you tearme he hath advanced the standard of Trade but we know it will be a great Detriment to us [. . .] therefore we injoyne you to use all the Art & Dilligence you can to bring our Goods to the old Standard.' Rich, *Copy-Book of Letters Outward*, p. 121.

13 Ray and Freeman, *Give Us Good Measure*, pp. 142–46 and pp. 163–97.

14 Specifically, paragraph 50 of the general letter of instructions for Fort Churchill ordered: 'That the warehouse-keeper do keep a warehouse book and enter therein every particular parcel of goods or skins that are traded with the Indians, and also the quantity and sorts of goods that is traded for such skins etc.' Davies, *Letters from Hudson Bay*, p. 255.

15 Davies, *Letters from Hudson Bay*, p. 255.

16 Davies, *Letters from Hudson Bay*, p. 255.

17 Examples are men's or servants' debt books, Indian debt books, inventories, etc.

18 Davies, *Letters from Hudson Bay*, pp. 225–42.

19 Critics of the company referred to this practice as the policy of 'sleeping by the frozen sea'.

20 E. E. Rich, *The Hudson's Bay Company, 1670–1870*, vol. 2 (Toronto: McClelland and Stewart, 1960), pp. 289–91.

21 An online biography of Colville is available at Archives of Manitoba/Hudson's Bay Company Archives [AM/HBCA] website: www.gov.mb.ca/chc/archives/hbca/biographical/c/colville_andrew.pdf.

22 In particular, Wedderburn was opposed to a precipitous expansion into the Athabasca District. Rich, *The Hudson's Bay Company*, p. 291.

23 Rich, *The Hudson's Bay Company*, p. 312.

24 This was accomplished in 1810. Rich, *The Hudson's Bay Company*, p. 292.

25 This list is based on my sampling of district reports for the period 1815–1825.

26 These reports are for the following trading years: 1815–1816, 1818–1820, 1820–1821, 1823–1824, 1824–1825 (two copies). In addition, there are reports for 1862–1863, 1875–1876 and 1886–1889.

27 A short biographical sketch of James Bird is available at AM/HBCA website: www.gov.mb.ca/chc/archives/hbca/biographical/b/bird_james_sr.pdf.

28 Fort Edmonton District Report, 1815, AM/HBCA B 60/e/1, folio 5.

29 Heron was from Donegal, Ireland. He joined the company in 1812 as a steward at York Factory. From 1815–1817 he was master of the Cumberland District. He served as District Chief at Edmonton from 1817 to 1812.

30 Fort Edmonton District Report, 1818–20, AM/HBCA B 60/e/3, 5.

31 According to Wedderburn's reforms, the company was to be administered in terms of two departments – the Northern Department and the Southern Department. The former department included most of Canada west of Hudson Bay and east of the Rocky Mountains. This included the following districts: York, Churchill, Saskatchewan and Winnipeg. The Southern Department included districts that adjoined James Bay. These were the Albany, Moose and Eastmain districts.

32 Fort Edmonton District Report, 1815, AM/HBCA B 60/e/1, folio 5.

33 Fort Edmonton District Report, 1818–20, AM/HBC B 60/e/3, folio 5 and Fort Edmonton District Report, 1820–21, AM/HBCA B 60/e/4, folio 5.

34 Fort Edmonton District Report, 18120–21, folio 5.

35 Fort Edmonton District Report, 18120–21, folio 5.

36 AM/HBCA B/60/e/4, folio 5.

37 I discuss this in A. Ray, *Telling It to the Judge: Taking Native History to Court* (Montreal-Kingston: McGill University Press, 2011), pp. 26–27.

38 It should be noted that the reports he filed for districts he had managed previously did not include extended commentaries on local First Nations tenure practices.

39 Ray, *Telling It to the Judge*, pp. 22–28.

40 Brown's discussion of Ack koo shaw, Cabbah and Caupin [Caspin] suggests the following socio-political structure. There was a nominal leader for all of the villages on the lake, which in effect comprised a regional group, perhaps a phratry, and two or more 'tribes', which included various lineage heads, who managed territories on behalf of their relatives. Brown's use of the term 'tribe' here is unclear. He does indicate that they included more than one village. So, perhaps, he is referring to different clans. Ack koo shaw belonged to one of the latter and Cabbah and Caupin to another.

41 Ray, *Telling It to the Judge*, p. 173.

42 These are: Fort Kilmaurs (Old Fort Babine) Post Journals, AM/HBCA, 1822–25, B 11/a/1–3 and Fort Kilmaurs (Old Fort Babine) District Reports for 1822 and 1826 AM/HBCA B 11/e/1–2.

43 They were of paramount importance because they provided the public forum for the passage of hereditary titles and responsibilities from one generation to the next.

44 This referred to the practice of sending company employees to camp with native hunters/trappers during the winter in order to obtain native peoples' furs before rival traders could do so.

45 A game of chance that involved sticks and teams of players was extremely popular among the native people of this area.

46 For example, he said of 'Dit chin neigh lan', who lived on 'Simpson's River', that he 'gains more furs at play than what he kills in hunting'. Regarding 'Hai its' of Babine lake, Brown said he was: 'a more expert gambler than hunter'. About 'Teel zie' of the village of Nass chick on Babine Lake, Brown commented that 'Between hunting and gambling this fellow generally procures more furs than any in the village". Ray, *Telling It to the Judge*, pp. 187–200.

47 A. Ray, *The Canadian Fur Trade in the Industrial Age* (Toronto: University of Toronto Press, 1990), pp. 75–76.

48 Hardisty had joined the company in 1849 and had served at various posts in the western interior of present-day Canada. In 1888 he was appointed as an acting inspector of the Northern Department. That same year he was appointed to the Canadian Senate. S.A. Smith, 'Hardisty, Richard Charles', in *Dictionary of Canadian Biography*, vol. I (1881–1890), www.biographi.ca/en/bio/hardisty_richard_charles_11E.html.

49 Beeston began his career with the company in the accountant's department in the London headquarters. He served there until 1881, when he moved to Red River, Manitoba. He served as the chief accountant for the Northern Department in 1882–1883 and as a junior chief trader in Winnipeg, Manitoba, from 1883–1888. In the latter year he became a chief trader and general inspector for the company.

50 This is a reference to heavy felted fabric of wool or wool and cotton that was used as a floor covering.

51 This was a medicine first patented in England in 1744. It was a mixture of various herbs and chemicals that was used for the treatment of various afflictions.

52 This was an effervescent powder of tartaric acid, sodium bicarbonate and salt that was used as a laxative.

53 Fort Francis Inspection Report, 1890, AM/HBCA B 105/e/17, folio 4. This discussion recalls similar commentaries in the London Inward Letters of the eighteenth century.

54 In the reforms of 1815, traders were supposed to discontinue using the MB standard, which expressed all prices in terms of prime beaver. They continued to use it in their dealings with their native clientele, however. In many areas the standard persisted into the twentieth century, albeit it was no longer used as a unit of account.

55 Fort Francis Inspection Report, 1890, AM/HBCA B 105/e/17, folio 9.

56 Fort Francis Inspection Report, 1890, AM/HBCA B 105/e/17., folio 10.

57 These are Louis Romanet's inspection reports of 1919 and 1920 for the Lake Superior District posts and those of the Lake Huron District, AM/HBCA A 92/19/5–17.

58 Ray, *The Canadian Fur Trade in the Industrial Age*, pp. 105–6.

59 Report on Mattice Post, Lake Superior District, 1919, AM/HBCA A 92/19/5, folio 5.

60 Report on Mattice Post, Lake Superior District, 1919, AM/HBCA A 92/19/5, folio 3.

61 Report on Mattice Post, Lake Superior District, 1919, AM/HBCA A 92/19/5, folio 4.

62 Report on Mattice Post, Lake Superior District, 1919, AM/HBCA A 92/19/5, folio 9.

63 Report on Mattice Post, Lake Superior District, 1919, AM/HBCA A 92/19/5, folio 5.

64 Report on Mattice Post, Lake Superior District, 1919, AM/HBCA A 92/19/5, folios 5 and 11.

# 7 Native labour and Imperial consumption on the periphery of Empire as revealed by the York Factory account books of the Hudson's Bay Company, c. 1869–1870[1]

*Frank J. Tough*

## Spatial and temporal context of fur trade bookkeeping

From the point of view of economic history, it is perhaps with some intellectual irony that one of the greatest collections of merchant accounts concerns a vast, but somewhat commercially insignificant, region on the periphery of global capitalism. Very few intensive studies of these records exist.[2] In respect of Native history and fur trade history, these records are seldom consulted. Ray's case concerning the utility of the source, made some three and a half decades ago, has largely been ignored and the results of such research have been met with silence.[3] A preference for narrative records and wide-open inferential conclusions characterises much of the recent work in these fields.[4] The bulk of existing fur trade literature does not provide a well-developed scholarly framework, and thus, this effort necessarily remains exploratory and iterative. As this chapter demonstrates, and unlike narrative sources, accounting records require a fair bit of processing before any reasonable observations are allowed (see Appendix A).

In a scholarly survey of the field of consumption studies for *The Oxford Handbook of the History of Consumption*, Frank Trentmann has presciently asserted that 'consumption is a mirror of the human condition' – a correspondence between how people ought to live and how they consume exists.[5] He defined *consumption* as consisting of 'a bundle of goods, practices, and representations', but suggested that consumption also 'concerned identity and social relations'.[6] At last then, consumption had stepped out of 'the shadow of production', the commodification thesis had been cracked, and research in cultural studies had reclaimed consumption as 'an active, creative and authentic practice'.[7] While informed by such insights, this chapter attempts to appreciate Native consumption as an outcome of a specialised labour process located on the periphery of the British Empire. This approach is consistent with Trentmann's desire for a 'greater integration of political economy with cultural inquiry' along with more micro-level analyses.[8]

This chapter will provide an analysis of a single, seemingly brief, Hudson's Bay Company (HBC) accounting record for York Factory or Kihchiwaskahikanihk (place of the great house) to the Cree. A document that discloses, with decent regularity, the goods obtained by Native tripmen (i.e. boatmen) for summer work performed by freighting cargoes between York Factory (57.001667, -92.305833), the main depot, and its inland depot of Norway House (53.990278, -97.815556).[9] This document records remuneration for two and a half seasons of freighting activity, at a point in time when the HBC and fur trade were undergoing a fundamental structural shift. In 1870, through negotiations with the Colonial Office and Canadian ministers, the HBC relinquished its claim to Rupertsland, and the territory came under the control of the Dominion of Canada.[10] Consequently, this piece of bookkeeping captures a fragment of a long-established and extensive accounting system at the end of the old fur trade, with a supply system focussed at the old entrepôt of York Factory, but before the pending changes of a new political economy associated with White settlement.

The Canadian fur trade entailed extensive operations; animal pelts trapped by Natives were collected at posts, transferred to district headquarters and then shipped, by Yorkboat to York Factory (in the case of the Northern Department). A reverse flow brought imported commodities to the remote corners of the fur country. York Factory was established in 1684 and for nearly two centuries it served as the major entrepôt for the north and west of present-day Canada. Through the HBC, Native trappers of a vast territory were connected to the London fur market and to a wide variety of worldly, merchant goods. The utility of trade goods, which was sometimes assumed as superior, is regarded as one of the main factors for Indian participation in this long-term enterprise.[11] As an industry, this was not a casual or an *ad hoc* operation, and the costs of operations and the value created were monitored; consequently, bookkeeping was reflected in the business records of the HBC.

A great expanse of difficult terrain was conquered by an ambitious mercantile determination to profit (or gain) by the exchange of imported manufactures for a raw material. The development and refinement, especially after 1821, of a transport system based on the Yorkboat and the displacement of the birch-bark trade canoe resulted in a more efficient use of labour.[12] Not only did this trade generate extensive economic activity associated with transport (e.g. boat building), but in turn, transport activities created local demand for other economic activities (e.g. obtaining wood).[13]

In order to understand the economic relationships (income and consumption) that might be discerned from this single account record, this chapter has been structured to: (1) outline the HBC Yorkboat transport system and describe the conditions of work inherent in the waterborne transport of a geological region known as the Canadian Shield, (2) provide an overview of the York Factory Tripmen Accounts of 1869–1871, (3) present some descriptive tabulations and (4) offer some initial insights and findings. As a case study, how this record was converted into digital data is explained in Appendix A.

## HBC Yorkboat transport system and labour conditions

Following the merging of the Hudson's Bay Company and the North West Company in 1821, the fur trade transport system was (1) consolidated around routes that made use of Bayside factories (e.g. York Factory, Moose Factory), and (2) the Yorkboat was adopted as the main mode for moving people and materials in HBC's territory. The birch-bark canoe, Indigenous know-how enlarged and modified by Montreal traders, was replaced by locally made wooden boats. As Canada's greatest economic historian, Harold Innis, observed: 'Dependence on the York boat rather than the canoe was symbolic of the increased importance of capitalism.'[14] A finely tuned system was created to unify the Mackenzie, Peace, Athabasca, Saskatchewan, Assiniboine, Red and Winnipeg river routes with the Hayes River. By and large, Montreal as a long-standing place of fur trade business, was bypassed after 1821; the links between the periphery and centre were strengthened through the long-established Bayside factories. Without such an innovative transport system, which eventually contributed much territory to the geography of the future Canadian nation state, this industry would have had to operate at much reduced scale.

Central to the overall functioning of the system was the relatively sizable and highly skilled pool of tripmen known as the Portage La Loche brigade. They were capable of travelling great distances by meeting the challenge of the short open water season. This brigade was recruited from the parish communities of the Red River Settlement, but their engagement entailed connecting the Red River Settlement sub-metropolis with the inland depot of Norway House, the Methey Portage (a bridge spanning the two continental watersheds), as well as, the district headquarters of Cumberland House and Île-à-la-Crosse (Ile a la Crosse), and finally, the Atlantic World's entrepôt of York Factory.[15]

At Norway House, cargoes for and from the HBC districts of Mackenzie, Athabasca, Caledonia, English River, Saskatchewan, Swan River, Red River and Lac la Pluie converged. A key link in this system was the Hayes River route between Norway House and York Factory. The Portage La Loche brigade were responsible for moving some of the cargo on this route, but Natives were hired at Norway House, Oxford House and York Factory to freight cargoes between Norway House and York Factory. Norway House served as an inland depot, a winter storage buffer, which allowed goods destined for the Athabasca and Mackenzie districts to be moved further up the transport system. The importance of this segment was noted by Innis: 'The route from York Fort [Factory] to Norway House was the basic short trunk line from which other routes branched to various departments [districts].'[16] The men hired at York Factory and Norway House could make two trips in the short open-water season. Apparently, the engagement of Indians as tripmen might date to 1832 when Island Lake District Indians were employed to transport 640 pieces.[17]

The movement of cargoes against the flow of the Hayes River must have been challenging.[18] For the crews recruited at York Factory, their trip began at sea level on the estuary of the Hayes River. Steadily, boats, cargo and crews climbed 219 metres to the Robinson Falls and its long difficult portage through swamps. The Echimanish River linked headwaters of the Hayes River with the upper reaches of the Nelson River. Their destination, HBC District Headquarters of Norway House, was situated on the Nelson River proximate to the northern end of Lake Winnipeg.[19]

Employment in Yorkboats demanded brutal exertions and in several respects it was far more demanding than freighting by canoe. Work entailed rowing the boats on lakes and rivers, but rapids (breaks in slopes) could be handled by: (1) attempting to shoot the rapids if heading with the current, (2) tracking the boat against the current through the rapids or (3) portaging the boat and cargo around rapids. If a Yorkboat could not be guided through rapids, it would be hauled and dragged, aided by straps and log rollers, across a portage, clearly, a more challenging task than shoulder hoisting the much lighter bark canoe. Similarly, a Yorkboat was harder to track up current than a canoe.[20]

The steersman commanded the crew and he loaded the freight onto the men's backs for carriage across the portages. The cargo was broken into packages called 'pieces', which weighed about 90–100 pounds (40.82–45.36 kilograms).[21] Pemmican,[22] an important commodity in terms of HBC cargoes, was packed into 90-pound bags. The Yorkboat had the capacity for 5,500 kilograms of weight.[23] The men, aided by portage straps, would carry two pieces (i.e. 180–200 pounds) on their backs at one time. Portage work was not the only arduous aspect of Yorkboat freighting. Willy Frog Ross, an Indian boatman employed on the northern Manitoba Berens River-Little Grand Rapids route, recalled that the oars were 'so large and heavy that it took a lot of muscle and strength to pull one all day long'.[24] Each oar weighed 18 kilograms.[25] Because the cargo ratio to crew for Yorkboats was greater than canoes, each tripman would then be responsible for more handling cargo than a typical voyageur. An empty wet Yorkboat weighed 1,360 kilograms, whereas a north freight canoe only weighed 136 kilograms.[26] Given hard usage, the life of a Yorkboat was limited to about four years and depreciated at 25 per cent per year. The number of portages on a route fluctuated with changing water levels. Generally, high water reduced portaging, but in turn, it could make low-lying swampy portages more difficult to traverse. Portage roads had to be cut and inadequate maintenance added to the discomfort. At the end of the long day there was very little rest. Cargo had to be readied for a quick departure, often as early as 4 in the morning.

Some of the most poignant observations of Yorkboat work come, not from HBC record keepers, but from local missionaries. In 1869, the Reverend H. Budd of The Pas mission compared hunting with boating: 'It will be quite a sport for these fellows to knock down the geese after 3 months working like slaves in these heavy boats.'[27] The Methodist missionary and Indian Affairs official John Semmens critically observed:

> Many a man in the North Land today had been crippled in these Portages and their families are in consequence objects of charity. Many a lonely grave evidences the severity of the work done on these Portages. One of my party after seeing the men carrying two hundred pounds across these swamps remarked that it was no wonder that so many widows were found at all the [annuity] pay stations when the husbands were compelled to work so distressingly hard.[28]

In a similar vein, the Reverend F.G. Stevens described the work done on northern Manitoba portages: 'One day in camp I was concerned to see a man having a bad lung hemorrhage. Next day he was working as usual. Right there I discovered that there were worse conditions of labour than negro slavery.'[29] He also recalled the Robinson Portage on the Hayes River between York Factory and Norway House: 'When carrying began the road was dry. When the work was done the way was muddy, wet with sweat dropped from the faces of the carriers.'[30] Stevens confirmed Semmens' observation, by stating 'many men were standing around doing nothing. These were pointed out to me – "They have hurt themselves carrying on the portages. Their lungs were affected. They will soon die"' and he was informed 'There are no men over fifty years of age at Island Lake.'[31] Ross provided an Indian recollection of this work:

> In those days each man had a hard task. Often sweat would be running down his face all day due to the heat and hard work. It was a hard way to make a living but many a time freighting was the only way to earn food to feed the families. Many a white man doesn't believe what a hard tough life we had in the olden days. Some think an Indian had a soft life but Ne-chee, Kesa-na-gun (Friend it was Hard).[32]

Although HBC records rarely dwell on the strain of Yorkboat work, the Cumberland House report for 1886 alluded to its difficulty and to the idea that some Indians were not conditioned to do this work. According to this report,

> The Chipewyan [Dene] Indians cannot be depended on for any kind of manual labour; they will not even work in the boat between here and there [Brochet]. They are physically weak and every time we employ them as boat men some of them are sure to fall sick on the trip – in fact so many have died whilst so employed that others are frightened.[33]

Yorkboats were not only used for HBC cargoes, but throughout the nineteenth century, missionaries and others were dependent upon this system. During the slow transition from HBC rule to control by Canada over the subarctic, this transportation system was used by government officials. For example, when Lieutenant-Governor J.C. Patterson toured northern Manitoba, he observed that Indians 'like this kind of work [freighting], and work late and early cheerfully. They are admirable voyageurs – in fact, the finest boatmen of their kind in the world.'[34] The extreme challenges of these labour conditions encourage questions concerning motivations for Native engagement as HBC tripmen.

## Overview description of the York Factory tripmen account book, 1869–1871[35]

During a survey of HBC accounting records, a York Factory tripmen account book for 1869–1873 attracted my attention. This record was catalogued as B.239/d/1219, in other words, it is the 1,219th accounting book in the York Factory series. This document was selected for digitisation because: it focussed on a particular aspect of the HBC business operations; a reasonable, but manageable span of time was captured in a single document; it relates to labour activity for a vital link in the HBC transport system; the document itself appeared orderly; and a quick perusal suggested that a narrow range of purchases had been made with the wages. Several non-essential types of commodities (e.g. coffee, chocolate) caught my eye. At first glance, what seemed to be a narrow range of goods suggested a manageable empirical project. What sorts of things the tripmen were purchasing with their hard-earned wages seemed of scholarly interest to economic history and might provide some insights about the willingness of men to engage in the risks and hardship associated with the movement of cargoes.

The York Factory tripmen account book covered the period from 2 August 1869 through 6 July 1871. Physically, the book contains 144 lined pages, eight blank pages, one page recorded 'sundries supplied Freight Brigade from Trading Room',[36] and thus, 135 pages provided information on the tripmen accounts. During the fur trade era, currency was seldom used to transact business. The payment/consumption of wages took the form of purchases from the HBC goods inventory. Normally, the HBC kept its accounts in the Made Beaver (MB).[37] However, this particular account was kept in the British system of pound/shilling/pence. The quantity and the cost of items purchased, along with fairly specific descriptions of the items were recorded. These details provide considerable information on consumption made possible by working in the HBC Yorkboats. The book recorded remuneration for five trips: one in 1869, two in 1870 and two in 1871. The book did not include an index of names.

The book contains 2,953 lines of data that record 2,364 entries against income. The total value of the transactions amounted to £730.51. Some non-goods purchase entries also occur: the payment of fur debts and donations to the Church Missionary Society were debited against the income from boat work. Over the period, £647.60 was expended on goods and £76.91 on fur debts, and £6.00 was donated to the Church Missionary Society. In broad categories, the payment for working in the boats was expended as immediate purchases, debt payment and gifts. This book used a separate page for each tripman and for each trip (engagement), and thus each account was limited to the value of the wages for a single round trip from York Factory to Norway House. This boat work generated 135 distinct accounts (16 in 1869, 61 in 1870 and 58 in 1871) or 135 separate engagements.[38] An entry/purchase refers to an item purchased on account of the wages. These purchases were for particular goods obtained by tripmen on credit of their wages. In digital form, each entry made up a single row of data. An account refers to a single transaction making up a number of purchases, made on a particular day, against the value of the wages from the employment of a single tripman.

At the top of each page, the name of the tripman, his position and the value of his labour (wage credit) were recorded as a heading. (A wage differential existed between guides, steersmen, bowmen and middlemen.) To illustrate the account set, William Wastesicout's purchases for 2 August 1869 are depicted in Figure 7.1. This image of a typical page from the tripmen account book has been transcribed as Table 7.1. The men were paid by the trip, and their purchases were made before starting out. With a few exceptions, purchases were made all at once; that is, their wage credit was expended in a single instance. These account credits tended to be for £8, £7, £6 or £5. The total value of all the purchases was simply debited against the wage credit for the trip.

In Table 7.1, the date that the purchases were made was recorded in two separate columns on the left side of the page (year, month and day). A wide column recorded the item purchases, a separate row was used for each purchase, and the quantity of each commodity purchased was specified. When needed, unit prices of the items were provided at the next column over. Many cryptic abbreviations were used to describe the trade items. The final column on the right side of the page recorded the total value of each item purchased. The last row on the page recorded the total value of the purchases. The total value of the purchases should, and in almost all cases did, equal the value of the wages for the trip. In other words, the wage credit and total transactions balanced in almost all instances.[39]

Based on this description, a number of basic questions can be asked of this document:

1) Who was employed?
2) When did they work?
3) How many were employed?
4) What employment positions existed?
5) What was the wage scale for each employment position?
6) How much were they paid?
7) How did the tripmen spend their wages (purchases and transfers)?
8) What sorts of goods did the HBC stock at York Factory?
9) What were the prices of the items that could be purchased?

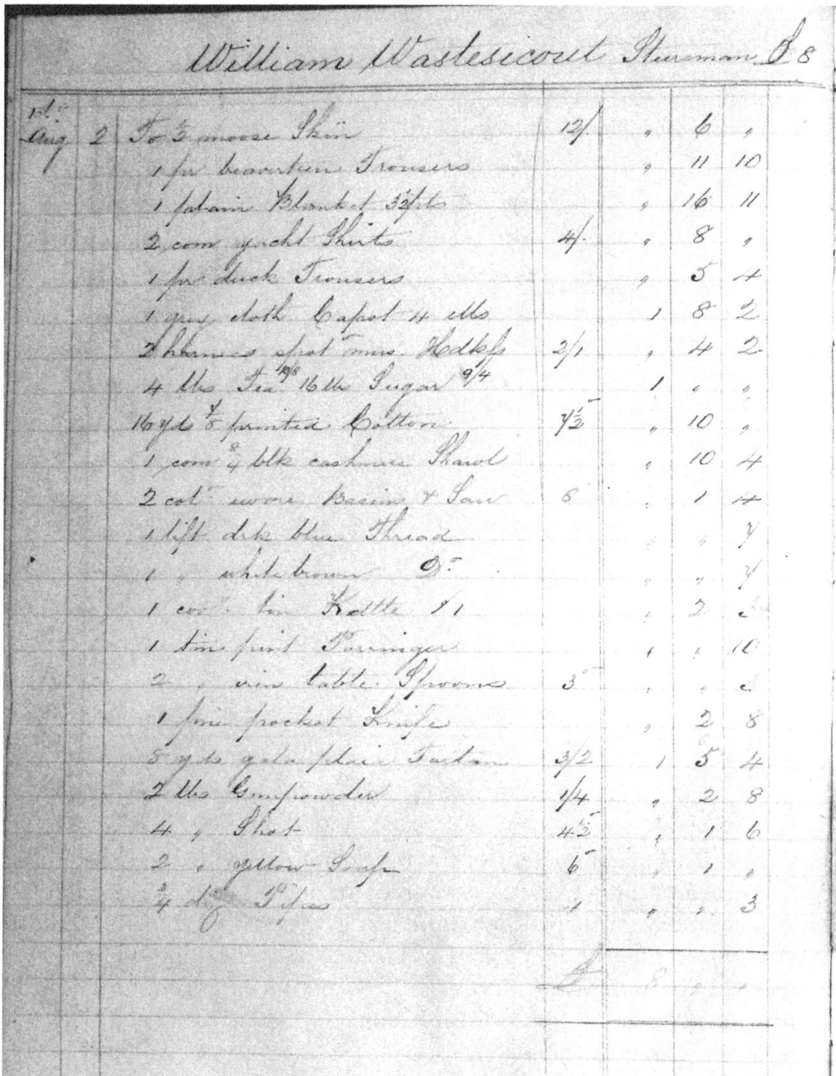

William Wastesicout Steersman Dr 8

| | | | | £ | s | d |
|---|---|---|---|---|---|---|
| 1869 Aug | 2 | To 3 moose Skin | 12/ | — | 6 | — |
| | | 1 pr beaverteen Trousers | | — | 11 | 10 |
| | | 1 fabain Blanket 3½ pts | | — | 16 | 11 |
| | | 2 com yacht Shirts | 4/ | — | 8 | — |
| | | 1 pr duck Trousers | | — | 5 | 4 |
| | | 1 grey cloth Capot 4 ells | | 1 | 8 | 2 |
| | | 2 spot mus Hdkfs | 2/1 | — | 4 | 2 |
| | | 4 lbs Tea 16 lbs Sugar | | 1 | — | — |
| | | 16 yds printed Cotton | 7½ | — | 10 | — |
| | | 1 com blk cashmere Shawl | | — | 10 | 4 |
| | | 2 cot wove Basins & Saucers | 8 | — | 1 | 4 |
| | | 1 dk blue Thread | | — | — | 7 |
| | | 1 white brown Do | | — | — | 7 |
| | | 1 cov tin Kettle | | — | 2 | 3 |
| | | 1 tin pint Porringer | | — | — | 10 |
| | | 2 tin table Spoons | 3 | — | — | 6 |
| | | 1 fine pocket Knife | | — | 2 | 8 |
| | | 5 yds gala plain Tartan | 3/2 | 1 | 5 | 4 |
| | | 2 lbs Gunpowder | 1/4 | — | 2 | 8 |
| | | 4 lbs Shot | 4½ | — | 1 | 6 |
| | | 2 yellow Soap | 6 | — | 1 | — |
| | | ¾ doz Pipes | 4 | — | — | 3 |
| | | | £ | 8 | — | — |

*Figure 7.1* William Wastesicout's purchases for 2 August 1869.

*Table 7.1* William Wastesicout's expenditures on steersman wages, York Factory, 1869.

| *1869* | *William Wastesicout Steersman £8* | *Unit price* | | *Amount cost* | | |
|---|---|---|---|---|---|---|
| *Date* | *Commodity* | *Shilling* | *Pence* | *Pounds* | *Shilling* | *Pence* |
| 02-Aug | To 1/2 moose Skin | 12 | | | 6 | |
| | 1 pr beaverteen Trousers | | | | 11 | 10 |
| | 1 plain Blanket 3 1/2 pts | | | | 16 | 11 |
| | 2 com yacht Shirts | 4 | | | 8 | |
| | 1 pr duck Trousers | | | | 5 | 4 |
| | 1 grey cloth Capot 4 ells | | | 1 | 8 | 2 |
| | 2 harness spot mens Hdkfs | 2 | 1 | | 4 | 2 |
| | 4 lbs Tea 19/8 16 lbs Sugar 9/4 | | | 1 | | |
| | 16 yds 7/8 printed Cotton | | 7.5 | | 10 | |
| | 1 com 8/4 blk cashmere Shawl | | | | 10 | 4 |
| | 2 col ware Basins & Sarr | | 8 | | 1 | 4 |
| | 1 lift dark blue Thread | | | | | 7 |
| | 1 lift white brown Thread | | | | | 7 |
| | 1 cov. Tin Kettle /1 | | | | 2 | 3 |
| | 1 tin pint Porringer | | | | | 10 |
| | 2 tin iron table Spoons | | 3 | | | 3 |
| | 1 fine pocket Knife | | | | 2 | 8 |
| | 8 yds gala plaid Tartan | 3 | 2 | 1 | 5 | 4 |
| | 2 lbs Gunpowder | 1 | 4 | | 2 | 8 |
| | 4 lbs Shot | | 4.5 | | 1 | 6 |
| | 2 lbs yellow Soap | | 6 | | 1 | |
| | 3/4 doz pipes | | 4 | | | 3 |
| | | | | 8 | | |

*Source*: HBCA B.239/d/1219 York Factory Accounts, 1869–1871

Given the structure and content of the information provided in the York Factory tripmen accounts, two basic subjects for inquiry became apparent: (1) could some labour participation parameters be discerned?; and (2) could the numerous transactions be aggregated and treated as a whole in order to discern some general consumption patterns based on the specific labour services that were provided by Native men of York Factory?

## Some findings about labour involvement

A simple perusal of the original document cannot tell us anything about the employment structure or organisation of labour. Generally, we know that the

Yorkboat labour was divided into positions of guides, steersmen, bowman and middleman, and that a crew typically totalled eight men, but sometimes Yorkboats had crews of ten. The largest group was the middlemen, who did most of the rowing.

Because steps were taken to digitise manuscript data (see Appendix A), some insights about the participation and incomes are possible from this accounting book. The participation of individual tripmen, as documented by this accounting book, is graphically reconstructed in Table 7.2. It is evident that the June trips employed more men. Also it is immediately apparent from numerical data, which a simple perusal of the document does not allow, that the potential total number of tripmen from York Factory was larger than the number that were engaged for any single trip. In other words, the potential labour pool was more than that regularly employed by the HBC. It also provides a simple visual reconstruction of individual engagement. A simple frequency of trip participation for the 43 men is depicted by Figure 7.2. This display is not a normal distribution, and in fact, the median modal class has the lowest value. Thirteen men constituted a core middleman group who engaged in four or five trips (Apelaguay, Anderson, Beardy, two Franks, three Kirknesses, Missawagun, Ouscan, two Spences and Weenask). Those who worked for four or five trips as bowsmen, steersmen or guides totalled five (two Keetchekeesicks, Massan, Missaygaun and Wastecout), although there were several other guides and steersmen. Thus, about 18 individuals made up the core labour pool for the York Factory-Norway House boatwork.

Different salaries were paid for the different positions in the boat brigades and the salaries in 1870 were lower than in 1869.[40] (In 1869, a guide was paid £9, a steersman £8, a bowsman £7 and a middleman £6 per trip, but each of these salary rates were reduced by one pound for the 1870 and 1871 trips.)[41] On a percentage basis, the difference between a guide and a middleman was significant. Figure 7.3 shows wage group frequencies for the duration of the information in the account book. Those who fell in the group that had earned £5 had made only one trip at the wage rate of a middleman. Those who were grouped at ≥ £26 tended to have been engaged for all five trips and/or were remunerated at the level of a middleman or higher. With respect to total incomes earned over the entire period, a similar absence of a normal distribution is evident. In fact, the frequency count of ten occurred for both the lowest and highest income groups. This distribution suggests that at York Factory the least engaged group was the same size as the most engaged group. Both frequency patterns reflect the degree of engagement in seasonal wage labour. Clearly, a sizeable group was able to specialise at boat work, and concomitantly, they were able to increase their ability to consume.

*Table 7.2* Individual engagement of York Factory tripmen, c.1869–1871.

| | *Year* | *August 1869* | *June 1870* | *July 1870* | *June 1871* | *July 1871* | *Trip count* | *Total salary* | *Position* |
|---|---|---|---|---|---|---|---|---|---|
| 1 | Albert Spence | | 5 | 5 | 5 | 5 | 4 | 20 | Midman |
| 2 | Baptiste Nepatabo | 6 | | 5 | 5 | | 3 | 16 | Midman |
| 3 | Ben Cooper | | 5 | | | 5 | 2 | 10 | Midman |
| 4 | Benjamin Wastesecout | | 5 | 5 | 5 | | 3 | 15 | Midman |
| 5 | Charles Gore | | 5 | | 5 | 5 | 3 | 15 | Midman |
| 6 | Charles Morris | | | | 5 | | 1 | 5 | Midman |
| 7 | David Anderson | 6 | 5 | 5 | 5 | 5 | 5 | 26 | Midman |
| 8 | David Brown | | | | | 5 | 1 | 5 | Midman |
| 9 | David Spence | | 5 | 5 | 5 | | 3 | 15 | Midman |
| 10 | Davie Bone | | | | 5 | | 1 | 5 | Midman |
| 11 | Dick | | 7 | | | | 1 | 7 | Steersman |
| 12 | Edward Frank | 6 | 5 | 5 | | 5 | 4 | 21 | Midman |
| 13 | Frederick Apelagaun | 6 | 5 | 5 | 5 | 5 | 5 | 26 | Midman |
| 14 | Georqe Dick | | | | 8 | | 1 | 8 | Guide |
| 15 | George Massan | | 8 | | 8 | 8 | 3 | 24 | Guide |
| 16 | George Ouscan/Uscan | | 7 | 7 | | | 2 | 14 | Steersman |
| 17 | Henry Stag | | | | | 5 | 1 | 5 | Midman |
| 18 | Jack Sewescum | | 5 | | | | 1 | 5 | Midman |
| 19 | Jack Squirrel | | | 5 | | 5 | 2 | 10 | Midman |
| 20 | Jacob Kirkness | 6 | 5 | | 5 | 5 | 4 | 21 | Midman |
| 21 | Jacob Weenask/Weenusk | | 5 | 5 | 5 | 5 | 4 | 20 | Midman |
| 22 | James Kirkness | | 5 | 5 | 5 | 5 | 4 | 20 | Midman |
| 23 | James Wastesecout | 6 | 5 | | | | 2 | 11 | Midman |
| 24 | James Isaac | | 5 | 5 | 5 | | 3 | 15 | Midman |
| 25 | James Ouchewap | | 5 | | | | 1 | 5 | Midman |
| 26 | James Waivie/Wavie | | 5 | | 5 | | 2 | 10 | Midman |
| 27 | John Beardy | 6 | 5 | 5 | 5 | | 4 | 21 | Midman |
| 28 | John Frank | 6 | 5 | 5 | 5 | 5 | 5 | 26 | Midman |
| 29 | John Kirkness | | 5 | 5 | 5 | 5 | 4 | 20 | Midman |

| | *Year* | *August 1869* | *June 1870* | *July 1870* | *June 1871* | *July 1871* | *Trip count* | *Total salary* | *Position* |
|---|---|---|---|---|---|---|---|---|---|
| 30 | John Missawaygun | 6 | 5 | 5 | 5 | 5 | 5 | 26 | Midman |
| 31 | John Ouscan | 6 | 5 | 5 | 5 | 5 | 5 | 26 | Midman |
| 32 | John Spence P | 6 | 5 | 5 | 5 | | 4 | 21 | Midman |
| 33 | Joseph Keetchekeesick | 7 | 6 | 6 | 6 | 7 | 5 | 32 | Bowsman |
| 34 | Keetchekaqaway | | 5 | | 5 | | 2 | 10 | Midman |
| 35 | Matthew Beardy | | 5 | | | | 1 | 5 | Midman |
| 36 | Mr. Spence | | 5 | 5 | 5 | | 3 | 15 | Midman |
| 37 | Petasetaw/ Petasetenay/ Petaseteway | | 5 | | 5 | | 2 | 10 | Midman |
| 38 | Peter Anderson | | | | 5 | | 1 | 5 | Midman |
| 39 | Sandy Hom | | | | | 5 | 1 | 5 | Midman |
| 40 | William Dick | | | | | 5 | 1 | 5 | Midman |
| 41 | William Keetchescik | 6 | 6 | 6 | 5 | 6 | 5 | 28 | Midman/ Bowsman |
| 42 | William Massan | 9 | 7 | 8 | 7 | 7 | 5 | 38 | Steersman/ Guide |
| 43 | William Missaygaun/ Mesaygagon | 7 | 6 | 6 | 6 | 6 | 5 | 31 | Bowsman |
| 44 | William Paunders/ Saunders | | 6 | | 6 | | 2 | 12 | Bowsman |
| 45 | William Wastescout | 8 | 7 | 7 | 7 | | 4 | 29 | Bowsman/ Steersman |
| 46 | William Wavey/ Waivie | | 6 | | 6 | | 2 | 12 | Bowsman |
| Total engaged | | | | | | | 132 | 731 | |
| No trip | | | | | | | | | |
| Midman | | | | | | | | | |
| Bowsmen | | | | | | | | | |
| Steersmen | | | | | | | | | |
| Guide | | | | | | | | | |
| Two positions listed | | | | | | | | | |

*Source*: HBCA B.239/d/1219 York Factory Accounts, 1869–1871

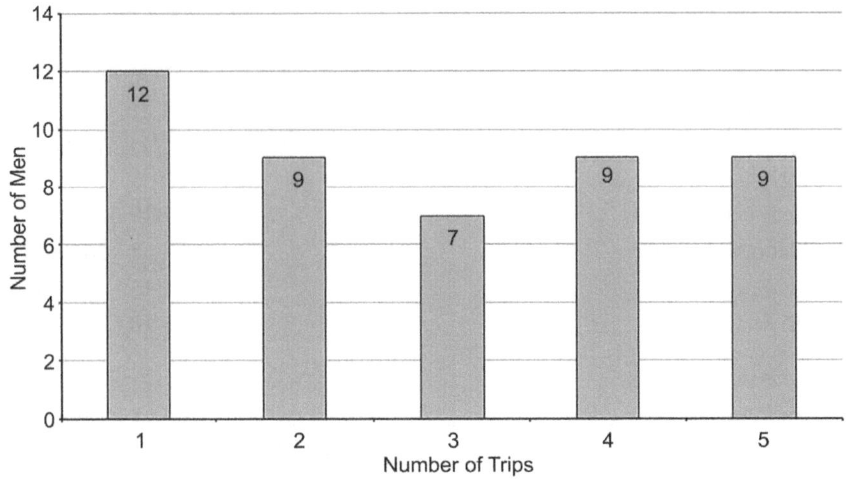


*Figure 7.2* Frequency of participation in York Factory-Norway House Yorkboat freighting, 1869–1871.

Source: HBCA B.239/d/1219 York Factory Accounts, 1869–1871

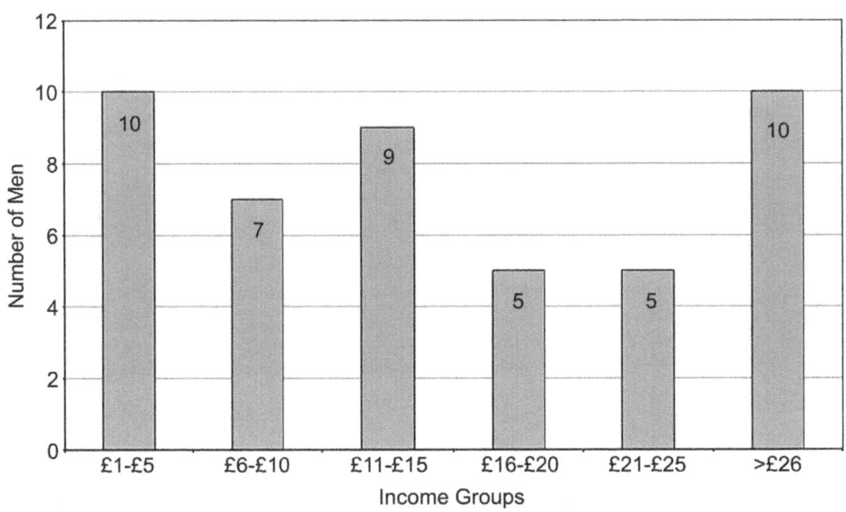


*Figure 7.3* Distribution of income from participation in York Factory-Norway House Yorkboat freighting, 1869–1871.

Source: HBCA B.239/d/1219 York Factory Accounts, 1869–1871

## Some findings about consumption[42]

Throughout the Northern Department, employment with the HBC also meant spending income in the company's store. Some encumbrances on the wages of the tripmen such as transfer to cover debts from the winter fur trade and donations to the Church Missionary Society meant that the entire wage credit was not spent on purchases at the time that it came to make a trip. Nonetheless, most of the wages were expended on goods (i.e. nondurable capital) and the HBC inventory at York Factory offered a sizeable variety of goods to purchase.

While some of these goods purchased by the tripmen are unfamiliar to present day non-specialists of nineteenth-century material culture, we were able to identify some of these oddly named goods by using reference sources and by checking 'online' sources. Most of the designations used in the tripmen accounts allowed for a basic identification with our commodity classes. Reconstruction of the consumption patterns of the Native workers in the fur trade required attempting to identify the specific qualities of the commodities sold/purchased.

A few key examples will suffice to illustrate the importance of ascertaining the technical meaning of designations used to identify HBC textile and clothing goods.

> *Beaverteen* trousers: 'Beaverteen – a heavily wefted fabric of the moleskin type used chiefly for heavy trouserings'; and 'a stout, solid colour, cotton twill cloth similar to Fustian. Napped on the Back and sheared after dyeing, it is used for hunting clothes, chiefly in the British Isles.'
>
> Blue *druggets*: 'A heavy cloth of wool, or of a mixture of wool and silk or wool and linen, used chiefly for clothing; a piece or length of this cloth.'
>
> *Gambroon* trousers: 'a twilled cloth of worsted and cotton or linen and cotton used for summer trousers; also a twilled linen used for linings'; and 'Union fabric, usually of cotton and wool, used for summer slacks and linings [. . .] British term for a group of fabrics made on plain or small twill weaves, and used for clothing. These cloths are union fabrics, and cotton, wool, worsted, and linen are the yarns used.'

Finally, the somewhat puzzling

> *Swanskin* drawers: 'a fine twill-weave flannel fabric'; and 'a flannel made with twill weave and closely woven. Used for Work clothes.'[43]

These technical descriptions provide some sense of the specific utility of the trade good.

On occasion, even a better known trade good such as the *capote* can be more fully appreciated by resorting to a technical dictionary for such a common fur trade garment known as the *capote*: 'A large, lose cloak with a hood attached;

made of heavy material, it is worn by women in cold climates'; but *capot* was also a type of fabric:

> A strong British or French cloth that is rugged, heavily fulled, and has a napped face similar to kersey and melton. It is often waterproofed or water repellent. Used for ulsters, peas jackets, other types of coating. Reworked or reused fibers are often used in the fiber content.[44]

Apparently, capotes were made from capot fabric.

During the early trade, the HBC developed the capacity to supply a good variety of commodities to the inhabitants of the HBC Territory.[45] To illustrate, an outsider's observation of the HBC store at Fort Edmonton (26 July 1859) suggests the surprising reach of British manufacturers. The Earl of Southesk offered a rare glimpse of the consumption possibilities during the era of the fur trade:

> I amused myself by looking through the store, that comprehensive place where everything required for the Indians or the Company's employés is procurable in greater or less abundance, – clothing, ammunition, blankets, groceries, pots and pans, crockery, knives, tobacco, and hundreds of *miscellaneous unexpected things*, all stowed away in an inviting orderly disorder.[46]

A similar sort of observation and impression about the trade could be made for York Factory. In fact, because York Factory was the entrepôt and main depot for the Northern Department, it is likely that even more choice in consumer products was available there than to the Indians and employees at Fort Edmonton. The Earl's wonderment at the range of 'everythings' in a far off corner of the Empire was indicative of the achievement of British merchants at generating and satisfying consumer demand and the ability to supply even tiny markets with British re-exports and manufactures. The variety of different kinds of the similar goods provides an interesting insight into mercantilism in the Canadian fur trade and the specifics of the exchanges made between those that produced raw materials and those that manufactured such goods or re-exported 'tropical groceries' (e.g. sugar) to distant markets.

In terms of the tripmen, and in contrast to my initial appraisal of the document, a variety of goods was available for purchase and a wide selection is indicated by the entries made in the accounting book. In fact, the York Factory tripmen account book for 1869–1879 itemised some 281 distinct commodities that were purchased/sold.[47] The distinction was based on how the HBC described its sales; thus a blue shirt and a white shirt were counted and inventoried as two different commodities. To illustrate several ranges of choice: 10 different kinds of shirts, 13 kinds of pants/trousers, 11 kinds of shawls and 13 kinds of handkerchiefs were purchased by the wages from arduous boat work. At least 30 different textiles amounting to 2,229.36 yards of fabric were purchased. Given the ethnic composition of the factory, 10 pieces of clothing and two textiles were described with the aid of the adjectives 'tartan' or 'plaid'. Ten pounds of coffee and 12 pounds of chocolate were purchased; however, in terms of consumption of foods from far away, 1,411 pounds of sugar and 368 pounds of tea were debited to the tripmen wages.[48] The sugar equated to 101,592 teaspoons. There is some variance on the number of calories in an ounce of sugar, but the estimated number of calories of sugar purchased by the tripmen at York Factory ranges from 1,625,472 to 1,862,520 calories.[49] (If the average daily individual calorie requirement in the severe subarctic clime was 5,000 calories, then the sugar purchased would supply one person between 325.1 and 372.5 days of caloric requirements.) If a pound of loose tea leaves makes 200 cups of tea, then the 368 pounds of tea would support 73,600 cups of tea, or enough tea for 201 people to have one cup of tea every day of the year.[50] The purchase of tea and sugar from the summer boat work during this two-year period seems to have satisfied a significant demand. As far as the supply and demand of tropical groceries was concerned, sugar and tea were well established, but like elsewhere, coffee and chocolate were exotic until the late nineteenth century.[51]

The range of consumer goods seems to provide a choice of different qualities of the same type of good; certainly there were serious price differentials. The cheapest shirt cost £0.125, the most expensive sold for £1.008 (1:8.06); the cheapest pants cost £0.442 and most expensive pants sold for £1.292 (1:2.92); the cheapest capot cost £1.121, the most expensive capot sold for £2.525 (1:2.25); and the cheapest shawl cost £0.204, the most expensive shawl sold for £1.00 (1:4.9), and the cheapest blanket cost £1.008 and the most expensive blanket sold for £1.125 (1:1.11). Given the magnitude of the price differentials for the same kind of good, the selection of expensive goods over cheaper goods infers that demand was shaped by a need greater than some basic functional utility. Also if a strong demand for European products existed among some Natives of the York Factory District, then they would have to supply labour for boat work since other sources of potential income (trapping, provisioning or temporary wage labour) were all tied to the Hudson's Bay Company. The desire to obtain differentiated and luxury goods was fulfilled by a willingness to work as a tripman.

Efforts to classify entries and purchases tend to reveal ambiguities, but without too much angst, these purchases were grouped into categories of goods, based on their basic utility. We grouped some 2,364 entries/purchases encompassing 281 goods into the following categories (1) hides and skins, (2) clothing, (3) textiles, (4) sewing goods, (5) food, (6) appearances, (7) household goods, (8) firearms and ammunition, (9) tobacco and pipes and (10) miscellaneous. Table 7.3 displays the expenditure of the total wage credit of the boatmen for the years 1869–1871 (i.e. five engagements) as classes of commodities. The table shows the breakdown between purchases, donations and debt. One per cent of the total wage credit was transferred to the local Church Missionary Society.

*Table 7.3* Allocation of York Factory tripmen income, 1869–1871.

| *Category* | *Total expenditures* | *Percent* | *Goods purchased* | *Percent* | *Imported goods purchased* | *Percent* |
|---|---|---|---|---|---|---|
| Transfers to other account | 76.91 | 10.53 | – | | – | |
| Transfers to Church Missionary Society | 6.00 | 0.82 | – | | – | |
| Skins and hides | 37.75 | 5.17 | 37.75 | 5.83 | – | |
| Clothing | 311.08 | 42.58 | 311.08 | 48.04 | 311.08 | 51.01 |
| Fabric | 127.30 | 17.43 | 127.30 | 19.66 | 127.30 | 20.87 |
| Sewing | 12.40 | 1.70 | 12.40 | 1.91 | 12.40 | 2.03 |
| Food | 98.26 | 13.45 | 98.26 | 15.17 | 98.26 | 16.11 |
| Appearance and hygiene | 24.61 | 3.37 | 24.61 | 3.80 | 24.61 | 4.04 |
| Household | 18.31 | 2.51 | 18.31 | 2.83 | 18.31 | 3.00 |
| Fire arms | 6.56 | 0.90 | 6.56 | 1.01 | 6.56 | 1.07 |
| Tobacco and pipes | 1.98 | 0.27 | 1.98 | 0.31 | 1.98 | 0.32 |
| Miscellaneous | 9.35 | 1.28 | 9.35 | 1.44 | 9.35 | 1.53 |
| Total | **730.51** | **100.00** | **647.60** | **100.00** | **609.85** | **100.00** |

*Source*: HBCA B.239/d/1219 York Factory Accounts, 1869–1871

Almost all of these transactions involved European manufactured goods or re-exports (e.g. sugar, tea, coffee and chocolate); however, most of the accounts begin with a purchase of half a moose (*Alces alces andersoni*) hide. Moose hides were an important product of the HBC Territory. In fact, hides or skins amounted to 6 per cent of the total earnings/wage credit spent on goods (see Table 7.3). This single purchase at 12 shillings, most likely used for apparel (moccasins), was not inexpensive. The York Factory country was not a good habitat for moose, but the company was in the position to supply its employees a commodity that fell into its bookkeeping designation of *Country produce*. The HBC transport system had the capacity to move not only European goods throughout its vast field of operations, but also to move a variety of country produce (e.g. pemmican, bark, flour, etc.) to districts of scarcity and need. Country produce, locally acquired materials (e.g. birch bark) or processed goods (e.g. pemmican) were produced by Indians and the Métis or by post labour. A wide variety of country products reduced the need to requisition expensive and consumable imports from the core such as food. Local procurement to sustain fur trade operations also freed up cargo capacity for goods that were imported, marked up and then traded. In the 1820s, the York Factory district had a standing requisition for some 150 moose hides from other districts.[52]

In the York Factory tripmen accounts, the HBC seemed to have been able to mark up the price of a moose hide significantly, since at the Red River Settlement in 1865, the price of a *whole* moose skin was 12 shillings.[53] Perhaps the commodification thesis has some selective relevance.

When only the imported goods purchased are considered, the broad expenditure patterns, and possibly consumption preferences, are indicated by Table 7.3. To a large degree, these categories correspond to my initial impressions of the accounting book. The processing of these data in a spreadsheet provides precision and some enhanced insights about consumption patterns. Summer wages from boat work satisfied rather particular needs and desires.

Some 51 per cent of the purchases were for ready-made clothes, fabric to make clothes amounted to 21 per cent, and items needed to sew accounted for 2 per cent (see Table 7.3). British dominance at producing woolens is reflected in the purchases made by York Factory tripmen.[54] These clothing and textile imports were not unique to the York Factory region. Bruce White has noted that, by value, cloth (32.9 per cent), clothing (9.4 per cent) and blankets (7.1 per cent) made up 49.4 per cent of the trade cargo of twelve Montreal canoe loads (c. 1780–1786) destined for the Great Lakes trade.[55] Similarly, Cory Willmott asserted that Native consumers in the Great Lakes 'valued cloth and clothing more than any other commodity'.[56] While the demand was comparable with these earlier periods, York Factory tripmen expended much of their wages on ready-made clothes.

Imported food amounted to 16 per cent of total imported-goods expenditure. Most of this category entailed the consumption of sugar and tea (both of these commodities are the result of the long-distance coordinating abilities of British merchants). Soap, jewellery and various combs made up the category of appearances. Household goods such as basins, spoons, saucers and knives accounted for 4 per cent of the salary expenditures. Two items which would generally be considered mainstays of the fur trade – guns and tobacco – generated very little demand during the open-water/summer freighting season. In fact, very few of these goods related to living off the land in the traditional mode of production. Although the 281 goods or 2,364 separate purchases can be collapsed into 10 categories of goods, in fact, the purchasing pattern of these tripmen was skewed heavily to imported clothing, textiles and food.

## From account ledger to economic history: some microanalysis findings

This section considers the patterns of consumption at York Factory for 1869–1871 and the consumption made possible by the boatwork necessary for sustaining the York Factory-Norway House corridor. This type of accounting record, which some academics might characterise as a simple, humdrum 'shopping list', actually has the potential to generate understandings about economic and social life. In fact, this bit of bookkeeping, along with other HBC records (e.g. Indian trading legers), captures individual household income and consumption based on exchange value. Consequently, some insights into the political economy of the relationship between an Indigenous population and a well-established European corporation are expected. The large mark-up on moose hides demonstrates that mercantilism not only gained through the organisation and control over long-distance trade, but it could also take a hold of local products, establish commodity relations and then turn a profit. From a broader perspective of changes brought by the fur trade, those that had possessed the skills to hunt or trap animals and process skins, hides and pelts ended up purchasing moose hides from the venerable HBC. However, since the environment of York Factory was not good moose habitat, purchasing these hides may have been a sensible choice.

Significantly, 11 per cent of this summer income was used to pay off fall/winter debts from the fall/winter trapping season. Several explanations might be suggested: (1) some trappers/tripmen took debts and then did not make the appropriate efforts to repay debt; (2) efforts at trapping and hunting were made, but resources were scarce; and (3) as a monopsony, actually a double monopolist (i.e. the HBC controlled the sale price of trade goods and the purchase price of furs), and that some unpaid debt was a rational outcome of an imperfect market. Regardless of the cause of these debts, freighting cargoes between York Factory and Norway House was one way to pay off the debt and to start off anew for the next cycle of production. The repayment of debt indicates a relationship of obligation. In this sense, wage labour and 'independent' commodity production were linked for some Native families during this era. Changes in consumption patterns supported changes in lifestyle.

The category 'food' makes up 15 per cent of the expenditures and the sugar purchased would have provided a large number of calories, but it would not have met the equivalent caloric needs over the period represented by the five trips. The fact that a mercantile concern like the HBC would offer a wide range of consumer goods indicates a capacity to integrate much needed Native labour through inducements to consume. York Factory was far from the London headquarters, but still the goods produced, or re-exported, from the metropolis generated sufficient demand to overcome geographical barriers and the so-called cultural obstacles devised mostly by modern-day ethnography. Nonetheless, this one small accounting record, which documents consumption based on a particular income generating activity, is consistent with Carlos and Lewis' study of HBC accounting records (c. 1716–1770) that indicates a demand shift in Indian consumption from producer goods towards household goods.[57]

Given that Yorkboat work was a physically demanding form of employment, requiring much exertion and considerable danger, and given that this population did not face any legal or technical barriers in accessing land and resources, how can their participation be explained? Were they coerced or were they enticed? While many of the goods had some practical utility, others had less. This partial reconstruction and examination of purchases indicates some quality and price differentials for the same kinds of good. For some, the consumption choices suggest an interest in metropolitan or European consumer tastes and/or a desire to enhance social power. Did some Natives of the York Factory region come to emulate HBC personnel with the advent of the fur trade? Moreover, as would be expected from commoditised labour, differential engagement meant differential consumption possibilities: Jack Sewescum's £5 for one trip as a midman can be compared to the more skill-based income of William Massan (guide/steersman) from his five trips that totalled £38.[58] Overall, this accounting book has to be seen as one very short moment in an incremental transition by which autonomous, self-supporting societies became integrated into a specialised commodity chain. It was one very tiny cog encapsulated in an immense mercantile exchange network that created and sustained a core and a periphery. Accounting records can tell us how many and at what prices certain goods were purchased, however, the specific and individual motives for desiring a particular commodity are not provided by such documents, although some inferences are possible based on the quality and utility of the good. The use of the York Factory Tripmen Accounts (HBCA B.239/d/1219) faces the same challenges. Although we do not yet know why the participation rate for boatwork varied, we can discern that contrasting purchasing powers would differentiate families.

The worldly consumption pursuits of Natives residing in the vicinity of York Factory, which had no doubt enhanced their material culture and may have induced, in Trentmann's terms, 'a rainbow of creativity, self-fashioning, exotic novelty, and (yes) pleasure',[59] were sustained by seasonal wage advances secured by Yorkboat freighting. The availability of such incomes was not unfettered. Initially, the post-1870 restructuring of the HBC fur trade had generated a provisional demand for Native labour and the settled community at the headquarters of the Northern Department increased. However, in the ensuing years large structural changes made York Factory economically and spatially obsolete as the link to the Atlantic World and local shortages combined to undermine the community that had come to make up York Factory.[60] A number of factors accumulated to make life dreadful at York Factory: declines in the availability of local and imported food; a marginal and overstretched environment set severe limits on procuring food and fuel; unsupportable population increases; the company's parsimonious responses to deprivation; declining fur prices; and successive contractions of the post economy, concomitant with a reduction in the scale of operations and the shrinking of the factory's hinterland as a result of the opening up of the fur country and changes to transportation modes. To illustrate, in 1888, post expenses ($9,503) had exceeded revenues ($6,390).[61] The archival record documented many accounts of contraction and severe destitution. This economic downturn had its toll. To illustrate, the HBC district report for 1889–1890 recorded the condition of the local population: 'Numbers have eaten their starved dogs, their snow shoes, and the refuse from their dust heaps, while several died from actual starvation.'[62] Observations during the spring of 1890 by Reverend G.S. Winter, stationed with the Church Missionary Society at York Factory, add horrific details to the HBC reporting:

> The poor people must have been starving indeed when they begged admission into the 'Blubber house' to take away [and] eat the leavings of the dogs' food. They even scraped the tanks to get off the putrid meat. A woman once visited her hooks, but found no fish. She was so fearfully hungry that she took up the bait and ate. A boy ate the bait set in a fox trap.[63]

The demand for Native labour and services did not generate an expansive commercialisation of the local economy.

This microanalysis of a small bookkeeping record contributes to some understanding of the importance of the relationship between the market and colonialism. The fur trade brought an engagement with the market and embryonic commodity chains. While at a very basic level, hybrid might be a functional way to describe the combining of European and Indian elements, a substantial economic re-orientation for Natives was required. Rational household choices made in seventeenth-century Holland and eighteenth-century Britain about the use of time, as Trentmann has educed, was a reflection of consumer behaviour that may infer that a domestic consumer revolution preceded the industrial revolution.[64] In this case study, however, a reallocation by York Factory Natives of their time from leisure and self-provisioning to exchange value activities (labour and the consumption of imported goods) did not set them on their merry way to a modern take-off or an industrious revolution.[65] Economic growth for this peripheral territory was largely a reflection of the needs of the metropolitan core. Yet a general and strong desire to consume by households in Holland, England and Rupertsland may have been similar.

## Appendix A: digitisation and spreadsheet techniques

This accounting record was photographed at the Hudson's Bay Company Archives (HBCA). The digitisation work on this document was carried out in the Métis Archival Project Lab (an archival research laboratory specialising in the digitisation of documents) at the University of Alberta. All of the accounting information for each tripman's engagement/account was entered into a separate Microsoft Word table. Since a Word table has no computational functions, why would we start data entry in Word instead of beginning directly with a Microsoft Excel spreadsheet? The Word table we developed was designed to mimic the appearance and structure of the original document as much as possible. (This intermediate step between document and digital data also circumvented the time-consuming chore of formatting and printing Excel worksheets.) Because the Word table can be made to resemble the original page of the account, it was easier to verify and correct the initial data entry. Hard copies of each account were used to verify and correct the digital data. The data were entered, verified and corrected by a different research assistant at each stage. All information for each tripman account was converted to digital text.

The Microsoft Word table data were then copied and pasted into various Excel spreadsheets that allowed tabulation and manipulation. Pivot tables procedure was used to compile and tabulate each purchase. For example, a basic profile (name, dates, positions, wages) for each account was compiled. A key table, which is referred to as the 'One Big List', was created by merging all of the lines of data rows/entries relating to expenditures/purchases. However, the individual transactions remained linked to the particular tripman. From the One Big List, the separate items purchased could then be grouped into separate classes of commodity purchases. (These commodity classes suggest patterns of expenditure and therefore, demand.)

The original accounting included some missing data; wage scales were not always provided in the headers, sometimes account totals were not provided, and sometimes unit prices were not given. These gaps could be filled in or calculated. Because 12 pence equals a shilling and 20 shillings equals a pound, addition and multiplication are complicated. Consequently, this cumbersome sterling/shilling/pence currency was converted to decimal pounds and our tabulations were done in decimal pounds.

Although not always completed, two calculations by the record keeper are evident in the account. Certain goods, such as yards of cloth, were purchased as multiple units, but priced by a unit of measurement – a total needed to be determined in order to debit the wages. Since the amount of items purchased should equal the wage credit, the purchases needed to be summed up in each account. In most cases, a total of all the transactions for a given tripman's account was provided. With respect to total purchases of multiple purchases of the same good, we tested reliability of the clerk's arithmetic by using Excel formula function (e.g. number * unit price). Account totals were also checked. Overall, the bookkeeping was accurate, although incomplete in places.

One necessary step in bringing some conceptual order to these data entailed sorting out who was employed (i.e. who made the purchases). Knowing how many individuals were engaged in this work during the accounting book's coverage would be a base statistic for other calculations and for understanding the engagements over time. While this might seem straightforward, the names were a mix of English and Swampy Cree. The phonetic spelling of Cree surnames meant that in some cases the usage of the surnames in this document was not based on standardised spelling (e.g. Missayguean and Mesaygagon). Sometimes only one name, either Christian or surname, was used (e.g. Baptiste instead of Baptiste Nepatabo). It also seems that even at this late date, some Cree were known by only a single name; as well, the record keeper made irregular use of European Christian names for some of the tripmen. The lack of an account index meant that we had to determine the variance of the accounts' names on a case-by-case basis. Often the similarity of spelling was adequate to make a connection.[66]

A single account was made for each engagement for each trip and running accounts/ledgers were not produced for the same individual over time. Thus, the possibility that two or three differing account headings kept during the duration of this record (i.e. five potential trips) may mean that the same individual was referenced by different headings (i.e. name). Consequently, throughout the duration of this document, in a few instances, each account does not necessarily refer to one unique individual. Clearly, this ambiguity represented a challenge to determining individual participation in the five separate trip hirings.

## Notes

1 This study was presented as 'Accounting for Hudson's Bay Company York Boat Labour, Ca. 1821–1871: Indications of Consumption', part of the panel 'Mercantilism and Accounting Records: Comparative Analysis of the Periphery-Core Structure and Its Impact on Indigenous Market Players' at the Sixteenth World Economic History Conference, Stellenbosch, Republic of South Africa (10 July 2012).

2 A. J. Ray and D. B. Freeman, *'Give Us Good Measure': An Economic Analysis of Relations Between the Indians and the Hudson's Bay Company Before 1763* (Toronto: University of Toronto Press, 1978). A useful analysis was made by A. M. Carlos and F. D. Lewis, 'Trade, Consumption, and Native Economy: Lessons from York Factory, Hudson Bay', *Journal of Economic History*, 61:4 (2001), pp. 1037–64.

3 A. J. Ray, 'The Early Hudson's Bay Company Account Books as Sources for Historical Research: An Analysis and Assessment', *Archivaria*, 1:1 (1975–1976), pp. 3–38.

4 In contrast, however, one of the sources used by Jarvenpa and Brumbach to assess 'the interplay of economic behaviour and ecological energetics' was outpost accounts; see R. Jarvenpa and H. J. Brumbach, 'The Microeconomics of Southern Chipewyan Fur Trade History', in S. Krech III (ed.), *The Subarctic Fur Trade: Native Social and Economic Adaptations* (Vancouver: University of British Columbia, 1984), pp. 147–85. Krech drew heavily upon HBC accounting records for the 1820s to understand the trade in the Mackenzie District. S. Krech III, 'The Trade of the Slavey and Dogrib at Fort Simpson in the Early Nineteenth Century', in *The Subarctic Fur Trade*, pp. 99–146. For non-HBC accounts, see B. M. White, 'Balancing the Books: Trader Profits in the British Lake Superior Fur Trade', in J. Fiske, S. Sleeper-Smith, and W. Wicken (eds.), *New Faces in the Fur Trade, New Faces of the Fur Trade: Selected Papers of the Seventh North American Fur Trade Conference, Halifax, Nova Scotia, 1995* (East Lansing: Michigan State University Press, 1998), pp. 175–92.

5 F. Trentmann, 'Introduction', in F. Trentmann (ed.), *The Oxford Handbook of the History of Consumption* (Oxford: Oxford University Press, 2012), p. 1.

6 F. Trentmann, 'Introduction', in F. Trentmann (ed.), *The Oxford Handbook*, p. 8, p. 13.

7 Trentmann also provided a useful schema for sorting out the literature on consumption: 'We can loosely identify three approaches that have been particularly influential. In one, consumption is about status, social hierarchy and inequality. In a second, it is about production and manipulation of taste and lifestyle in capitalist society. In a third it is about symbolic communication between individuals and groups.' F. Trentmann, 'Introduction', in F. Trentmann (ed.), *The Oxford Handbook*, p. 1, p. 17, p. 11, p. 9.

8 F. Trentmann, 'Introduction', in F. Trentmann (ed.), *The Oxford Handbook*, p. 16.

9 Decimal degrees of longitude and latitude were obtained from http://www4.rncan.gc.ca/search-place-names/unique/.

10 For details, see F. J. Tough, 'Aboriginal Rights versus the Deed of Surrender: The Legal Rights of Native Peoples and Canada's Acquisition of the Hudson's Bay Company Territory', *Prairie Forum*, 17:2 (1992), pp. 225–50.

11 A. Goldsworthy Bailey, *The Conflict of European and Eastern Algonkian Cultures 1504–1700*, 2nd ed. (Toronto: University of Toronto Press, 1969). Originally published in 1937, it is an early study concerning the impact of trade goods. With respect to the spiritual qualities of European trade goods, see C. Martin, 'The Four Lives of a Micmac

Copper Pot', *Ethnohistory*, 22:2 (1975), pp. 111–34. Important depictions of the quantitative volume of trade over time at York Factory is found in A. J. Ray, 'Arms, Brandy, Beads and Sundries', in *Indians in the Fur Trade: Their Role as Trappers, Hunters, and Middlemen in the Lands Southwest of Hudson Bay, 1660–1870* (Toronto: University of Toronto Press, 1998), pp. 72–93.

12 One comparison of canoes and Yorkboats suggests significant labour efficiency was gained by adopting the Yorkboat. The Northern Canoe had of crew of five to seven and they handled four to five pieces of cargo each, whereas the large Yorkboat had a crew of nine and they handled eleven piece of cargo each. D. F. Johnson, *York Boats of the Hudson's Bay Company: Canada's Inland Armada* (Calgary: Fifth House, 2006), p. 179.

13 F. Tough, 'To Look for Food Instead of Fur': Local Economies – Indian Bands and Company Posts', in *'As Their Natural Resources Fail': Native Peoples and the Economic History of Northern Manitoba, 1870–1930* (Vancouver: University of British Columbia Press, 1996), pp. 14–43; and L. Parker, 'Re-Conceptualizing the Traditional Economy: Indigenous Peoples' Participation in the Nineteenth Century Fur Trade in Canada and Whaling Industry in New Zealand' (PhD dissertation, University of Alberta, 2011), pp. 161–201.

14 H. A. Innis, *The Fur Trade in Canada: An Introduction to Canadian Economic History* (Toronto: University of Toronto Press, 1999), p. 387.

15 For details of the organisation of this system, see Innis, *The Fur Trade in Canada*, pp. 289–92; and for the transport configuration after 1870, see Tough, 'As Their Natural Resources Fail', p. 48.

16 Innis, *The Fur Trade*, p. 292.

17 Innis, *The Fur Trade*, p. 308.

18 The differential in the HBC rates for a piece of cargo in July 1830 indicates the difficulty in Yorkboating upstream on the Hayes River. For York Factory to Norway House (upstream) 15s (shillings) was allowed for each piece, whereas from Norway House to York Factory (downstream) 5s were allowed for each piece. Based on this pricing, freighting against the current required three times the effort. R. Harvey Fleming (ed.), *Minutes of Council: Northern Department of Rupert Land* (Toronto: Champlain Society and Hudson's Bay Record Society, 1940), p. 257.

19 Canada, Energy, Mines and Resources, Maps of the National Topographic System, 1:250,000, Hayes River 54C, 2nd ed. (1988); Gods River, 2nd ed. (1987); Knee Lake 53M, 3rd ed. (1988); Oxford House 53L, 5th ed. (1988); and Cross Lake 63I, 3rd ed. (1989).

20 Alexander Henry observed on 17 October 1810 at Rocky Mountain House: 'This afternoon the H.B. boat arrived; these poor fellows have suffered much in the cold water, snow and ice, having to track [cordel] continually. Their boats are not constructed for pulling up the current as our canoes are.' E. Coues (ed.), *New Light on the Early History of the Greater Northwest: The Manuscript Journals of Alexander Henry [the Younger] Fur Trader of the Northwest Company, and of David Thompson, Official Geographer and Explorer of the Same Company, 1799–1814; Exploration and Adventure Among the Indians on the Red, Saskatchewan, Missouri, and Columbia Rivers*, vol. 2 (Minneapolis: Ross and Haines, 1965), p. 654.

21 Innis asserted that the HBC would increase the weight of pieces 'from 90 to 100 and 105 pounds'. Innis, *The Fur Trade*, p. 310.

22 Pemmican, an Indigenous food that became one of the most desired mainstays of fur trade, was made from pounded dried bison mixed with grease and berries. This highly portable food was a concentrated mix of energy and protein. Pemmican was an essential ration at many northern posts and for Yorkboat crews.

23 Johnson, *York Boats of the Hudson's Bay Company*, p. 179.

24 Archives of Manitoba, F.C. Leach Papers, MG1 A14, no. 10, Willy Frog Ross, 'York Boats' (Hereafter AM).

25 Johnson, *York Boats of the Hudson's Bay Company*, p. 179.

26 Johnson, York Boats of the Hudson's Bay Company, p. 183. However, Podruchny reported that six men were required to portage the larger *canot du maître* and that these canoes weighed between 650 and 1,500 pounds, noting that 'A canoe could be especially

difficult to carry when the ground was uneven because the weight of the canoe would be distributed unevenly'. C. Podruchny, *Making the Voyageur World: Travelers and Traders in the North American Fur Trade* (Lincoln: University of Nebraska Press, 2006), p. 126.

27 Library and Archives Canada, Church Missionary Society, Microfilm Reel A-99 (6 September 1890) (Hereafter CMS, A-99).

28 Library and Archives Canada, Public Records of the Department of Indian Affairs, Record Group 10, vol. 4009, file 249,461, pt. 1A (24 October 1910).

29 United Church of Canada Archives, personal papers of Frederich George Stevens, 'Autobiography of the Rev. Frederich G. Stevens', p. 8 (Hereafter UCCA, Stevens).

30 UCCA, *Stevens*, p. 8.

31 UCCA, *Stevens*, p. 10.

32 AM, Leach Papers, MG1 A14, no. 11, Ross, 'York Boats'.

33 HBCA, B.49/e/12, Cumberland House District Report (1886), ff. 37–38.

34 Canada, Sessional Papers, 1898, Annual Report for the Department of the Interior, 1897, Report of the Lieutenant-Governor of Keewatin, no. 13, p. 4.

35 Unless otherwise indicated, all numerical references are from HBCA, B.239/d/1219, York Factory Accounts 1869–1871.

36 This page listed the gear, tools and supplies provided for the trip.

37 Generally, HBC accounting records were kept in Made Beaver (MB), a numéraire representing the ideal value of a prime beaver pelt. Other fur pelts, provisions, labour and European goods were priced in MB.

38 On a couple of occasions it appears that the purchasing was carried out on separate dates, but for the same trip engagement.

39 Only eleven accounts did not balance in this manner.

40 In the 1820s, the scale of wages was higher than that earned by the Natives of York Factory: Steersmen = £22; bowsmen = £20; middlemen = £17. Fleming, Minutes of Council, p. 227. Innis associated 'the general problem of overhead costs of transportation' with the problem of personnel and wages. He noted that 'For the handing of freight on the trunk route from York Factory to Norway House overhead was shifted to an increasing extent to the Indians and later to Red River settlement'. Innis, *The Fur Trade*, p. 308.

41 In HBCA, B.239/d/1219, the prices of goods did not change.

42 Unless otherwise indicated, all numerical references are from HBCA, B.239/d/1219, York Factory Accounts 1869–1871.

43 Descriptions found at: www.encyclo.co.uk/define/Beaverteen; http://oed.com/view/Entry/57991; jsessionid=E00CAE41CEDB33FB912D2A079E21B563?redirectedFrom=drugget#eid; and http://chestofbooks. com/reference/Dictionary-of-Dry-Goods/Gambroon.html; and www.thefreedictionary.com/swanskin; and G. E. Linton, *The Modern Textile Dictionary Fully Revised and Expanded* (New York: Duell, Sloan, and Pearce, 1963), p. 71, p. 143, p. 413 and p. 906.

44 Linton, *The Modern Textile Dictionary*, p. 135.

45 On the need to adapt European trade goods to the real needs of Subarctic Indians and that Indians were shrewd not gullible consumers, see A. J. Ray, 'Indians as Consumers in the Eighteenth Century', in C. M. Judd and A. J. Ray (eds.), *Old Trails and New Directions: Papers of the Third North American Fur Trade Conference* (Toronto: University of Toronto Press, 1980), pp. 255–71.

46 The Earl of Southesk [James Carnegie], *Saskatchewan and the Rocky Mountains: A Diary and Narrative of Travel, Sport, and Adventure During a Journey Through the Hudson's Bay Company Territories, 1859 and 1869* (Edmonton: M.G. Hurtig, 1969), p. 131 [emphasis added].

47 The identification of 281 commodities here only refers to the purchases for boat work; the entire inventory at York Factory would reflect a much greater range of goods.

48 On the growth of British tea imports and the ability of English merchants to control a triangular trade network involving Britain, China and India, see T. Chung, 'The Britain-China-India Trade Triangle (1771–1840)', *Indian Economic and Social History Review*, 11:4 (1974), pp. 431–41.

49 I have used a 12-ounce pound, whereas a 16-ounce pound would increase the magnitude of sugar consumption in this account book. The conversion of sugar weight to calories was found at http://wiki.answers.com/ and http://wiki.answers.com// calories-nutrition/usda/granulated-sugar.

50 To get a sense of how much tea could be consumed form tea leaves, I consulted: www.statisticbrain.com/tea-drinking-statistics/.

51 Trentmann notes that in the seventeenth century, coffee and chocolate were exotic, but had 'mutated into national mass products by the end of the nineteenth'. Trentmann, 'Introduction', p. 17.

52 Fleming, *Minutes of Council*, p. 167.

53 J. J. Hardgrave, *Red River (np: 1971)*, p. 505 [emphasis added], citing the Northwestor (18 November 1865). In the early 1820s, for the purpose of inventories and transfers, a large moose skin was valued at 3s 9d, and a small moose skin was 3s, however, with a more firmly established monopoly by 1827, the HBC valued a large moose at 2s, and 1s for a small moose skins (July 1927), Fleming, *Minutes of Council*, p. 162, p. 195.

54 On the importance of British woollens to the North American fur trade, see C. Willmott, 'From Stroud to Strouds: The Hidden History of a British Fur Trade Textile', *Textile History*, 36:2 (2005), pp. 196–234.

55 B. M. White, 'Montreal Canoes and Their Cargoes', in B. G. Trigger, T. Morantz, and L. Dechene (eds.), *Le Castor Fait Tout: Selected Papers of the Fifth North American Fur Trade Conference, 1985* (Montreal: Lake St Louis Historical Society, 1987), p. 170.

56 Willmott, 'From Stroud to Strouds', p. 203.

57 Carlos and Lewis, 'Trade, Consumption, and the Native Economy', p. 1061.

58 HBCA, B.239/d/1219, York Factory Accounts 1869–1871, ff. 3, 4d, 23d, 30d, 43 and 60d.

59 Trentmann, 'Introduction', p. 7.

60 A fuller explanation of the post-1870 changes to York Factory can be pursued with A. J. Ray, 'York Factory: "The Crises of Transition, 1870–1888"', *The Beaver Outfit*, 313:2 (1982), pp. 26–31; and F. Tough, '"Dependent on the Company's Provisions for Subsistence": The Decline of Kihchiwashahikanihk (York Factory)', in *As Their Natural Resources Fail*, pp. 63–74.

61 HBCA B.239/e/11, York Factory District Report, 1888, fol. 2.

62 HBCA B.239/e/13, York Factory District Report, 1889, fol. 2.

63 CMS, A-116 (30 April 1890).

64 Trentmann, 'Introduction', p. 15.

65 See J. de Vries, 'The Industrial Revolution and the Industrious Revolution', *Journal of Economic History*, 54:2 (1994), pp. 249–70; for an institutional approach to this question, see J. L. van Zanden, *The Long Road to the Industrial Revolution: The European Economy in a Global Perspective, 1000–1800* (Leiden: Brill, 2009).

66 Furthermore, for any trip, the total crews should approximate multiples of eight. Moreover, if two similar names existed for the same trip engagement, then we assumed that these were two different individuals with similar names. The problem of account name variances was expressed between different trip engagements.

# 8 Conclusion

## Accounting, money and mercantilism in European exchange, 1500–1900

*Richard W. Unger*

From the end of the Middle Ages to the late nineteenth century, world commerce grew rapidly. The European share of that trade grew even more rapidly. Shipping goods of all sorts over diverse distances made inroads in markets within Europe and around the world. The growth in commerce reoriented economic and social relations in almost all parts of the globe. Merchants, their agents and shippers brought new commodities to local populations and developed enduring trading relations with people of varied backgrounds, languages and cultures. Those European traders and their representatives brought with them accounting practices and the concepts inherent in such record keeping. The written accounts of transactions, no matter their original purpose, by their nature provide a variety of information and not just about the prices of goods bought and sold. Embedded in them is information about what happened to the participants, whether people of European background or Indigenous peoples, when contact, interchange and exchange took place. As with any period there are problems of defining categories to encompass the aspects of the age. That makes for problems of precision in understanding and summarising what happened, especially over such a lengthy period of time with more and more varied people and peoples involved. Mercantilism is one term, often used though rarely explained, that fails to describe with any accuracy. Whatever the phenomenon was, it is misunderstood and so, for that matter, is the more general concept of accounting.

The practice has deep roots in the general sense of reckoning and numeration. There seems to be, if not a universal need, at least a common desire to rank, to note the relative size of objects, people, even ideas. Languages have comparatives and superlatives to fulfil that function. Counting serves to give some greater precision in the exercise of examining relationships of size, scope and scale. The process of accounting can and does degenerate. The creation of metrics that do not measure what they claim to measure or the misuse of data to achieve desired results makes the exercise a sham and creates little more than just another tool for propaganda. The use of figures to intimidate people who have neither skill nor interest in examining where the numbers come from, how they are gathered or what they might mean has the same effect. The promotion of the idea of strength in size – that more numbers are better, that big data must by definition give useful results – can also obscure all the problems to do with accounting. Since the seventeenth century, at least in English, the word has taken on a more restricted meaning. It came to describe, and now primarily describes, reckoning in general but the keeping and verifying of financial records. It is that more narrow sense that gives it unique status and creates the qualities which make the sources valuable for the study of both the present and the past.

It was common for people involved in business to keep some sort of records of their transactions. The variation was in the extent and complexity of what they chose to write down. In a world where credit is common, having accurate record keeping is something desirable for all those involved. In cases where there were numerous small transactions between two parties over time, say in a retail store, payment in a lump sum is simpler, especially where small change is in short supply. Paying retailers weekly or monthly was the equivalent of the credit card, the seller supplying the credit. If the seller brings together all the charges and gets payment in a lump sum for the total, then record keeping is something desirable for both parties. For complex transactions involving multiple participants carried out over time, as with investors in an enterprise, then reports about the state of the operation were even more than desirable. They became a central feature of the business. The larger the enterprise, the greater the number of investors, the greater the distances involved, the more durable the enterprise, the more important record keeping became.

In high medieval Europe, as business expanded, merchants big and small developed increasingly sophisticated accounting procedures. Italy was a leader in most matters commercial. Signs of standard practice appeared there in the High Middle Ages. By the fifteenth century, there were books detailing what records to keep, how to integrate them and how to use them effectively.[1] Examples of record books from small traders up to large international banking establishments survive. They indicate that accounting practice was not consistent. Some merchants were better than others in maintaining accurate and reliable accounts. That was equally true as Italian practices spread northward. By the sixteenth century, merchants throughout western Europe used established ways of keeping records to a greater or lesser extent. As the scope of trade expanded in the wake of voyages of exploration, those practices followed Europeans overseas. Governments and the large trading companies that emerged in the seventeenth century took on the accounting methods that started in the counting houses of medieval Italy. The East India Company, for example, produced extensive and increasingly complex records to track its transactions. More important, those records of bigger institutions, unlike the account books of small-scale traders, often survive, offering historians a mass of raw material.

Accounting records can yield a wide variety of information. The problem for researchers is to decide what in fact those books of figures do show. Accountants, an anachronistic term, generally prepared those records for narrow purposes, but the products of their hands can yield an abundance of information about the economy, consumption patterns, cultural norms and social relations. Though practices became more standardised over time, there were still wide variations in the scope of the records. Though there were differences, one thing does seem to have been consistent. After examination of a broad range of accounts of merchants and businessmen in pre-modern Europe, it seems clear that they got the books to balance. That was done without computers or electronic calculators and only with the aid, at most, of a counting table with small tokens moved around to show the data and to make doing the sums simpler.

From 1500 to 1800, in general, the European economy, despite some difficult decades, enjoyed considerable growth. Expansion was broadly based spanning different sectors. Trade and exchange for much of the period increased the most dramatically in volume and value and had the greatest impact on the rest of the economy. In the Middle Ages agriculture accounted for over 90 per cent of output. That sector held on to that large share down through much of the nineteenth century, though the booming commercial sector took on a larger proportion over time. The late eighteenth and the nineteenth centuries saw the start of the Industrial Revolution in northwestern Europe. It diffused slowly from there. Even as manufacturing output rose, however, commerce continued to expand. Trade fed industrialisation by supplying factories with necessary raw materials and markets for their finished products. The era just before industrialisation was one of more merchants carrying on more trade. Starting in the early nineteenth century, the period came to be called one of mercantilism.

A precise and exact or even just a useful definition of the term mercantilism has eluded historians. Like many labels invented after the fact and for political purposes, the term gets used extensively but almost indiscriminately and rarely with any thought invested by the user in what it might mean. Sadly, there are many terms invented by historians which were not known to contemporaries and are used as if everyone knows what they mean when in fact really no one knows. It is true that in the years from 1500 to 1800, the fastest growing sector of the European and world economy was trade. As it took an ever more important place in the economy, merchants came to have a sharply increasing role in society. Traders also took on a more prominent place in politics, both as actors and as people favoured by the politically powerful, since traders generated income and wealth. The greater political influence of men involved in commerce had its roots in the Middle Ages in the governments of Venice and, to a lesser extent, Florence, Genoa and many other towns in northern Italy. Though, over the long term, many of the merchant-involved governments in those towns collapsed, there was in the seventeenth century a new example of a state where traders held the levers of power. The success of the Dutch Republic was the envy of governments throughout Europe in the seventeenth century. The rise to its unprecedented prosperity and international political power was an inspiration for a range of largely defensive policy choices made by jurisdictions all over the continent. One result of the changes in European politics is the confusion of the era of commercial expansion, where merchants more frequently entered the political arena with a body of government policies that emerged in the course of the late sixteenth through the mid-eighteenth century.

The roots of 'mercantilism' as the name for an era in the history of the economy are in a short chapter of *An Inquiry into the Nature and Causes of the Wealth of Nations* by Adam Smith published in 1776.[2] The much lauded and little read proponent of freer trade did not use the word mercantilism but did talk about what he called the mercantile system. For him, it was one of a number of systems, including, for example, the agricultural system derived from the ideas of his French contemporaries, the Physiocrats. He compared those systems to his own ideas about proper government policy. Smith was not an economist since the title and the concept did not exist in his lifetime. Rather, his work was in the field of political economy, as the intellectual exercise was called well into the twentieth century. In his own and in previous centuries, politics and economy were known to be closely intertwined. Smith, in his chapter on the mercantile system, listed a set of policies, which he thought were counterproductive. It was his view that individuals should be allowed to pursue their own gain, a path that would yield in the end the greatest benefit for the nation. Smith believed that people have a natural tendency to truck, barter and exchange. By exercising that impulse, by trading goods they could specialise and so use their talents to their fullest. Incidentally, they would also tend to think of better ways to carry out their specialised tasks and so improve technology.[3] Gradually, in Britain and in other countries in the nineteenth century, Smith's ideas came to dominate. The government practices he deplored became lumped together into something called mercantilism, which was by definition bad for the economy.

There was never anything like a 'mercantilist dogma'; no theoreticians before Smith, who produced some generalised theory for the policies of governments, the way Smith did for what came to be called liberalism. There was neither a coherent, dominating body of thought nor much a way of systematic thinking about the economy before the eighteenth century. There was certainly no ideology of mercantilism. The efforts of many historians to give some coherence to that chaotic and inconsistent collection of ideas and government actions have failed. It is not clear whether the term mercantilism applies to ideas or policies, or when it might have prevailed and where. The Swedish economic historian Eli Heckscher's monumental and massive two-volume summary simply titled *Mercantilism*, first published in Swedish in 1931 and followed by the first German edition in 1932, a further revised German edition in 1935 and then an English translation in the same year, did not resolve the issue of defining the phenomenon. Despite subsequent efforts by other scholars, it is still not clear what might qualify as mercantilism and what might not.[4] 'Mercantilism [...] has long been marked by profound and persistent – some might say interminable – disagreement about the meaning, scope, and temporal and geographical applicability of that elusive, many-sided concept.'[5] That lack of clarity or order condemns writers to struggle with describing the many facets of economic policy and practice through the years from 1500 to 1800.

Heckscher and others concentrated on the prevailing policies of the period. More recently, efforts to find broader goals in comments on economic matters have yielded a list of some very general characteristics of economic writing from the sixteenth through the eighteenth centuries. Many who dealt with the subject were concerned with the economy as a system with interdependent parts. Some also perceived differences in the pace of economic growth in different parts of Europe and so questioned why that was the case, delving then into more general questions about balances of payments, social structure, patterns of investment and prevailing social norms.[6] The success of some states like Venice in the sixteenth century and the Dutch Republic in the seventeenth, combined with the relative decline of others, most notably Spain but also Italy, raised questions about the sources of economic success. Discussion among writers often centred on trade and manufacturing and their promotion, though those were far from the only preoccupations. The overarching issue was economic development.[7] There may have been some common problems addressed during the era called mercantilist, but there was no consistent body of ideas, specific or general, to emerge from the varied and often disconnected expressions of interest in economic development or underdevelopment.

The roots of many of the often-cited aspects of mercantilism were in actions by towns in late medieval Italy and the Low Countries.[8] Those practices, mostly to do with trade between towns and the nearby countryside and among towns, spread through western Europe from the seventeenth through to the early nineteenth century. Though by no means consistent, there were some recurring areas of the economy, which attracted government attention. There were issues about money, that is, what constituted money and how it was used and how it was accounted for. There were problems of how governments were to tax what and at what rates. Taxation expanded dramatically in the period, so there was extensive scope for action. There were questions around the promotion of domestic industries and barriers to deter imports. More generally, there was the issue of the proper reach of government. Over time, it proved easier for the state to coerce people living within its borders and beyond, so political force became ever more a part of economic policy. That capability, combined with the boom in long-distance trade, gave European states the incentive to extend their reach to other parts of the world through setting up of colonies. Often those overseas outposts, no matter their form, were expected to supply goods for the mother country. For most parts of the world and for most of the period down into the nineteenth century, the colonies were little more than trading posts, isolated settlements typically on the coast with small numbers of Europeans acting as intermediaries in commercial exchange. Only slowly did settler colonies emerge, almost exclusively in the western hemisphere, but even there, the largest number of immigrants over the seventeenth and eighteenth centuries came, involuntarily, from Africa. The European colonies, whether in Asia, Australia, Oceania or the Americas, put Europeans and the European economy in contact with populations new to them. The people they met and dealt with had different practices, traditions and, most important for the economy, different consumption patterns.

Europeans did not export markets to other parts of the world, but they brought their own business practices with them. As a result, they served to change the character of exchange in the places they went to. That was most obvious in Asia, where there were well-established states regulating trade and producing legal tender. There, as in other parts of the world, there was trade and some form of money, which could serve in the negotiation of trade. Money, by definition, is a medium of exchange and a store of wealth. It can take many forms. Europeans brought their own type of money with them and their own ways of dealing with those currencies.

Merchants and traders in thirteenth-century Italy were faced with a variety of different coins from different jurisdictions, some civic, some noble, some ecclesiastical. The authority of the state to issue money had fragmented along with the Roman Empire, which had held the exclusive power to mint coins. The fragmentation presented a problem for the keepers of accounts. One of their principal tasks was to make comparisons of payments across all transactions they recorded. That was always the case. Multiple coinages meant different units of payment, which had to be made comparable. Exchange rates between various currencies existed, but they would fluctuate and governments, especially in the fourteenth century, discovered they could profit by re-minting the coinage and holding back a share of the precious metal for their own benefit. The people who kept financial records created a standard, often mythical or out-of-date, money and converted all transactions into that money of account. The practice is the same as the twenty-first-century one of large multinational corporations. They produce annual reports in the currency of their home country even though many of the transactions took place in different media. The exchange rates they choose influence the bottom line as did the conversion rates that medieval accountants used.

The problem of dealing with the complex monetary regime that existed in late medieval Europe also prevailed in a number of places beyond the continent in the years between 1500 and 1800. In seventeenth-century China, the accounts of one Jesuit missionary living in a small town near a large commercial centre reveal how a foreigner handled transactions in what to him was a very foreign land. His records show that even for small payments people used silver. Having adequate quantities of small change was a recurring problem for making payments up to the twentieth century. China, which had a highly sophisticated economy, seems to have solved the problem to a significant degree. At least that is what the records of one European strongly suggest. The specifics of payments the missionary included in his books also undermine general conclusions about the use of silver in China in the period. How much silver circulated in China in the fifteenth through to eighteenth centuries has long been a matter of discussion. World silver supplies grew rapidly in the sixteenth and seventeenth centuries thanks to improved technology of extraction and to the exploitation of sources, first in Japan and then new, rich mines in what is now Mexico and Bolivia. Despite claims of a great impact on prices in Europe because of an influx of American silver, it is clear that large quantities of the metal found their way to the Far East to pay for the products of the diverse and sophisticated Chinese economy.[9] It has proven extremely difficult to quantify the flow of silver into China. If missionaries, fitting into the daily life of one small city, admittedly in a part of the country close to big trading towns, used silver, then it suggests that the metal from overseas had penetrated deeply into the Chinese economy. While the finding may not force revision of any general theory about the role of specie in China in the period, the accounting source does indicate that there are reasons for concern about prevailing views of China in the world silver trade and of the role of silver in China.

The case of those Jesuit missionaries also shows Europeans' accommodation to the local monetary regime. The same was true of Dutch immigrants dealing in furs in the valley of the Hudson River at about the same time. There was in both places some method of measuring the relative value of trade goods. The presence of more than one currency is no surprise. In Europe, typically many different coinages were in circulation even as late as the seventeenth century. When New Netherland was a colony, there were voices in the mother country calling for freer trade and less regulation of the economy, a prelude to a fully articulated theory in the hands of Adam Smith. There were, at the same time, protectionist policies in the Dutch Republic, which continued down to Smith's day.[10] It is no surprise that the two conflicting tendencies that existed at home would also arise in the colony. No matter the theories that were circulating, what predominated in New Netherland was finding practical solutions to immediate problems. Pragmatic considerations prevailed when it came to buying and selling as well as to government monetary policy. In the North American Dutch colony, there was not so much a conflict between Europeans and Indigenous peoples in how they understood money. For the people on either side of bargains in the Hudson River Valley, neither money nor beaver pelts had some intrinsic value but they both had value in exchange. Neither coins nor skins deteriorated much over time, so they could be held, if necessary, in the hope of an increase in what might be got by trading them away. The two currencies that existed, guilders and sewant, had an exchange rate or relative price just like beaver pelts and European manufactures. Sewant appears to have fallen out of use over time as coins became more abundant and as Europeans became more numerous. An account book from the region dated to the mid-eighteenth century supports that impression. The lack of extensive earlier accounts makes it hard to know precisely how people used the two currencies in the colony. There is certainly a lack of clarity about the power and effectiveness of government policy, since it seems to have been overruled more than once by what people found to be the most efficient practices. The best way to carry on exchange seems to have shaped government policy, with preconceptions brought from their homeland by the Europeans being of lesser importance. The Dutch colony and its English-ruled successor suggest that preconceptions could quickly be undermined by circumstances on the ground. The need to survive and thrive in a hostile, unfamiliar environment gave great force to practical considerations.

In West Africa, by the late eighteenth century, the use of money of account was a well-established practice. Different ports of call used different units, but the principle was the same. All parties accepted the notional method of reckoning value, thus making exchange simpler. The practice also made the task of the accountant not only easier but also possible. The accountant had to record prices of all goods traded for the sake of comparison. It did not matter if traders incurred expenses or received income from sales in France, West Africa or the Caribbean. The accountant had to find a mutually agreed way to record what happened. Most of all the accounts had to be in a form that their superiors, in this case the investors, could understand and preferably easily understand. That imperative does raise the possibility that the records were designed as much or more for the audience than to show what happened. There was and is always a question of honesty. That is not the only reason for treating accounts with the same judicious eye required of historians in dealing with any sources.

Before there was silver from the New World to fuel international trade from the Americas to Europe and to Asia, there was silver added to European stocks from mines in Saxony, Bohemia and Hungary. Signs of some limitation in specie supplies in the fifteenth century disappeared even before gold and silver began to make their way across the Atlantic not long after Columbus' voyages. Governments were always interested in silver. They inherited from Roman law control over what came out of the ground, and the charges they imposed on people extracting mineral riches could yield sizeable royalties. Authorities, as a result, insisted on oversight of the mining of precious metals. Though governments may well have been more interested in royalty income than in supplying a reliable means of exchange, they did the latter as best as they could as part of their responsibilities. The need for regulation and oversight for government regulation meant there had to be careful accounting. In general, the expanding role of the state from the late Middle Ages meant better accounting procedures. There was an interest in standardising the ways of recording and measuring the effectiveness of reporting. Governments needed good accounting and, thus, they needed good accountants. The books produced to report to political authorities may look very good and better over time, but their accuracy was and is always a subject of doubt. For a merchant, keeping records for himself that are to be seen by no one else unless he had to go to court, getting the numbers right was of primary importance. Making the books straightforward and easily penetrable was the primary task of the purser on a trading voyage. For government employees, accuracy of reports might be a detriment to their welfare. Typically, corruption is ignored, but the possibility existed not only for those working for governments but also for people employed by the large trading companies where oversight might be an ocean away. The potential for misrepresenting the flow of business so that some funds would end up in the hands of record keepers could have been considerable. The exact extent of corruption will never be known. Efforts to eliminate theft through oversight, better accounting or by catching cheaters indicate corruption existed, but how common it was is immeasurable. The thieves' purpose was to produce accounts that masked what they stole. Large international trading companies, like the Hudson's Bay Company, appear to have had ways to minimise theft, though that did not stop them from careful surveillance, which was one of the ways they kept down dishonest payments.

The extent of European commercial expansion, the creation of global and increasing domination of high seas shipping in the years after 1500 has left the impression of a world where Europe was at the centre and the people and places Europeans dealt with were peripheral. Of course the geography did not change suddenly. Europe and the rest of the world were in the same places as before Columbus, and Vasco da Gama showed how all-sea routes might be used to create a global seaborne trading network. Being at the centre is, of course, a matter of the observer's vantage point. The way the emperors of China treated other Asians, Europeans and Africans shows that their view of what was peripheral was different from that of contemporary Europeans and, for that matter, of historians who see Europe at the centre of the history of the period. That view is certainly anachronistic. It reads back into the pre-modern world what came to be the case in the wake of the Industrial Revolution. Then, Europeans enjoyed tremendous advantages over other producers around the world because of what they could make and at what costs. As manufacturing became more efficient through the eighteenth and nineteenth centuries, those people who traded with Europeans gained. Prices for European goods fell, so their trading partners paid less in grain, furs, pelts or whatever might be on offer relative to the imports from Europe. In addition, all consumers gained because goods available typically increased in variety and quality. Some features of that world economy and European comparative advantage had appeared even before the Industrial Revolution.

A few advantages already existed as early as the twelfth century for the traders who supplied goods made in Europe. The range of wares for which prices were lower than those of competitors increased over time. By improving shipping efficiency and capabilities, Europeans carrying those goods, including specie, came to dominate long-distance carrying trades in most of the world from the fifteenth century onward. For that reason they were largely traders, functioning mainly through their trading posts, supplemented in places like the New World, Australia and New Zealand, with mining camps and settlements producing foodstuffs for traders. Where there was sizeable settlement, in the tropical and subtropical Americas, it was to produce agricultural goods, principally sugar, for export to Europe. The loss of Indigenous populations to disease made economically necessary the forced settlement of people from the other side of the Atlantic to raise crops for European markets. That trade in human beings, like all the other high-seas exchanges, expanded and became more formalised over time. In the first instance, the traders, when they arrived, needed to ingratiate themselves into existing economies. They did not manage, with few exceptions, colonial economies but rather fit into existing structures and then, over time, tried to shape the economies of those places where they were able to establish some political power. The new rulers established authority, sometimes extensive and sometimes rather limited, at the expense of other Europeans and of the locally powerful.

The years up to the mid-nineteenth century were in various parts of the world an age of merchants and trading, of buying, shipping and selling. Success for Europeans depended on the ability to meet the needs and wants of people they encountered. In Africa, French traders, there to buy slaves to work the plantations in the Americas, had to meet local demand. Market intelligence was critical for their commercial success. Traders were at the mercy of local demand. They had to shift and adjust the kind and range of goods they sent to West Africa to get the maximum buying power in coastal slave markets. Captains kept meticulous, detailed records of what they sold in exchange for slaves. They and their investors used that information, recorded in accounts, to keep up with consumer trends and so to enhance their profits, if there were any. Slavery and slave markets existed before Europeans arrived, but their presence and the great demand for labour to exploit the potential of agriculture in the western hemisphere created a re-orientation of the local economy and the expansion of one sector, slaving, presumably to the detriment of others. The pattern recurred in other parts of the world where Europeans did business.

The problem of meeting local demand was one that was typical of managing distant markets. The poor quality of communication, the long delays in the transfer of information and the very different cultural norms Europeans encountered presented serious management problems. Difficulties of trying to ensure sales at some considerable distance away, critical to the success of business, existed in the Middle Ages. Communication improved over time. It proved possible to move information faster in the eighteenth than in the thirteenth century. The improvements facilitated better management and also made possible the extension of business operations to far-flung places. In Canada, the Hudson's Bay Company had to decide on the stock of goods held at its posts well in advance of their sale. Keeping records of what was sold and to whom gave guidance to the company as to when to replenish stores and when to adjust supplies to accommodate changing tastes. The presence of European suppliers and rising incomes among local populations, through specialisation and exchange, made for shifts in consumer demand. Over the long term, patterns of change became clear to managers in Britain; they also become clear, through the accounting records, to historians scouring them for data. The books indicate an expanding range of consumer goods, changes in consumption and in the value of goods in the minds of buyers and sellers.

There was, alongside those long-term directions taken in the stocking of supplies and their sales, a short-term situation faced by locals on the ground. In small stores, trading posts or on markets in West Africa, people had to make decisions on the spot about what to buy and sell at what price. The Hudson's Bay Company, for example, might set prices but factors, the accounts suggest, had some latitude in negotiating what exchanged for what. While to varying degrees Europeans enjoyed advantages of coercive power when it came to making a deal, with both parties interested in finding a satisfactory price, it came down to a matter of haggling and bargaining. Consistently from New York to New Zealand and from Africa to Hudson's Bay, reports are of Indigenous people able to participate in bargaining, and they do so effectively. The evidence serves to support Smith's expectation of a desire among people to truck, barter and exchange. Trading goods one for another, one of them often being money in some form, though, could be and was combined in many places and cases with other sorts of relations. Gift giving, for example, was always a way to negotiate dealing with others. It had varying importance over time and apparently declined relative to buying and selling over time. At least that is what the accounting records suggest. Certainly market or market-like transactions did not supersede all exchange activities or even all relations between Indigenous peoples and Europeans. However, the supposed barriers to business transactions should be seen as 'so-called cultural obstacles devised mostly by modern-day ethnography' and a product of myth-making.[11] Who might benefit from the myth is not clear. While the skills that Indigenous peoples showed at haggling, bartering and dealing with currencies may be a surprise to historians, that wonder may not have been shared by Europeans who carried out transactions of various sorts with those Indigenous peoples.

No matter who was involved or the nature of the transaction, it was necessary to have some accounts, even if only a mental record. European participants in the trades were very often interested in producing written accounts consistent with established practices at home. They needed to make them for their political superiors or for the owners or investors in the enterprises of which they were a part. For trading companies, the accounts were important and understood as a tool of planning, management and a key to financial success. The Hudson's Bay Company, for example, changed its methods of record keeping in 1814–1815 as part of rethinking how it was going to do business. In this case, as in others, the stark numbers could be accompanied by descriptions, making the accounting sources even richer if harder for researchers to use. The accounts, whether in words or numbers, were often more precise and clearly defined than the discussion of them by historians who are left trying to piece together what happened out of the reports to superiors.

Keeping accounts always presented problems of comparing apples and oranges. The problem of comparing goods was much like the problem of comparing currencies. Specific trades presented their own unique practical problems. Methods used to deal with slaves indicate an extreme case of the difficulties accountants faced. The people, whom French captains were buying, were not by any means a uniform commodity. Drawing up the accounts was not a matter of calculating a price on a human being. It was rather the need to have some basis of comparison to know what goods would be needed for exchange. For the enterprise, profit and loss was the difference between what was paid for the trade goods that left France and what was received from the sale of the sugar and other agricultural goods brought into the home port at the end of voyage, less all expenses of the voyage. Slaves, though unique personally and as objects of trade, did present problems typical of measurement in dealing with transactions. Difficulties with beaver pelts were different; still, they had rates of exchange, prices that could be denominated in goods. That was exactly what factors in forts or store owners did.

> The fur trade brought an engagement with the market and embryonic commodity chains. While at a very basic level, hybrid might be a functional way to describe the combining of European and Indian elements, a substantial economic re-orientation for Natives was required.[12]

The same was true of all trades where Europeans intruded themselves into local economies. It would be wrong to think that Europeans did not have to re-orient themselves and their ways of doing business when they dealt with Indigenous peoples. The money used and prevailing accounting practices show that, in fact, Europeans did adjust.

Money meant power for governments in early modern Europe. The cost of deploying fighting forces, be it on land or at sea, rose dramatically from the sixteenth century onward. Government efforts to ferret out more sources of tax income started already in the Middle Ages. Trade was a favourite target for the authorities.[13] Finding funds became more pressing as armies got bigger and gunpowder weapons became a requirement for success. The need to increase state incomes to pay the costs of maintaining the fiscal-military state was a driving political force.[14] It is all too easy to see many of the practical considerations governments faced in covering their military and naval costs as part of some larger concept and then call that loose collection of policies, along with some ideas expressed by proponents of acquisitive nascent states, mercantilism. Economic policy, if the hodgepodge of state actions could be given such an elevated title, was driven by the need or desire to put more cash in the hands of governments. The similarities of those policies in different parts of western and central Europe do at least leave the impression or generate hope of finding some larger ideas lurking somewhere in the background.

It is undoubtedly true that among Renaissance politicians there was a sense that they had a great deal of freedom of action. Princes could often behave despotically, though the many revolts of the period, some successful, suggest that there were significant limits on how much coercive power was wise to use. The concept of mercantilism seems to piece together the general political situation, the ability of states to act to some degree on whim, with the rising cost of armies and navies driving a search for more tax income. Those elements add up to nothing more than a mercantile system which even Smith, who first identified the phenomenon, did not think was universal or supported by some general theory. One general principle he did attach to the mercantile system was that national wealth consisted of gold and silver.[15] Some of Smith's predecessors did talk about the need to have specie flow into the country and from that came the idea that there was a belief that the precious metals had some intrinsic value. Thomas Mun, for example, wrote in the 1620s about England having a balance of payments surplus so that silver would come into the country.[16] There are problems with claiming that he just wanted silver. His goal was to earn the metal by trade and then to ship it to the Far East, where it was more prised than in Europe. For him, the value of silver was not intrinsic but instrumental, a means to expand English trade and increase the wealth of the kingdom. The same understanding of precious metals was true for governments that collected and even hoarded silver. They knew that when war came, as it very frequently did among European states in the period, they would need all they could get their hands on to pay for the costs of fighting.

Specific instances, again and again, indicate a strong pragmatism among agents in the world economy from 1500 to 1900. Cases show governments as well as traders groping to find efficiency and power as levers to increase income. Records of transactions, no matter how extensive and where they came from, indicate over time a pattern of searching for effective ways to do business or, in the case of governments, to tax. Mercantilism, a concept that tries to lump together that varied collection of efforts to solve immediate problems, simply is too imprecise to be a useful tool for analysis. Just as it is wrong to see a context for the economy defined by a specific and consistent body of ideas and policies, so it is wrong to see the trade that went on outside Europe, often far from its shores, as peripheral. For those engaged in transactions on both sides, certainly the trade was far from peripheral. It was central to their survival or, at the very least, to whatever prosperity they knew. Those exchanges might take place far from the major port towns of Europe but they were still an essential, even critical part of the complex web of economic relations, which European commerce constructed in the centuries after 1500. Trades were interconnected and interdependent so all exchange contributed to prosperity and economic growth.

Numerous European records of doing business fortunately survive, although there are problems with the use of them. The reasons for survival are diverse. Goals may have been similar and general principles behind the accounts may have been similar. Individual practice, however, varied and variation over time was common. The records come from specific times and places, and so it is impossible to generate any global data from them. The sources are to a degree anecdotal and to make more of them requires a lot of estimation or just simple guess work. There is no reason to claim that the existing sample is representative of what was normal or even typical. With all those limitations the accounts remain extremely valuable for finding out about many features of the lives of the people involved. The records are especially valuable in the case of relations between Europeans and the people of very different numbers and character they met around the world, people who typically have left no financial records. Europeans needed their own accounts to measure and compare, to report to superiors and plan future action. It would be wrong to think that the people they traded with did not have some of the same needs. How Indigenous peoples carried out their accounting is not known from their own sources. Their lack of formalised accounting procedures and record keeping may well have put them at a disadvantage. That impression, though, may be a result of the character and quality of the accounting records that Europeans kept, which generate a false impression of superiority in negotiating relationships. Indigenous peoples did not go over to formal or written accounting with records preserved, but there is evidence that just as Europeans adopted habits and practices and traditional ecological knowledge of the people they met, so Indigenous peoples adopted, to varying degrees, imported habits and practices. At least the records that survive can give some hints about how the Europeans' trading counterparts measured those transactions.

The highly ordered columns with standard categories, the representation of goods and people in money terms treating all objects as similar and to be bought and sold, suggests a precise and considerably restricted way of perceiving the world. They leave the impression of something like an obsession with money. That all those who prepared and inspected accounts and all those described in them shared those views is certainly not the case. Accounts served specific purposes for specific people. To those ends, participants restricted their thinking and actions. That the records reflect only a part of the lives of authors and users turns up in the accounts themselves. In the same way, the instrumentality of money, like the instrumentality of trade and exchange, comes through in various ways in the dry numeration of the lives of people who are in the books. Such nuances in the numbers may make the accounting sources hard to use but may also make them valuable for teasing out the character of life for people meeting and exchanging, and not just exchanging goods, from the sixteenth through to the nineteenth century.

The surviving accounts show accommodation of Europeans to differing economic regimes. The case of Jesuit missionaries in China shows Europeans inserting themselves into the local monetary regime. Sets of accounts from other places around the world indicate the same successful insertion of Europeans into prevailing norms. That is what accounts were supposed to report. Europeans had to adapt because of their goals and the circumstances in which they found themselves. They adjusted to the practices they found in order to be successful in whatever enterprise they were engaged. There was mutual accommodation, with all parties being forced to one degree or another into re-orientation. The account books of those accommodations record the successes, the instances when parties could find mutual ground. They also show, now and again, that haggling and bargaining did not produce a positive result. The accounting records above all suggest what the character of management of those interactions was like for all parties. They may be tedious for historians to deal with, but, in the right hands, they can produce a broad range of information about how people lived, functioned and dealt with others, no matter how different they were when they first encountered each other.

## Notes

1 E. S. Hunt and J. M. Murray, *A History of Business in Medieval Europe, 1200–1550* (Cambridge and New York: Cambridge University Press, 1999), pp. 62–63, pp. 157–58, pp. 239–42.
2 A. Smith, *An Inquiry into the Nature and Causes of the Wealth of Nations*, ed. E. Canaan (New York: Modern Library, 1937), book IV, chapter 1, pp. 398–419. Smith probably got the term from the Marquis de Mirabeau's Philosophie Royale of 1763; see L. Magnusson, *Mercantilism: The Shaping of an Economic Language* (London and New York: Routledge, 1994), p. 25.
3 R. W. Unger, 'Warships, Cargo Ships and Adam Smith: Trade and Government in the Eighteenth Century', *The Mariner's Mirror*, 92:1 (2006), pp. 42–44.
4 For example, C. W. Cole, *French Mercantilism, 1683–1700* (New York: Columbia University Press, 1943); D. C. Coleman, 'Mercantilism Revisited', *The Historical Journal*, 23 (1980), pp. 773–91; R. B. Ekelund and R. D. Tollison, *Politicized Economies: Monarchy, Monopoly, and Mercantilism* (College Station: Texas A and M University Press, 1997); L. Magnusson, *Mercantilism: The Shaping of an Economic Language* (London and New York: Routledge, 1994); L. Magnusson (ed.), *Mercantilist Economics* (New York: Springer, 1993); D. Ormrod, *The Rise of Commercial Empires: England and the Netherlands in the Age of Mercantilism, 1650–1770* (Cambridge, UK, and New York: Cambridge University Press, 2003); A. Wakefield, *The Disordered Police State: German Cameralism as Science and Practice* (Chicago: University of Chicago Press, 2009).
5 A. W. Coats, 'Concluding Reflections', in Magnusson (ed.), *Mercantilist Economics*, p. 259.
6 For example, see C. Perrotta, 'Early Spanish Mercantilism: The First Analysis of Underdevelopment', in Magnusson (ed.), *Mercantilist Economics*, pp. 17–58.
7 E. S. Reinert and S. A. Reinert, 'Mercantilism and Economic Development: Schumpeterian Dynamics, Institution-Building and International Benchmarking', in K. S. Jomo and E. S. Reinert (eds.), *The Origins of Development Economics: How Schools of Economic Thought Have Addressed Development* (New Delhi, London and New York: Tulika Books, 2005), pp. 8–12, pp. 16–18. The interest in relative economic development, though, did not set them apart from later writers on economics.
8 E. F. Heckscher, *Mercantilism*, vol. I, trans. M. Shapiro, ed. E. F. Söderlund (London: Allen and Unwin Macmillan; New York: Macmillan, 1955), pp. 128–36.
9 W. Barrrett, 'World Bullion Flows, 1450–1800', in J. D. Tracy (ed.), *The Rise of Merchant Empires: Long-Distance Trade in the Early Modern World, 1350–1750* (Cambridge: Cambridge University Press, 1990); T. Brook, *Vermeer's Hat: The Seventeenth Century and the Dawn of the Global World* (New York: Bloomsbury, 2008).
10 W. D. Voorthuijsen, *De Republiek Der Verenigde Nederlanden en het mercantilisme* (Den Haag: Nijhoff, 1965).
11 See F. Tough in this volume.
12 See F. Tough in this volume.
13 R. W. Unger, 'Trade, Taxation and Government Policy in the High Middle Ages', *Viator*, 46:3 (2015), pp. 195–217.
14 R. Bonney, *The Rise of the Fiscal State in Europe, c. 1200–1815* (Oxford: Oxford University Press, 1999); J. Glete, *War and the State in Early Modern Europe: Spain, the Dutch Republic and Sweden as Fiscal-Military States, 1500–1660, Warfare and History* (London and New York: Routledge, 2002).
15 Smith, *An Inquiry into the Nature and Causes of the Wealth of Nations*, p. 418.
16 T. Mun and J. Mun, *England's Treasure by Forraign Trade, or, the Ballance of Our Forraign Trade Is the Rule of Our Treasure* (London: Printed by J. G. for Thomas Clark, 1664). The book was published by his son but not until 23 years after his death.

# Index

Note: **Boldface** page references indicate tables. *Italic* references indicate figures.

For Product Safety Concerns and Information please contact our EU representative GPSR@taylorandfrancis.com Taylor & Francis Verlag GmbH, Kaufingerstraße 24, 80331 München, Germany